ASEAN-India
Strengthening Partnership and Post-Pandemic Future

THIRTY YEARS OF ASEAN-INDIA RELATIONS

ASEAN-India
Strengthening Partnership and Post-Pandemic Future

Edited by
Prabir De
Suthiphand Chirathivat

AIC
ASEAN-India Centre at RIS

RIS
Research and Information System
for Developing Countries
विकासशील देशों की अनुसंधान एवं सूचना प्रणाली

ศูนย์อาเซียนศึกษา
จุฬาลงกรณ์มหาวิทยาลัย
ASEAN STUDIES CENTER
CHULALONGKORN UNIVERSITY

KW
KNOWLEDGE WORLD

KW Publishers Pvt Ltd
New Delhi

ISBN   978-93-91490-47-8   Hardback
ISBN   978-93-91490-63-8   eBook

Published in India by Kalpana Shukla

KW
KNOWLEDGE WORLD

KW Publishers Pvt Ltd
4676/21, First Floor, Ansari Road
Daryaganj, New Delhi 110002
Phone: +91 11 43528107
Marketing: kw@kwpub.in
Editorial: production@kwpub.in
Website: www.kwpub.in

Contents

PART I
SECTION I: Changing Landscape of Global Order and ASEAN-India Relations in the Post-COVID-19 Period

SECTION V: Way Forward

PART II
Sixth Roundtable of ASEAN-India Network of Think Tanks (AINTT) 20-21 August 2020

Foreword

ASEAN has been at the forefront of India's Act Policy. ASEAN-India relations have stood the test of time and have matured from sectoral partnership in 1992 to a full-fledged dialogue partnership in 1995, summit level partnership in 2002 and eventually turning into a strategic relationship in the year 2012. The year 2018 marked 25 years of ASEAN-India relations. India and ASEAN are going to celebrate the 30 years of their bilateral relations in 2022.

Over the years, ASEAN member states and India have cooperated on multiple areas ranging from economic activities to connectivity issues. The amelioration in ASEAN-India relations have been a part and participle of the conjoined efforts of several agencies and institutions. Think-tanks from ASEAN and India are one such agency which has aggravated the pace of cooperation between the two regions. The coming together of think-tanks of the two regions provides a way forward for deepening ASEAN-India cooperation.

In recent times, the Covid-19 pandemic has brought the world economy to its knees. Several ASEAN countries are experiencing a fresh wave of infections. India faced with a brutal second wave in early 2021. ASEAN-India cooperation stands a chance in shifting the scales in its favour through deeper economic integration. Previous roundtables of AINTT have discussed and emphasised on ironing out connectivity issues and strengthening people to people connectivity.

The ASEAN-India Centre (AIC) at RIS has been collaborating with think-tanks from the ASEAN member states from 2012 onwards, and has come up with successive roundtables of the ASEAN-India Network of Think-Tanks (AINTT). The platform serves as an anchor for strengthening economic, socio-cultural and people to people ties between ASEAN and India. The AINTT holds an annual roundtable with much fanfare and engages contributors from think-tanks, academia, policy makers, business representatives, etc.

The sixth roundtable of the ASEAN-India Network of Think-Tanks, held on 20-21 August, 2020, in virtual format, witnessed discussions around a wide range of issues concerning the ASEAN-India partnership. The thrust of the roundtable was on cementing ASEAN-India cooperation post-Covid-19. The roundtable saw discussions around a host of issues, organised into five sessions. The contributors presented their views on topics such as global value chains, the fourth industrial revolution, ASEAN Outlook on the Indo-Pacific (AOIP) and the Indo-Pacific Oceans Initiative (IPOI), etc. The proceedings of the sixth roundtable present a detailed account of the discussions we had in the sixth roundtable of the AINTT.

I take this opportunity to thank the RIS team led by DG, Prof. Sachin Chaturvedi. In particular, I would like to appreciate the efforts of my senior colleague, Prof. Prabir De, and his team at AIC, in bringing forth this volume of sixth roundtable of the ASEAN-India Network of Think-tanks.

I am hopeful that the proceedings of the sixth roundtable of AINTT will act as a valuable reference point for policy makers, academics and practitioners.

Mohan Kumar
Chairman, RIS

Preface

It is well-known that RIS since 1992 has been providing analytical support for strengthening ASEAN-India partnership. As part of this endeavour, ASEAN-India Centre was set up at RIS in 2013. The process of organising Roundtables of ASEAN-India Network of Think Tank (AINTT) since then to engage with think-tanks, policy makers, academicians and representatives from business and industry circles for exchange of ideas on various aspects of ASEAN-India relationship.

Over the years, extensive efforts have been made for evolving comprehensive partnership with academic community between India and ASEAN. The Sixth Roundtable of AINTT was held in the backdrop of the whole world grappling with the unprecedented health care challenge owing to COVID-19 pandemic. The issues that came up for intensive discussion included changing landscape of global order and ASEAN-India Relations in the post-COVID era; emerging value chains and opportunities for ASEAN and India in the post-COVID era; and new normal and significance of 4IR on ASEAN-India Partnership and future collaborations. In view of realising the vision of an open, free, inclusive and rule-based Indo-Pacific region, there was also a session on ASEAN outlook on Indo-Pacific and Indo-Pacific Oceans initiative (IPOI): complementarities and cooperation.

The present volume contains proceedings of the Sixth Roundtable for the benefit of all those who are connected with the process of deepening ASEAN-India partnership. We thank the Ministry of External Affairs, Government of India for its support and to the RIS Governing Body and the Chairman for their guidance and support. We also compliment the editors Dr Prabir De, Coordinator, AIC at RIS and Dr Suthiphand Chirathivat,

Chairman, Chula Global Network and Executive Director, ASEAN Studies Center, Chulalongkorn University, Thailand, for bringing out the volume.

Sachin Chaturvedi
Director-General, RIS

Acknowledgements

This volume "ASEAN-India: Strengthening Partnership in the Post-COVID-19 Period" has been edited by Dr. Prabir De, Professor and Coordinator, ASEAN-India Centre (AIC), Research and Information System for Developing Countries (RIS) and Prof. Suthiphand Chirathivat, Executive Director, ASEAN Studies Centre (ASC), Chulalongkorn University, Bangkok. This volume also presents the proceedings of the sixth Roundtable of the ASEAN-India Network of Thinks-Tanks (AINTT), which was held on 20-21 August 2020 via video conferencing.

Editors are grateful to Dr. Mohan Kumar, Chairman, RIS and Prof. Sachin Chaturvedi, Director General, RIS for their support in organising the sixth roundtable and bringing out this volume.

Editors are grateful to Ms. Sreya Pan, Research Associate, AIC at RIS for her useful research and editorial assistance. Editors are also thankful to Ms. Thitiya Saramul, Academic Officer, ASEAN Studies Centre of Chulalongkorn University, Bangkok; Dr. Durairaj Kumarasamy, former Consultant, AIC at RIS; and Dr. Nida Rahman, Young Professional, RIS for their administrative and editorial assistance.

We would like to thank the ASEAN Studies Centre (ASC), Chulalongkorn University, Bangkok and the Ministry of Foreign Affairs of the Kingdom of Thailand and the Ministry for organising the sixth Roundtable of the ASEAN-India Network of Think Tanks (AINTT). We gratefully acknowledge the support extended by the Ministry of External Affairs (MEA), Government of India in organizing the Sixth Roundtable of AINTT.

We would like to thank Dr. Rajeev Ranjan Chaturvedy, Visiting Fellow, S. Rajaratnam School of International Studies (RSIS), Nanyang Technological University (NTU), Singapore; Ms. Komal

Biswal, Research Scholar, Jawaharlal Nehru University (JNU), New Delhi; Ms. Urvi Dhar, Intern, AIC at RIS and Ms. Geeta, Intern, AIC at RIS for the rapporteuring and project assistance. This publication has been benefitted from work done in support by the RIS Faculty and Administration.

We are grateful to Ms Kalpana Shukla and Mr Sushanta Gayen, KW Publishers for their support in bringing out this volume.

Views expressed in the volume are those of the participants of the 6th AINTT and do not reflect the views of the Government of India or ASEAN countries, ASEAN Secretariat, Research and Information System for Developing countries (RIS) and ASEAN-India Centre (AIC). Usual disclaimers apply. For any further queries, please contact prabirde@ris.org.in or suthipand.c@chula.ac.th.

List of Contributors

Pradeep Chauhan, Director General, National Maritime Foundation (NMF), New Delhi.

C. Uday Bhaskar, Director, Society of Policy Studies (SPS), New Delhi.

Ramesh Kodammal, Chairman of Goldtex Group of Companies, and Chairman, ASEAN-India Business Council (AIBC), Kuala Lumpur.

Carole Ann Chit Tha, Professor (Retd.), Member, Myanmar Institute of Strategic and International Studies (Myanmar-ISIS), Yangon.

Fukunari Kimura, Professor, Faculty of Economics, Keio University and Chief Economist, Economic Research Institute for ASEAN and East Asia (ERIA), Jakarta.

Joefe B. Santarita, Dean, Asian Center, University of the Philippines, Dilman, Manila.

Amita Batra, Professor, School of International Studies (SIS), Jawaharlal Nehru University (JNU), New Delhi.

Nanigopal Mohanta, Director, Centre for Southeast Asian Studies, Gauhati University, Guwahati.

Jayant Menon, Visiting Senior Fellow, Institute of Southeast Asian Studies (ISEAS)–Yusof Ishak Institute, Singapore.

Balaji Parthasarathy, Centre for Information Technology and Public Policy, International Institute of Information Technology, Bangaluru.

Rupa Chanda, RBI Chair Professor in Economics, Indian Institute of Management (IIM), Bengaluru.

Tham Siew Yean, Visiting Senior Fellow, ISEAS-Yusof Ishak Institute, Professor Emeritus, Universiti Kebangsaan Malaysia, Singapore.

Saon Ray, Senior Fellow, Indian Council for Research on International Economic Relations (ICRIER), New Delhi.

Lau Sim Yee, Professor, Reitaku University, Tokyo.

Premesha Saha, Associate Fellow, Observer Research Foundation, New Delhi.

Lau Sim Kim, Professor, Wollongong University, Australia.

Suthiphand Chirathivat, Executive Director, ASEAN Studies Centre (ASC), Chulalongkorn University, Bangkok.

Prabir De, Professor, ASEAN-India Centre (AIC), Research and Information System for Developing Countries (RIS), New Delhi.

List of Tables, Figures and Annexure

Tables

Figures

List of Abbreviations

3D	Three Dimension
4IR	Fourth Industrial Revolution
ADB	Asian Development Bank
ADPC	Asian Disaster Preparedness Centre
AEP	Act East Policy
AFTA	ASEAN Free Trade Agreement
AI	Artificial Intelligence
AIBC	ASEAN-India Business Council
AI-DCPC	ASEAN-India Disease Control and Prevention Center
AIFTA	ASEAN-India Free Trade Agreement
AINTT	ASEAN-India Network of Think Tanks
AMS	ASEAN Member States
AOIP	ASEAN Outlook on Indo-Pacific
ASEAN	Association of Southeast Asian Nations
BBIN	Bangladesh-Bhutan-India-Nepal
BCIM	Bangladesh-China-India-Myanmar
BIMSTEC	Bay of Bengal Initiative for Multi-Sectoral Technical and Economic Cooperation
BRI	Belt and Road Initiative
CDRI	Coalition for Disaster Resilient Infrastructure
CECA	Comprehensive Economic Cooperation Agreement
CLMV	Cambodia-Lao PDR-Myanmar-Vietnam
CPEC	China-Pakistan Economic Corridor
CPTPP	Comprehensive and Progressive Agreement for Trans-Pacific Partnership
EAS	East Asia Summit
EEC	Eastern Economic Corridor

EOC	Emergency Operations Centre
ERIA	Economic Research Institute for ASEAN and East Asia
FDI	Foreign Direct Investment
FIPIC	Forum for India-Pacific Islands Cooperation
FOIP	Free and Open Indo-Pacific
FTA	Free Trade Agreement
FTZ	Free Trade Zone
GDP	Gross Domestic Product
GST	Goods and Services Tax
GVC	Global Value Chain
IAID	Indonesia-Africa Infrastructure Dialogue
ICT	Information and Communications Technology
IITM	Indian Institute of Technology, Madras
ILO	International Labour Organisation
IORA	Indian Ocean Rim Association
IP	Intellectual Property
IPOI	Indo-Pacific Oceans' Initiative
IT	Information Technology
ITC	International Trade Centre
LTTD	Low Temperature Thermal Desalination
MFN	Most Favoured Nation
ML	Machine Learning
MNE	Multinational Enterprise
MRA	Mutual Recognition Agreement
MSME	Supporting Micro and Small and Medium Enterprise
NAM	Non-Aligned Movement
NDMA	National Disaster Management Authority
NIOT	National Institute of Ocean Technology
NTM	Non-Tariff Measure
OECD	Organisation for Economic Co-operation and Development
ORE	Ocean Renewable Energy
PSA	Port of Singapore Authority

QUAD	Quadrilateral Security Dialogue
RCEP	Regional Comprehensive Economic Partnership
RIS	Research and Information System for Developing Countries
SAGAR	Security and Growth for All in the Region
SDGs	Sustainable Development Goals
SMEs	Small and Medium-sized Enterprises
SOM	Senior Officials Meeting
TPP	Trans-Pacific Partnership
TRIPS	Trade-Related Aspects of Intellectual Property Rights
UNCLOS	United Nations Convention on the Law of the Sea
UNCTAD	United Nations Conference on Trade and Development
USA	United States of America
WEF	World Economic Forum
WHO	World Health Organization
WTO	World Trade Organization

1. Introduction

Prabir De and Suthiphand Chirathivat

The Association of Southeast Asian Nations (ASEAN) and India are bound together by their shared history and culture. Relation with ASEAN is one of the cornerstones of India's Foreign Policy. There has been steady progress in the ASEAN-India relation since the Look East Policy (LEP) was initiated in 1992 and the Act East Policy (AEP) in 2014. Over time, the ASEAN-India partnership has crossed many milestones one after another. In 2018, ASEAN and India commemorated 25 years of dialogue partnership and 15 years of Summit level partnership. The Commemorative Summit was attended by the Leaders from all the 10 ASEAN countries and came out with the Delhi Declaration, the guiding roadmap of the ASEAN-India partnership. In 2022, ASEAN and India will complete their three decades of dialogue partnership.

The world since 2020 is reeling under the COVID-19 pandemic. Apart from the Public Health challenges, the pandemic has thrown up several socio-economic challenges. The lock-downs, closures, social distancing and travel restrictions have disrupted major economic activities and resulted in huge losses in livelihoods. The impact of the economic crisis is deep-rooted and spans over all the sectors of economy. There remains a significant degree of uncertainty on the severity and duration of the global outbreak and the trajectory of the global economic recovery once the outbreak has been contained. With the global economic landscape shift, ASEAN and India need to work more closely to explore in a post-Covid world order new sources of growth and prosperity.

Opportunities of Collaboration

The COVID-19 pandemic has far-reaching implications for the world. The pandemic is also posing an anti-globalisation and anti-multilateralism threat. In such a situation, ASEAN and India can collaborate to promote a more inclusive, responsive and participatory international governance architecture.

The COVID-19 outbreak has disrupted established value chains in scale and severity. However, the rise in demand as a result of lock-downs for new products and services, presents an opportunity for both ASEAN and India. The economic complementarities between ASEAN and India can provide for a move towards sustainable and resilient supply chains driven by technology that will help the region emerge healthier from the pandemic. Sectors like pharmaceuticals, healthcare, education, green energy, and traditional medicine offer new opportunities. Besides, if facilitated, production and services networks in digital connectivity, e-commerce, cross-border delivery services, logistics business, tourism, start-ups, etc. may emerge as important components of the ASEAN-India economic portfolio.

The 4th Industrial Revolution (4IR) is an emerging concept deriving from technological advancement and disruptive developments in the industrial sector worldwide in the past few years. Artificial Intelligence, Machine Learning, Robotics, Internet of Things, Blockchain along with the pool of ASEAN-India young generation savvy with digital knowledge hold a great potential for the future of ASEAN-India Strategic Partnership. The application of AI and ML has helped ASEAN countries and India to control the spread of the COVID-19.

The 'Indo-Pacific' is gaining the centre stage of the international relations and diplomacy. The use of the expression 'Indo-Pacific' has been increasingly prevalent in regional and global discourse. The "ASEAN Outlook on the Indo-Pacific" resonates with India's Indo-Pacific Oceans Initiative (IPOI) as articulated by the Indian Prime Minister at the 14th East Asia Summit, not only in positioning ASEAN-centrality as a foundational tenet of the Indo-Pacific, but also as a vital principle for promoting cooperation in the Indo-Pacific region, with ASEAN and ASEAN-led mechanisms.

What follows the ASEAN-India cooperation is the key to economic stability, competitiveness, growth and integration in the Indo-Pacific region. In the rapidly changing times, the ASEAN-India Strategic Partnership must embed new ideas to remain active.

AINTT Roundtable

With an objective to provide policy inputs to governments on future direction of cooperation, ASEAN-India Centre (AIC) at Research and Information System for Developing Countries (RIS) and ASEAN Studies Centre (ASC) of the Chulalongkorn University organised the 6th AINTT roundtable in virtual format in 2020. The AINTT roundtable was established at the 7th ASEAN-India Summit in Thailand in 2009. The forum serves as a high quality research platform and provides long-term perspectives to further strengthen the ASEAN-India Strategic Partnership. The 6th AINTT roundtable was held through digital interface on 20-21 August 2020 in partnership with India's Ministry of External Affairs and Ministry of Foreign Affairs of Thailand. The ASEAN-India Centre (AIC) at RIS and ASEAN Studies Centre (ASC) at Chulalongkorn University were the organising partners. The roundtable focussed on strengthening ASEAN-India relations at a time when COVID-19 pandemic has created uncertainty at an unprecedented level.

Takeaways

The AINTT roundtable, divided into five thematic sessions, was jointly inaugurated by the Deputy Prime Minister and Foreign Minister of Thailand H.E. Mr. Don Pramudwinai and India's External Affairs Minister H.E. Dr. S. Jaishankar. H.E. Dato' Lim Jock Hoi, Secretary-General of ASEAN also addressed the inaugural session. Scholars and experts from ASEAN and India met and made their points on the roundtable discussion. Following key recommendations emerged as important avenues for strengthening ASEAN-India relations:

(i) Towards Building Trust/Cooperation amidst Unprecedented Uncertainties

- The roundtable underlined extraordinary post-COVID 19 challenges faced by countries and urged them to work together and look for "collective solutions" to emerging challenges.

- Diplomatic style is very important for India. Though it is not threatening, the Indian government may like to focus on building more trust and to enhance its soft power. It will help improve India's ability to do right things and to contribute.

- SHARE or Supply Chain Connectivity; Human Security in all dimensions; Academics; Regionalism; and Environment was suggested as a framework for ASEAN-India engagement in post-COVID.

- Despite monumental disruptions, India-ASEAN common aspirations have nurtured our connections. There are many common elements in our visions for the region. ASEAN Outlook on the Indo-Pacific, India's Act East Policy and Indo-Pacific Oceans Initiative are aimed to bring stability and prosperity in the region.

- The US-China trade war has generated common challenges, which provides common grounds for going forward. Further, think-tanks of India and ASEAN should come out with fresh and implementable ideas such as maritime summits, Indo-Pacific infrastructure meet, disaster management collaboration, and strengthening of existing mechanisms can help in deepening the India and ASEAN cooperation. Platforms like maritime law workshop and maritime security workshop should start between India and ASEAN to strengthen maritime cooperation.

- ASEAN and India need to have a new mindset through constructive dialogue and consultation, information sharing and people-to-people linkages. Subregional cooperation requires special focus such as BIMSTEC, MGC, etc., and incorporating Brahmaputra river civilisation as a part of

MGC. All existing mechanisms between India and ASEAN should be used optimally.

- ASEAN and India must focus on completion of its 4th ASEAN-India POA and both the partners need to elevate their partnership from strategic to comprehensive strategic partnership.

(ii) COVID-19 Cooperation

- India and ASEAN can work together to develop affordable vaccines and other lifesaving medicines or medical kits, low cost ventilators and training of healthcare workers. In case a vaccine is developed in some other country but could be manufactured in India under license, India could take the lead to persuade other nations through the WHO/WTO to relax the IPR related patent conditions for manufacture of the vaccine in India (which incidentally has the largest manufacturing capacity for vaccines in the world) so that the vaccine could be supplied to third countries at a reasonable rate without wastage of time.

- ASEAN and India shall establish ASEAN-India Covid Control and Prevention Centre for Public Health Emergency and to provide healthcare for the COVID-19 affected victims, which would help knowledge sharing and dissemination in the region.

(iii) Supply-Chain/Connectivity/Trade/Investment

- ASEAN and India should re-engage, re-intensify and build trust to forge close relationships and take advantage of the two markets to increase trade. Review of ASEAN-India FTA to further reduce the trade barriers and build enhanced industrial linkages would broaden and diversify the trade pattern.

- ASEAN and India should promote trade in food and agriculture and facilitate private sector investment in agro-food products to serve global and regional markets, particularly in the Covid crisis period.

- ASEAN and India have unmet trade potential and offer scope to expand GVC participation in the sectors such as electrical and electronic items, agriculture and agro-based products, pharmaceutical, medical equipment and digital services in manufacturing in COVID-19 period. To improve the GVC participation, India should engage in 'Assembling in India' as a part of the 'Make in India' strategy and improve manufacturing capacities in network products to enhance the scope for intra-industry trade and low-cost logistics. Besides, digitisation could provide opportunities for MSMEs in integrating the manufacturing and services sectors, thereby unlocking GVC potential.
- FDI linked manufacturing should be encouraged, which may enhance FDI linked exports, and deepen India's engagement and participation with ASEAN and the world.
- Develop time-bound roadmap along the lines of the deliverables of MPAC 2025, which shall include not just 'hard' and 'soft' infrastructure, but also new initiatives to facilitate maritime tourism and maritime partnership through the safe movement of ships of all kinds, addressing maritime security problems, security implications of climate change, environmental degradation and pollution and other cross-border challenges. Two immediate solutions are proposed: first, development of cruise-ship tourism by reducing tariffs (GoI has reduced tariffs by 70 per cent), and, second, encouraging Ro-Ro shipping.

(iv) Digital/New Economy

- Agriculture emerged as one of the most important sectors for cooperation. Digital technologies need to be introduced in the field of agriculture. India's 'Digital Village' programme in CLMV should also include agriculture. Capacity in digital techniques and platforms in the field of agriculture should be enhanced. It also requires creating a pool of 'Digital Talents'. India may consider extending necessary assistance to Myanmar and other ASEAN countries for developing the digital infrastructure and providing digital solutions for agriculture, education, e-government platforms.

- Recommendations to bring India-ASEAN e-commerce to the next higher level: (i) sustainable Fintech, helping people can do financial transactions just by using a smart-phone; and (ii) set up an ASEAN-India e-Commerce Online Market. This will allow India and ASEAN to sell directly their products, thus strengthening MSMEs' participation.

- India should work with ASEAN countries in developing Start-ups ecosystem and to find innovative and regional solutions to common challenges.

- One possible recommendation is to identify and solidify how to deploy technological advances of 4IR from area of commerce/trade into the other areas of cooperation most importantly e-education; e-health; e-government (including AI for social good) and deploy digitalisation into the non-mainstream areas such as agriculture and food processing. India can also help to reduce the digital divide within the region.

- COVID-19 has fast-tracked the process of digital connectivity in a remarkable way. However, it has also generated growing cyber threats. Hence, cyber security should be one of the priority areas of cooperation between India and ASEAN.

(v) Sectoral Cooperation

- Collaborative initiatives/actions shall be taken between India's NDMA and ASEAN's Coordinating Centres for Humanitarian Disaster Management (AHA Centre) for managing disasters and learning from each other's experience. Coalition for Disaster Resilient Infrastructure is another avenue for ASEAN countries to work along with India.

- India and ASEAN shall form the Blue Economy Task Force to deal with plastic debris, hydrological surveys, marine degradation related projects particularly those caused by human activities like illegal fishing, illegal construction islands, destruction of marine life and coordinated patrolling in high seas to prevent such illegal activities including trafficking of humans, drugs and other goods, IUU fishing, etc.

- Think-tanks of India and ASEAN need to work on the current status of marine pollution that concerns the Indo-Pacific region particularly to find how much of the waste generated by COVID-19 is dumped in nearby water.
- India and ASEAN can come together through Coast Guards to supply offshore coast guard vessels, to build PTPAL, to conduct collaborative cleaning exercises, to foster exchange of officers through training programmes from naval war colleges and defence universities of India to ASEAN, developing information sharing centres, making India participate in ASEAN Coast Guard Law Enforcement Forum, etc.
- Emphasis should be given to India-ASEAN Renewable Ocean Initiative, a confluence of IPOI and AOIP, by investing in technology and stimulating innovation through PPP to unlock the potential of ocean energy to create a reliable source for the future and to reduce carbon footprints. India may consider developing new projects such as Solar Park.

(vi) Indo-Pacific Cooperation

- India needs to spell out details of the Indo-Pacific Oceans Initiative (IPOI) and also accommodate ASEAN's invitation to join RCEP.
- Commonalities in various Indo-Pacific visions should be spelled out with actionable agendas.

Background of the Book

This edited volume presents a set of 15 research papers, which were presented at the 6th AINTT roundtable. Divided in five major sections, this volume reviews some of the achievements of ASEAN-India relations while completing three decades of partnership, and presents a set of new agenda for the fourth decade. It also underlines the desire of the ASEAN countries and India to diversify and further strengthen the relations in the third decade. This volume is also published to commemorate the thirty years of ASEAN-India relations. We hope that this book will be liked by many in India and abroad as an important reference book on ASEAN-India relations in post COVID-19 period.

PART I

SECTION I: Changing Landscape of Global Order and ASEAN-India Relations in the Post-COVID-19 Period

2. ASEAN-India: Strengthening Partnership in the Pandemic Times

Amita Batra

Introduction

The once in a lifetime predicament that the pandemic is making us realise the importance of the ASEAN-India partnership. As we put our minds to seeking solutions, both in the field of medicine as well as in the field of economics, it is realised that we need to be innovative. However, equal focus also needs to be given to how the global economic order is also undergoing a change simultaneously and how the India-ASEAN partnership can prove to be relevant at this juncture. The central focus of this paper is on issues relating to multilateralism, regionalism, ASEAN centrality and the contribution that the regional partnership can make to the global economic order. Also, the paper reflects briefly on how India needs to align itself with the ASEAN so as to be able to further its national policy objective of self-reliance while at the same time contributing to maintaining ASEAN centrality in the regional context.

Multilateralism in the Present Scenario

As for the global economic order, while many of the changes that we see today – protectionism, trade nationalism and the threat to multilateralism, as such, have been evident over the last decade and much before the pandemic. The pandemic has only accelerated the pace of change. But while it does so, the urgency of the moment also brings forth imperatives to work on concrete solutions. The first and foremost in this context is the idea of multilateralism and global trade dynamics. Global trade has been hugely impacted by the pandemic. There is a change, both in the nature and magnitude of global trade. The difficult but inevitable response of almost all countries across the world to the pandemic has been in terms of partial, phased or complete lockdowns and shutdown of the economies. National borders being sealed and restrictions on travel have led to an unprecedented decline in global trade, both in goods and services. Trade in goods and services started to decline in the first quarter of 2020 itself. The decline in the second quarter was more evident relative to that in the first quarter. Trade in goods is estimated to have declined, year-on-year, by 18 per cent in the second quarter and services trade by 21 per cent in the same period.[1] With this historical decline, there has also been a progressive move towards trade-restrictive policies. Many countries restricted movement of essential commodities across borders including medicines and food. Interestingly though, the restrictive trade policies have been accompanied soon after, by growing flexibilities too, as more and more industrial production turned towards manufacturing pandemics related commodities such as PPEs and ventilators. While broadly restricted, trade cooperation was forthcoming gradually in essential medical equipment like medical equipment, masks, food items, etc.

However, in the fight against the pandemic what requires probably the most attention and solutions is the vaccine and related manufacturing capabilities. As vaccine is most likely to be the only or at least the main channel of respite from the virus, the world needs to cooperate to manufacture and make available the vaccine as a public good. It is only if the vaccine is viewed as a 'public good' that vaccine availability can be ensured for all. In this context, India-ASEAN partnership assumes significance. With regard to shared medical technology, knowledge and distribution, regional cooperation may be imperative. The big issue that we need to tackle in the sharing of manufacturing technology and know-how for the vaccine is, however, the question of intellectual property (IP) rights and ownership of this technology. It would be imperative to introduce flexibilities, even if, of a temporary nature in the existing agreements that we already have, at the multilateral forum or design fresh agreements with the required flexibility clauses in the IP context. The most obvious institutional platform to achieve this flexibility in intellectual property ownership rights would be the international/ multilateral trade body – the World Trade Organization (WTO).

Internationally, at the WTO, flexibilities under the TRIPS that is in terms of public health issues have been incorporated earlier and so that should be the basis of seeking the same again this time for the pandemic and vaccine manufacturing. However, the difficulty lies in the ability of the multilateral forum to be able to make this possible, to undertake negotiations towards the objective or to be able to impress the idea of knowledge sharing on international manufacturing firms and their host economies, particularly the advanced economies of the EU and the United States. Does the multilateral body have the requisite capabilities to undertake the task? This is where, therefore, the issue of revival of multilateralism and that of the multilateral institution, the WTO really comes in as a prior and as an objective of the India-ASEAN partnership. This is one important issue that we need to pay attention to and think about at this stage, well ahead of when it becomes available.

As is well known, multilateralism has been and remains under considerable pressure. During the years of the Trump presidency, in particular post-2017, the rise of trade tensions between the US and China that were reflected in unilateral discriminatory policies such as tariff escalation clearly led to undermining of the multilateral institution. The US policy of correcting its trade imbalances through bilateral tariff escalation was clearly in violation of the MFN principles which are fundamental to the concept and working of multilateralism. In addition, the US by delaying appointments on the appellate panel of the dispute settlement body (DSM) rendered ineffectively. The DSM has been at the core of protecting the other principle of multilateralism-free and fair trade.

Regional Partnership under Multilateralism

The regional partnership of India and ASEAN needs to work towards revival of multilateralism. This has to be a major objective that the regional partnership needs to strive for bringing back the spirit and body of multilateralism. While free trade agreements and mega-regional agreements carry on the business and trade agenda of large corporations, it is only multilateralism and the WTO that can take forward global trade in a free and fair manner, while serving and protecting the interest of the lesser developed nations. It is necessary that like-minded countries, that have had faith in multilateralism, must at this point, come forward and come together to revive multilateralism. India and ASEAN from the region must lead these efforts. Together, the two countries must formulate and lead proposals for IPR flexibilities at the WTO to make vaccine availability for all a reality. The pandemic necessitates that all of the global community be vaccinated and that is possible only if vaccine technology is shared with lesser developed nations.

Beyond multilateralism, for India itself, it is also important to think and respond to regional developments. As the regional context continues to be dominated by supply chains, regional trade and movement of inputs/intermediates will be directed by regional trade agreements. This will remain so, and mega-regional trade agreements will continue to be used as prime trade instruments, particularly when the multilateral rules are not fully effective given the weaknesses in the multilateral system. In Asia, the RCEP is the regional comprehensive economic partnership and the CPTPP, the comprehensive and progressive trans-pacific partnership are the two dominant mega-regional trade agreements.

India has withdrawn from the RCEP in November 2019 just as it was close to finalization. The CPTPP is the TPP minus the US. The United States withdrew from the TPP in 2017 soon after the President assumed power. So, we have two mega-regionals in Asia – the RCEP and the CPTPP. From the first, India has withdrawn and from the second, the United States has withdrawn its membership. Given this situation, it would be pertinent to reflect on whether the region is according greater leverage to China to exercise its influence on trade rules-making in the region. After all, the RCEP would be dominated by China as its largest trading economy. In addition, it is also true that the ASEAN economies have a large degree of interdependency vis-à-vis China. They are part of a dense regional network of supply chains. Furthermore, it may also be recognised that the United States is not really able to provide an alternative as an anchor or alternative in the region to counter the BRI, that is the other connectivity network that China has long initiated. The BUILD Act of the US and the amount of money committed by the United States under the BUILD Act may just be too small for the ASEAN countries or the region to accept the United States as an alternative at all in the region. The United States needs to do much more. In the absence of both, India and the US in the region, therefore, and with China concretising its participation platforms in the region, the scope for extending its economic influence in the region would be much more. ASEAN and India need to come together on this front too. And for this purpose, it may be essential to rebuilding, re-establish the idea of ASEAN centrality.

Focusing ASEAN-India Relation and ASEAN Centrality

It is important for India contributing to continued use of the idea of ASEAN centrality in the region, so as to not give leverage or not allow a particular country to extend its influence beyond the justifiable. India and ASEAN need to work on structuring and strengthening their relationship to prevent any further push forwards by any single country in the regional context and for all to abide by a rule-based regional order.

The other aspect that India needs to focus on with regard to the ASEAN relationship is participation in regional supply chains. With an increase in Chinese labour costs and reorientation of the Chinese growth model towards domestic consumption, supply chain shifts have been evident to some extent away from China. Some pre-existing consolidation of supply chains has also been apparent in the

ASEAN region. This may be further accelerated by the pandemic. The pace and quantum of supply chains relocation is most likely to gather pace. This relocation would involve other emerging market economies in the region. Thus far, relocation within the ASEAN has been the more obvious trend. A major movement towards India has not been quite evident. Therefore, what is it that would help India attract these shifting regional supply chains should be on India's economic policy agenda. As a big opportunity to create both manufacturing competitiveness and jobs, integrating with regional supply chains would be a facilitating mechanism. India needs to work this out with the ASEAN countries. While much would depend also on the strength and timeline of Chinese recovery, both in terms of health as well as economics, India's own business and trade environment would be equally important. The pandemic will alter not just the locations, but also the nature of supply chains. What was efficient supply chains earlier, that is just in time supply chains-minimum recovery, minimum inventories, etc. will undergo a change possibly towards more resilient but perhaps higher-cost supply chains.

Concluding Remarks

Notwithstanding the nature of change, this is an opportunity for India. India has to seek ways to exploit this opportunity somehow or the other by integrating with what we would see as one of the more dynamic regions ASEAN and East Asia. ASEAN is going to be a dynamic region both in terms of the way it has dealt with the pandemic and we expect it to come out of the pandemic better than many other regions in the world. The need of the hour would be to shape appropriate industrial policies that would be conditioned not by an inward-looking, import-substituting model but by an export push model and push to trade as a means to growth. The ASEAN countries experience helps understand the significance of outward-oriented growth. India-ASEAN partnership should be able to harness these lessons for planning post pandemics.

India-ASEAN partnership can go a long way in helping ameliorate the adverse consequences of the pandemic in terms of global and regional trade as also in terms of economic growth.

Note
1. Impact of the COVID-19 on trade and development: Transitioning to a new normal, UNCTAD, 2020.

Reference
UNCTAD (2000). "Impact of the COVID-19 on Trade and Development: Transitioning to a New Normal". United Nations Conference on Trade and Development (UNCTAD), Geneva.

3. Changing Landscape of Global World Order and India-ASEAN Relations through India's Northeast

Nani Gopal Mahanta

Introduction

After the end of the Cold war, perhaps for the first time, the entire world has been witnessing major structural changes having far-reaching consequences in the international political economy of public health, livelihood, functioning of global institutions, supply chain, security architecture and so on. The changes are visible mainly on four fronts. First, there could be a shift from the centrality of geo-trade and geo-commerce of globalisation period to a geo-strategic world with significant reliance on geo-technology. Secondly, there is a retreat from globalisation to nationalisation, and again, from regionalisation to sub-regionalisation and subsequently to localisation. Thirdly, transformation from the US-dominated global order to a China-centric political economy. 'China's Salalmi slicing' and 'wolf-warrior' diplomacy may continue as the world, more specifically South and South East Asia, is groaning under the pandemic crisis. Fourthly, even in ASEAN region, the geo-strategic and security issues will become critical in the post-COVID-19 period as static or negative economic growth will significantly shy away from the ASEAN nations from security expenditure or build-up, which might provide China to leverage its hegemonic tactics in south china and east china sea thus causing significant insecurity to the nations in the region.

Some of these changes have occurred even before the onslaught of COVID-19; however, pandemic has precipitated these developments. In this context, the article presents India's foreign policy shift in Section 2. Section 3 discusses India-ASEAN cooperation. Finally, the conclusion is drawn in Section 4.

India's Foreign Policy Shift from 'Asian Solidarity' to 'ASEAN Solidarity'

In choosing India's previous foreign policy options of NAM, South East Asia played a critical role in developing 'Asian Solidarity' through 'Bandung Conference' (howsoever short-lived) and now ASEAN is becoming India's most important foreign policy thrust after the decline of SAARC. India's foreign policy options in South Asia and Central and West Asia is gradually shrinking.

Critics are sceptical about the USA's profound ambivalence in many issues. Some of the issues where the USA had either withdrawn or shown ambivalent positions are – Paris Climate Change; not attending the last ASEAN summit meet in Thailand in 2020,[1] withdrawing from Iran nuclear deal; WTO;[2] WHO; withdrawal from Pacific Rim Nations or Trans-Pacific Partnership,[3] etc.

The USA has to show to its strategic partners that USA's unwavering commitment to Indo-Pacific will continue. On the other hand, USA's departure from Obama's plan in Iran and in those areas not only put India into great foreign policy embarrassment, but also facilitated China's entry into the region in a major way. Now the situation is such that the Chabhar-Zahidon Railway line critical project might go to China. One writer calls this as a 'Dravidi Pranyam' to encircle "Gwadar port". China, thus, got access to Afghanistan market as well as Central Asia as the US had withdrawn from the nuclear deal and it became imperative for Iran to come closer to China as a balancer.

India's Critical Position vis-à-vis China and the US

In terms of positioning herself, India has three policy options in the light of global changes that have been occurring may be for the last one year.

i) With QUAD and Indo-Pacific security architecture – join the USA centric security order;

ii) Strategic balancing with China. That would perhaps mean joining with BRI and also in CPEC, Chabhar-Zahidon project, and the BCIM, which has a significant impact in the North-eastern region of the country.

iii) Remain excluded from all strategic and security bloc with independent choices – as India was adopting during NAM with a tactical advantage to lean towards any as per circumstances. However, it must be kept in mind that the dynamics of big powers in the post-pandemic situation are entirely different.

India-ASEAN Cooperation through India's Northeast

The North-eastern region is said to be the pivot or engine of the Act East Policy (AEP), but the area is not getting adequate benefit from the Act East Policy. Even now Act East remains Delhi-centric. The positioning of the region is very significant from a geo-strategic point of view. Only 2 per cent of the landmass is connected with India and the rest of the boundaries which is more than 5182 km international border is shared with South and South-East Asian countries like Bangladesh (1596 km), Nepal (97 km), Bhutan (455 km), China (1395 km) and Myanmar (1640 km).

Unfortunately, the region's trade share with ASEAN is hovering around 1 to 1.5 per cent of total trade for the last ten years. Most of the trade happens through the port of Kolkata. Therefore, except for the big projects like Trilateral Highway and Kaladan Multi-modal project, which are to be completed in 2022; the region since 1993 is yet to see major policy benefits. If we really want Northeast India as the entry point of 'Act East Policy' along with Kaladan Multi-Modal project and Trilateral Highway, we need to gear up the North-eastern) states in terms of its human resources, public health, inter-regional connectivity – like railway, highway and waterways.

Situation at Border Points

At a time when the discourse on operation mechanism of AEP and its implications is getting its momentum, already initiated measures like formalisation on cross-border trade and the subsequent imposition of GST on traded items are creating conflicting trends. It is premature, but only true to opine that attempts to formalise are leading to more complexities in the Northeast. We can consider the case of Zokhawthar in this regard. Until 2015, Zokhawthar recorded the highest volume of international barter trade in northeast India. The period from 1994 to November 2015 was considered as the booming period for barter trade volume. The formalisation of trade in Zokhawthar became effective in December 2015. The sudden restriction on this age-old trend has deserted Zokhawthar. From Zokhawthar to Tidim (53 km) and Tahan (200 km) in Myanmar, majority of people belong to the Zomi community. As they affiliate to the same cultural communities in Mizoram, people cross the river to meet their relatives without a visa or other valid document. It has become more liberal after Aung San Su Kyi took over the Republic of Myanmar. Therefore, they realised it better to avoid complex formal trade through Zokhawthar.

Community to Community Relations: Critical in Northeast India

A survey of border in Manipur and Myanmar sector in 2013 was opposed by Manipur's Tangkhul, Kuki and Naga communities. Protests from people living in the Moreh, Chorokhunnou and Molchan areas forced the authorities to refer the matter to Manipur government. The fencing would restrict a huge tract of land to Myanmar and would prevent their traditional communication. Govajang is one such village and in 2009, the officials of both India and Myanmar conducted a joint survey for erecting a fence in the area.

There are following five routes that connect the region with Myanmar and subsequently with other regions of South East Asia.

i)   Nampong (Pangsau Pass) at Arunachal Pradesh with Pangsu Land Custom System (LCS) in Myanmar

ii) Moreh-Tamu LCS in Manipur

iii) Zokhawthar (Champai)-Rih LCS in Mizoram

iv) Avangkhu-Somara LCS in Nagaland.

v)   To this, one can add two more border trade points – first is Zorinpuri in the southern portion of Mizoram on the Kaladan route. The second one supplementing Moreh is Behyang-Chikha on the Tiddim road (south of Churchanpur in Manipur).

These are traditional connecting points between the tribes of the region with the ethnic tribes across border. Except the Moreh-Tamu border, other border points, which are not in proper condition, need immediate attention of the government.

Conclusion
India-ASEAN Cooperation in Future: A Few Critical Areas

The three-decade India-ASEAN relationship comes to a new tangent where we need to find areas for future cooperation. The following section identifies a few critical areas of cooperation between India and ASEAN to enhance collaborative association.

i)   India cannot expect ASEAN to play a very pro-India or pro-QUAD security role as ASEAN more or less traditionally plays the role of balancer with some existential notion of autonomy between big power players in the region. They would play a middle strategic position. However, it is expected that ASEAN would be more affirmative in favour of freedom of navigation, free trade, human rights, etc.

ii) Although India slowly was accepted as a potential leader in the region, however, the COVID-19 outbreak and continuous sharpening high curve made many believe that India would be constrained by the pandemic to play a leadership role in the region. As Prof Alan Chong of S Rajaratanam School of International Studies argues – the COVID-19 pandemic will act as a major irritant for India to assume the role of leadership in the region. This is especially very significant as ASEAN has almost become Covid free and countries like Lao PDR, Cambodia, Thailand, and Vietnam have opened up their economies.

iii) Completion of projects on time[4] is most critical and commitment made as term loan or LOC and their timely disbursement is also very critical in enhancing the image of India as serious player in the region. We must see that what had happened in Chabahar in Iran must not be repeated in ASEAN.

If we really want northeast India as the entry point of "Act East Policy" along with Kaladan multi-modal project and Trilateral Highway, we need to gear up the Northeastern states in terms of its human resource training, public health, inter-regional connectivity like railways, highways and waterways so that the region becomes competitive to get attention of Southeast Asia.

Notes

1. Trump administration skipped the meet two years in a row at a critical time when the South East Asia region grapples with China's increasing assertiveness in South China Sea.
2. "For the first time since 2005, lawmakers from both parties and both houses of Congress are pushing to pull the United States out of the trading body it helped create and which was the culmination of decades of post-war efforts to boost free trade and economic integration." "US Effort to depart WTO gathers Momentum" by Keith Johnson.
3. Trump administration withdrew in 2017.
4. Majority of the projects taken in Myanmar and Southeast Asia regions are far behind schedule.

Reference

Johnson, K. (2020). "US Effort to depart WTO gathers Momentum", *Foreign Policy*. 20 May. https://foreignpolicy.com/2020/05/27/world-trade-organization-united-states-departure-china

4. Disease Control and Prevention

New Avenue for the ASEAN-India Cooperation in Post-COVID Era

Lau Sim Yee and *Lau Sim Kim*

Introduction

At the time of writing, the world already is infected with more than 21.83 million Coronavirus cases. While there were roughly 14.56 million recovered, the deaths are more than 773,000. They are 67.9 per cent and 3.5 per cent of infected cases, respectively. The US is leading in this "marathon race of COVID-19", but sadly with more than 5.5 million infected cases and worst still with more than 173,000 deaths.[1] Living with the pandemic is not "Game of Thrones" that the storyline twists here and there among competing claimants.

From containing the outbreak to total elimination of pandemic is full of complexity. Preventing foreign visitors from entering a country and at the same time establishing quarantine facilities is not easy. Entry refusal is politically correct but diplomatically incorrect. Quarantine is a necessary evil but humanely wrong. They are not the best countermeasures, but they are understandably acceptable even though there are people who disagree. Just as important, developing medicine for curing Coronavirus is time-consuming not only in research and development but also in clinical trials before it can be prescribed to the rising number of infected people over time. The complexity needs concerted efforts from all countries concerned.

Against this background, this chapter aims to examine why it is crucially relevant for enhancing the ASEAN-India relations not only in tackling COVID-19, but also in strengthening disease control and prevention in post-COVID-19 era. Also, this chapter plans to suggest specific modalities in undertaking the task, which is of extreme importance for member countries of the Framework Agreement on Economic Cooperation between India and the ASEAN.

Globalisation and COVID-19

While the ongoing pandemic is well-reported and updated in media, but its linkage with globalisation has not attracted serious discussion. This situation is the inconvenient truth. Technological change has driven and will continue to accelerate globalisation, in which the intensity of cross-border exchanges of goods, services and capital has risen amazingly in the last quarter of century. Moreover, movement of people across national boundaries has increased rapidly. These two forces have indeed flattened our planet. Equally serious, the quest for a higher level of living standards has lifted our income but it has also triggered a spectrum of events such as intensified mass production and consumption spanning the globe. Both aspects also induce cross border movement of people. Positive results from travellers and the host are well discussed but stories about illicit activities such as human trafficking, money laundering, smuggling of precious stones and drugs and spread of human-to-human infectious diseases are, unfortunately, mostly kept under the carpet.

A few important premises such as nation-state, market economy, humanitarian requisites such as fundamental human rights, civil society, fairness of distribution, social justice, social well-being in individual health and hygiene have become obscure. It has become doubtful whether everyone understands the same meaning, even those related to the inside. This question is not only necessarily caused by differences in civilisation, culture, and values, but also by the meaning of the word "sustainable social well beings".

No one wants to dispute that globalisation means openness. This process at least implies to the extent of borderless economy. The supporters insist that openness or free trade pushes up competitiveness, but they have not examined its shadow sufficiently. The shadow comprises a situation where government losses room for manoeuvring policy intervention to support some citizens who are affordable to surf along with globalisation waves but infected contiguous diseases abroad. Equally critical, if not more, there are also some citizens who are poorer but infected with contiguous diseases at home. Hence, while government encourages openness, on the one hand, it lost control of better governance that add misery to vulnerable people who live in the sovereign territory on the other hand.

Dani Rodrick shows that the nation-state, democratic politics, and deep integration are in a triangular relation, but these ideals also create a "trilemma" in political economy. Openness brings about deeper integration with the rest of the world. Democratic politics promote policies that support openness and enhanced competitiveness in international marketplace. However, nation-state is the foundation for democratic politics, but it is against immoral and unethical competition that produces a large share of the have not that defeats the greater good of fairness, equality, social well-being within the sovereign territory. Hence, two elements can be mutually inclusive but not three. Democratic politics enhances deep integration and vice versa but nation-state does not respond to deep integration because it is obliged to support a large group of vulnerable citizens – both with and without globalisation. Nation-state and democratic politics are also mutually inclusive if deep integration with the rest of the world is not included[2].

Involvement in activities related to those issues still gives diversified opinions to the extent of disagreement instead of "agree to disagree." This is not only truly unproductive but sometimes it is the inconvenient truth of globalisation that is often being avoided in public policy and discourse. Even when the inconvenient truth is spoken out but still the discussion often has left unclear with what kind of priority is to be undertaken for achieving sustainable social well being. Even if there was an agreement on the type of mechanism for enabling who and how to realise the undertaking, one still could not overlook the fact that, quite often, it did not resolve convincingly because in fact, that is by itself an inconvenient truth.

The question to ask is how can governments, international organisations, scientists, medical and health professionals, and the like work together to contain and then to arrest COVID-19 in the coming months? The inconvenient truth must not obstruct the mission. The goal instead is clear although the roadmap still requires well-defined milestones for accomplishing it. The journey ahead might be a long and winding one but prevention no doubt is of an utmost important effort, to begin with. Louis Pasteur said: "When meditating over a disease, I never think of finding a remedy for it, but, instead, a means of preventing it." Furthermore, in the post-COVID-19 days, with hindsight, to deal with another disease of equivalent scale of Coronavirus, a stronger cooperation between countries and among a group of countries requires forward-looking with specific – in enhanced institutional, in organisational, and in technical capability – in disease control and prevention. We shall examine the relationship between globalisation and pandemic or a large scale outbreak of life-threatening diseases.

Is there a Causality?

This section analyses the relationship between international travellers or tourists and COVID-19 in terms of infected cases and death. This analysis selected 51 countries (see Table A4.1 in Annexure). This investigation focuses on the relationship between international travellers, infected cases, and deaths. Figure 4.1 shows the relationship between infected cases and deaths. This scatter diagram illustrates that the US and Brazil are both above average values of infected cases and deaths. This is not surprising because they are two front runners in this "marathon".

Results in Table 4.1 are quite indicative. This regression explains about 87 per cent of the relationship between deaths and infected cases. The estimated coefficient, viz., infected cases is statistically significant below 1 per cent. The Independent variable in Table 4.1 shows the estimated coefficient suggesting that a 100 infected cases increment influences a rise of about 3 deaths. The estimated coefficient may be higher because as shown in Figure 4.1, the US and Brazil are both higher than mean of infected cases and deaths. We have conducted a robust regression test as shown in Figure 4.2. Normalised residual squared is the difference between the predicted value and the actual (or observed) value. Leverage means the distance between independent variable and its mean. A high leverage point can influence the estimation (i.e., the estimated coefficient).

Figure 4.1: Scatter Diagram of Infected Cases and Death

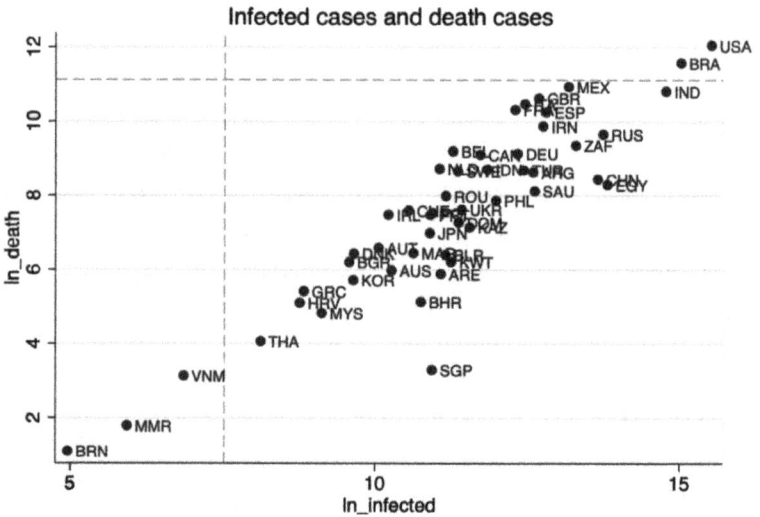

Note: vertical and horizontal dash line is mean of infected cases and deaths, respectively.

Table 4.1: Regression Results (I)

Dependent Variable: Death	Coef.	Std. Err.	t	p> ltl
Infected	.0297	0.0016	18.50	0.000
Constant	888.86	1,755.8750	1.08	0.287

Note: Adj. R-squared = 0.8699, F-value = 340.10.

Figure 4.2: Robust Regression of Deaths and Infected Cases

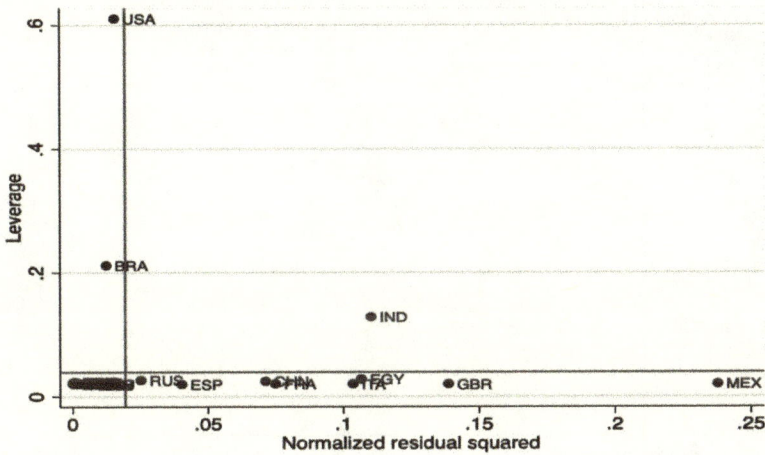

Source: Authors' own.

Table 4.2 shows the regression explaining about 88 per cent of the relationship between deaths, tourists, and infected cases. The estimated coefficients suggest that an increase of 1 million tourists influences 300 deaths, whereas a 1,000 increment of infected cases affects 27 deaths. The latter is quite close to the estimated result shown in Table 4.1. The former hints that mobility in globalisation has a bearing on the spread of Coronavirus. When compared with the analytical sample shown in Table A4.1 (about 1.14 billion tourists), the estimated coefficient for infected cases has about half of the explanatory power. Figure 4.3 shows the robust regression result, which clearly indicates more countries than those in Figure 4.2 have leveraged in this sample.

Table 4.2: Regression Results (II)

Dependent Variable: Death	Coef.	Std. Err.	t	p> ltl
Tourist	0.0003	0.0008	3.50	0.001
Infected	0.0271	0.0017	16.47	0.000
Constant	-3,326.875	3173.375	-1.53	0.1323

Note: Adj. R-squared = 0.8815, F-value = 178.55.

Figure 4.3: Robust Regression of Deaths, Tourists, and Infected Cases

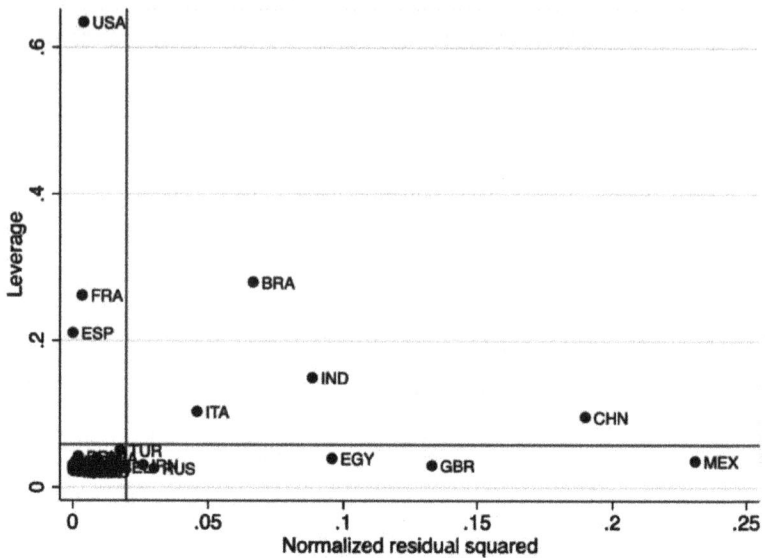

Source: Authors' own.

Present COVID-19 Situation in ASEAN and India:
Fact and Implication

Table 4.3 shows the basic facts of Covid-19 pertaining to ASEAN and India. There were about 148 million (11 per cent of the world total) international tourists who visited these 13 countries (in 2018). There are roughly 2.95 million (20.3 per cent of world total) infected cases as of 16 August 2020. The deaths are approximately 59,000 (about 8 per cent of the world total).

The scatter diagram (Figure 4.4) has three distinct groups: India, Indonesia, and the Philippines are quite far away from the means of infected cases and deaths; Malaysia and Singapore are situated above the mean of infected cases but lower than the mean of deaths; Thailand, Vietnam, Myanmar, and Brunei are all below the means of infected cases and deaths. The first group of countries have done relatively well in either complete lock-down or strict movement control.[3] But, population size, giving non-existence of medicines and vaccines, inevitably caused quite many deaths in each respective

Table 4.3: The ASEAN-India Tourists, Infected Cases and Deaths (Person)

Country	Tourist	Infected	Death
Lao PDR	3,77,000	22	0
Brunei	2,78,000	142	3
Cambodia	62,01,000	273	0
Indonesia	1,58,10,000	1,37,468	6,037
Malaysia	2,58,32,000	9,175	125
Myanmar	35,51,000	374	6
Philippines	71,68,000	1,57,918	2,600
Singapore	1,46,73,000	55,661	27
Thailand	3,81,78,000	3,376	28
Vietnam	1,54,98,000	951	23
sub-total	13,09,59,000	3,65,360	8,913
India	1,74,23,000	25,89,208	50,084
Total	14,83,82,000	29,54,568	58,997

Source: Same as Table A4.1.

Figure 4.4: Scatter Diagram of the ASEAN-India Infected Cases and Death

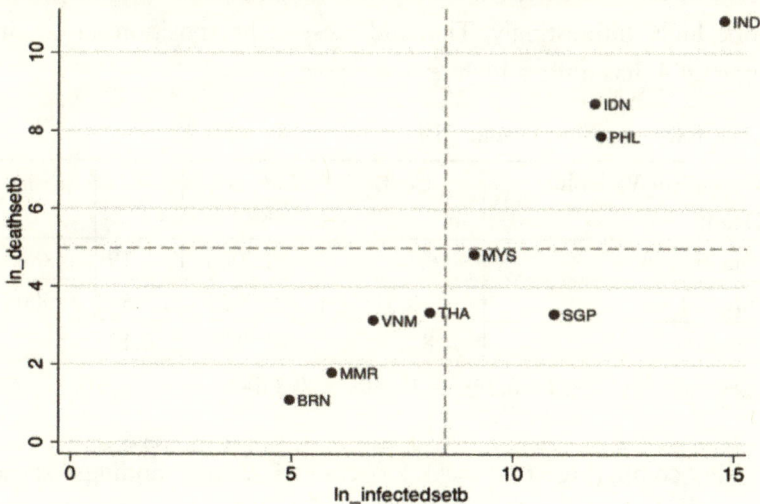

Source: Authors' own

country. Lower deaths in Malaysia and Singapore are the result of imposed movement control and strict quarantine measures.[4] However, pockets of infected clusters have caused many infected people. In the third group, Thailand and Vietnam have done well in containing the spread,[5] whereas Myanmar and Brunei are not seriously affected because of their lesser exposure to globalisation waves.

Our regression results are quite interesting too. The model explains about 99 per cent of the relationship between deaths, inbound international travellers, and infected cases. The estimated independent variable – infected cases – is statistically significant at 1 per cent, whereas international inbound travellers are not statistically significant. The former suggests that a 1,000 increment of infected cases influences about 19 deaths. This is about 10 lesser deaths than the estimated results of 51 countries shown earlier. International inbound travellers do not influence death cases because of strict border controls.

Statistically, India and Indonesia may have influenced substantially on the estimated results. Figure 4.5 shows the leverage point of India, whereas normalised residual square of Indonesia is quite high. Interestingly, Thailand, despite her position shown in Figure 4.4, has quite a high leverage point.

Table 4.4: Regression Results (III)

Dependent Variable: Death	Coef.	Std. Err.	t	p > |t|
tourist_setb	6.65e-06	0.0004	0.19	0.856
infected_setb	0.0193	0.0052	37.65	0.000
constant	81.7259	610.7531	0.13	0.897

Note: Adj. R-squared = 0.89934, F-value = 718.64.

In comparing two sets of countries, the findings show international inbound tourists did not affect deaths in the ASEAN-India regional group. This implies the border control and the strict domestic movement restriction in each country in the last few months

Figure 4.5: Robust Regression of Deaths, Tourists, and Infected Cases in the ASEAN-India

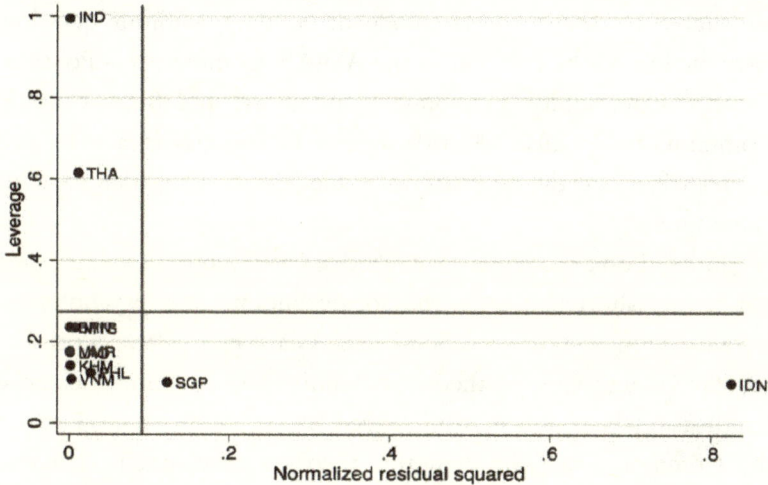

Source: Authors' own.

have helped to contain the spread of COVID-19. Many countries in another set have lifted the restrictions earlier than necessary. Consequently, instead of reinvigorating economic activities and freer mobility for normalising social interactions among citizens, it is quite apparent that the re-emergence of transmission has become alarming. The uncertainty has not diminished yet. Regardless, it is not an exaggeration in saying it is politically incorrect to ignore the clear and present danger created by the invisible COVID-19.

ASEAN-India: Prospects for Closer Integration

ASEAN was established on 8 August 1967. Since then, notwithstanding the First-Second divide, the collapse of the Berlin Wall, this regional group has grown with leaps and bounds. The accessions of Vietnam, Lao PDR, Myanmar and Cambodia in 1990s have elevated the intensity of integration in the last two decades. Their sails were not necessarily smooth. Occasionally, tides were high, and wind was strong. Every member country is pushing deeper and wider regional integration with pragmatic approach based on market-based principles. Each country also adheres to the principle of non-interference. Equally crucial, this group of countries abides by "agree to disagree". The code of conduct, without question, have facilitated the creation of the ASEAN Community – Political-Security Community, Economic Community, and Socio-Cultural Community – in 2015. A wide variety of regional fora is created for transforming the diversity to "One Vision, One Identity, One Community".[6]

India's Look East Policy, launched in 1991, has not only reignited but it has shortened both the socioeconomic and psychological distance with countries in Southeast Asia region. French oriental scholar George Cœdès' theory of "Indianized Kingdom" claimed Southeast Asia region was influenced by Indian civilisation before the Common Era. Although this theory was eloquent, it could not explain the spread of Theravada Buddhism in the continental Southeast Asian countries (Myanmar, Thailand, Cambodia, Laos). Instead, strong influence of "Pali-ism" (Pali Canon) caused these countries to spontaneously be receptive to Indian civilisation in the 4th and the 5th Century.[7] From this historical context, India indeed has rediscovered the long lost cultural and trade linkages with Southeast Asia.

Impressive Indian diplomacy and long historical relationship have cemented the establishment of the "Framework Agreement on Comprehensive Economic Cooperation between the Republic of India and the Association of Southeast Asian Nations" (Framework Agreement) on 1 July 2004.[8] The Framework Agreement led to the creation of the ASEAN-India Free Trade Agreement (AIFTA) on 1 January 2010.[9]

Since then, trade flows between ASEAN and India have picked up notably. The total trade value of this group of countries in 2019 was US$ 3,590 billion, which equates to about 9.5 per cent of total world trade.[10] This is a substantial share from a group of 11 countries. Indian exports to and imports from the ASEAN in 2019 was US$ 33.80 billion and US$ 57.49 billion, respectively. India's trade deficit was US$ 23.7 billion, quite an alarming situation. On

Table 4.5: Total Trade in 2019: the ASEAN and India (US$ billion)

Country	Import	Export
Brunei	5.10	7.04
Cambodia	23.97	19.24
Indonesia	170.73	167.00
Lao PDR	5.80	5.81
Malaysia	204.91	238.09
Myanmar	18.58	18.00
Philippines	117.25	70.93
Singapore	358.97	390.33
Thailand	216.80	233.67
Vietnam	253.44	264.61
India	478.88	323.25
Total	**1,854.43**	**1,737.98**

Source: World Development Indicators, World Bank.

the contrary, the ASEAN's exports to and import from India was US$ 360.9 billion and US$ 337.20 billion, respectively (see Table A4.2 for the intra-ASEAN-India trade). ASEAN's trade surplus was equivalent to India's trade deficit. Therefore, the Indian government is presently asking for the reduction of trade deficit from her counterparts in Southeast Asia. Although this is an alarming situation, but this regional grouping must not let it blur their quest for a deeper and a broader economic integration in the spirit of the Framework Agreement.

Total exports balance total imports in theory. The deficit between India and the ASEAN is compensated by the former's surplus with other countries or regional groups. In this respect, the parties concerned must work together in levelling the imbalance. Otherwise, everyone is "not seeing the wood for the trees", which will defeat the spirit enshrined in the Framework Agreement.

More importantly, trade of itself and by itself are not the sole purpose for a closer integration between ASEAN and India. There is a broad spectrum of mutually beneficial cooperative issues that require equal attention as in the trade front. In this regard, stronger ASEAN-India relations in general, and especially pushing for new cooperation in disease control and prevention in the post-Covid-19 era is surely mutually beneficial.

Disease Control and Prevention in the Post-COVID-19 Period

- ASEAN and India have defined the objectives of Framework Agreement:[11]
- Strengthen and enhance economic, trade and investment co-operation between the parties;
- Progressively liberalise and promote trade in goods and services as well as create a transparent, liberal and facilitative investment regime;
- Explore new areas and develop appropriate measures for closer economic co-operation between the parties; and
- Facilitate the more effective economic integration of the new ASEAN Member States and bridge the development gap among the parties.

The parties are working diligently in achieving them in the last decade. The ferociousness of invisible COVID-19 is unparalleled in recent history. Thus, mutual exploration for specific fields of cooperation is not in the radar. It is certainly "better late than never" to work together in determining what kind of modalities for cooperating in disease control and prevention in the post-COVID-19 era. We must not ignore there are many known unknowns in life-threatening diseases or viruses. For this reason and others, it is politically, socioeconomically, and morally right for member states of the ASEAN and India to iron out the details in realising this area of cooperation.

ASEAN has a regional setup known as "The ASEAN Emergency Operations Centre Network for Public Health Emergency" (ASEAN EOC Network). It falls within the purview of the ASEAN Health Ministers Meeting, under the umbrella of the ASEAN Socio-

Cultural Community. In addition, each member state has a national organisation for working closely with the ASEAN EOC Network. From the early stage of COVID-19, the ASEAN EOC Network has contributed enormously to data collection, information sharing, expertise and experience sharing among member states and many other dialogue partners such as China, Korea, Japan, Australia, France, the EU and others. It also disseminates information regularly for raising awareness and strengthening information flows of disease control and prevention.

To stimulate construction deliberation among the parties, this paper proposes the establishment of the "ASEAN-India Disease Control and Prevention Center (AI-DCPC)". In this respect, member states of ASEAN and India not only can expand the ASEAN EOC Network, but also add new specific response measures in establishing a permanent, action-oriented, information and expertise sharing, strengthening hard and soft institutional and organisational infrastructures, capacity building human resources (including leadership in disease control and prevention) both at national and local levels in each member country. Equally important, the proposed AI-DCPC can solicit cooperation from the established institutions of the same kind in each dialogue partner (such as Australia, China, the EU, Korea, Japan, Russia, the US).

There remains a broad spectrum of specific issues of greatest concern such as financial and human resources, medical and health experts, and others that require detailed study. This task is beyond the scope of this paper, but we intend to study it in not the foreseeable future.

Concluding Remarks

This article has examined, alas narrowly, the imperative and urgent subject matter that is of extreme relevance to the home of 2 billion citizens. The main intention is to raise the awareness of urgency in establishing a regional centre in the form of hub with extended pipes to each member states of the ASEAN-India regional group.

The COVID-19 will persist beyond 2020. Even when this pandemic is contained, everyone must remain resilient in facing new challenges that are life-threatening in coming period. We will certainly feel rewarded with new hope if this paper generates new interests in academic and public discourse of minimising uncertainty of the mercilessness of any invisible enemy like Coronavirus.

The journey to the realisation of the proposed AI-DCPC is likely to be long and winding one. However, we are confident that the committed dedication from individuals, institutions and the business community will surely lay down specific milestones towards the goal. The transformation from unknowns to known without question will make our livelihoods healthier, safer, and rewarding.

Annexure

Table A4.1: Tourists, Infected Cases and Deaths (person)

Country	Tourist	Infected	Death
United States	79.75	5.53	172.61
Brazil	6.62	3.32	107.30
India	17.42	2.59	50.08
Egypt, Arab Rep.	11.20	0.99	4.00
Russian Federation	24.55	0.92	15.62
China	62.90	0.84	4.63
South Africa	10.47	0.58	11.62
Mexico	41.31	0.52	56.54
Spain	82.77	0.36	28.62
Iran, Islamic Rep.	7.30	0.34	19.49
United Kingdom	36.32	0.32	41.36
Saudi Arabia	15.33	0.30	3.37
Argentina	6.94	0.29	5.64
Italy	61.57	0.25	35.39
Turkey	45.77	0.25	5.96
Germany	38.88	0.22	9.29
France	89.32	0.22	30.41
Philippines	7.17	0.16	2.60

Indonesia	15.81	0.14	6.07
Canada	21.13	0.12	9.02
Kazakhstan	8.79	0.10	1.27
Ukraine	14.10	0.09	2.04
Dominican Republic	6.57	0.09	1.44
Sweden	7.44	0.08	5.78
Belgium	9.12	0.08	9.94
Kuwait	8.51	0.08	0.50
Romania	11.72	0.07	2.95
Belarus	11.50	0.07	0.60
United Arab Emirates	21.29	0.06	0.36
Netherlands	18.78	0.06	6.17
Poland	19.62	0.06	1.87
Singapore	14.67	0.06	0.03
Portugal	16.19	0.05	1.78
Japan	31.19	0.05	1.09
Bahrain	12.05	0.05	0.17
Morocco	12.29	0.04	0.63
Switzerland	10.36	0.04	1.99
Australia	9.25	0.03	0.40
Ireland	10.93	0.03	1.77
Austria	30.82	0.02	0.73
Denmark	12.75	0.02	0.62
Korea, Rep.	15.35	0.02	0.31
Bulgaria	9.27	0.01	0.50
Malaysia	25.83	0.01	0.13
Greece	30.12	0.01	0.23
Croatia	16.65	0.01	0.17
Thailand	38.18	0.00	0.06
Vietnam	15.50	0.00	0.02
Myanmar	3.55	0.00	0.01
Cambodia	6.20	0.00	0.00
Brunei	0.28	0.00	0.00

Source: https://data.europa.eu/euodp/en/data/dataset/covid-19-coronavirus-data (retrived on 14 August 2020).

https://www.worldometers.info/coronavirus/(retrived 14 August 2020)

Table A4.2: The Intra-ASEAN-India Trade in 2019 US$ billion)

Country	India	Brunei	Cambodia	Indonesia	Lao PDR	Malaysia	Myanmar	Philippines	Singapore	Thailand	Vietnam	Total Exports
India		0.057	0.204	4.515	0.029	6.269	0.507	1.636	10.739	4.332	5.513	33.799
Brunei	0.581		0.000	0.039	0.000	0.612	0.000	0.119	0.967	0.552	0.199	3.068
Cambodia	0.047	0.020		0.043	0.000	0.165	0.002	0.085	2.099	2.048	0.902	5.411
Indonesia	15.564	0.131	0.619		0.031	8.942	0.873	6.758	12.929	6.213	5.150	57.210
Lao PDR	0.003	0.000	0.017	0.002		0.015	0.002	0.000	0.015	2.407	1.055	3.515
Malaysia	10.408	0.605	0.602	7.737	0.023		0.668	4.387	33.036	13.480	8.383	79.328
Myanmar	0.957	0.001	0.017	0.183	0.003	0.263		0.124	0.327	3.229	0.228	5.331
Philippines	0.557	0.009	0.026	0.821	0.002	2.179	0.048		3.832	2.972	1.270	11.715
Singapore	14.894	0.640	2.270	17.305	0.088	21.606	3.387	6.935		15.354	12.961	95.440
Thailand	7.034	0.118	6.949	9.463	2.916	10.677	2.171	7.249	7.657		11.608	65.843
Vietnam	7.446	0.115	4.311	3.842	0.451	4.726	0.625	3.860	3.647	5.010		34.034
Total imports	57.490	1.694	15.015	43.950	3.544	55.453	8.283	31.152	75.246	55.597	47.268	

Source: https://comtrade.un.org/data/ (retrieved 13 August 2020.

Notes

1. https://www.worldometers.info/coronavirus/ (accessed on 17 August 2020). However, at the time of revision, infected cases have exceeded 91 million – more than 4-fold increase in less than half a year. There are 90 million recovered cases, with 2.5 million deaths representing 2.7 per cent of total infected cases. The US was, sadly, leading with more than 26 million infected cases and even worse, about 380,000 deaths (accessed on 10 January 2021).
2. Dani Rodrick (2012) *The Globalization Paradox: Democracy and the Future of the World Economy*, W. W. Norton.
3. *South Morning China Post*, Free Malaysia Today, New Straits Times, New York Times, *The Economist* and other news medias.
4. Ibid.
5. Ibid.
6. https://asean.org/storage/2012/05/7.-Fact-Sheet-on-ASEAN-Community.pdf (accessed on 15 August 2020).
7. Kiriyama Noboru and others (2019) *A History of Southeast Asia* 2nd Edition (in Japanese), Yuhikaku.
8. https://asean.org/?static_post=framework-agreement-on-comprehensive-economic-cooperation-between-the-republic-of-india-and-the-association-of-southeast-asian-nations-2 (accessed on 14 August 2020).
9. https://www.asean.org/wp-content/uploads/images/2015/October/outreach-document/Edited%20AIFTA.pdf (retrieved on 14 August 2020).
10. https://www.trademap.org/ (accessed on 14 August 2020)
11. https://asean.org/?static_post=framework-agreement-on-comprehensive-economic-cooperation-between-the-republic-of-india-and-the-association-of-southeast-asian-nations-2

References

Kiriyama, N. et al., (2019). *A History of Southeast Asia*, 2nd Edition (in Japanese), Yuhikaku.

Rodrick, D. (2012). *The Globalization Paradox: Democracy and the Future of the World Economy*, W. W. Norton.

News Portals:
The Economists, various issues
Free Malaysia Today, Malaysia
New Straits Times, Malaysia
New York Times, US
South Morning China Post, Hong Kong

URL resources:

Source: https://data.europa.eu/euodp/en/data/dataset/covid-19-coronavirus-data (retrieved 14 August 2020).

https://www.worldometers.info/coronavirus/(accessed on 17 August 2020).

https://www.trademap.org/ (accessed 14 August 2020).

https://asean.org/storage/2012/05/7.-Fact-Sheet-on-ASEAN-Community.pdf (accessed on 15 August 2020).

https://asean.org/?static_post=framework-agreement-on-comprehensive-economic-cooperation-between-the-republic-of-india-and-the-association-of-southeast-asian-nations-2 (access on 14 August 2020).

https://asean.org/?static_post=framework-agreement-on-comprehensive-economic-cooperation-between-the-republic-of-india-and-the-association-of-southeast-asian-nations-2.

https://www.asean.org/wp-content/uploads/images/2015/October/outreachdocument/Edited%20AIFTA.pdf (retrieved 14 August 2020).

5. Changing Landscape of Global Order and ASEAN-India Relations in the Post-COVID-19 Era

Carole Ann Chit Tha

Introduction

The dominant feature of today's world is no more multipolarity but multiplexity marked by complex global and regional linkages. We are witnessing the fast-changing geopolitical and geo-economic environment, which raises concerns about how we can adapt and cope as major powers become more assertive and active in the region. The global structure is gradually shifting away from the post-Cold War "unipolar moment" towards a new order, be it bipolar, or so-called "multiplex order". Great power politics may be constant throughout world history, but it does not reappear in the same way and for the same reasons. We cannot keep using the 19th century European lens to describe the 21st century realities in Asia, Southeast Asia, and the world. The rise of some powers and of Asia as a region does not mean others are declining. It represents a move towards a more even distribution of power. The power distribution in the region is changing. The principle questions are how it is changing and how the region will deal with the changes.

Against the backdrop of the COVID-19 pandemic, we noted the growing uncertainties resulting from the changing geopolitical dynamics in the regional and global landscape and these ways have detrimental ramifications for the region. The emergence of the unprecedented COVID-19 pandemic and its subsequent political and socio-economic ramifications, the rise of geopolitical fragmentation, major powers rivalries, the global economic downturn as well as the non-traditional security threats are the challenges of the global as well as the region. The general response in the region to the evolving changing situation is best described as strategies of "engagement" and multiple "partnerships" rather than the narrower "hedging, balance of power, or traditional alliances approaches". The concept of "balance of power" no longer adequately describes the changing economic and political relationship in the region.

Southeast Asian countries are moving toward a mature and resilient form of multilateral integration taking an approach of "threatening none" through a process of mutual confidence and transparency. We need to call for concrete cooperation that would stimulate the development of mutual trust. The key challenge is whether major powers can commit to cooperation and then implement it. How do states build the will to cooperate? And what if mutual trust takes decades to grow between historic opponents? ASEAN members prefer "Strategic Partnerships" to alliances. Moving beyond managing differences and capitalising on common interests requires a "Strategic Vision" of a new equilibrium for the region. We need to assess how ASEAN is stretching out its relations with dialogue partners especially within the existing ASEAN-India dialogue mechanism. Can ASEAN and India mutually fulfil each other's needs and interests in the post-COVID-19 period looking into the emerging issues of political, economic and socio-cultural dimensions and the strategic changes of a regional and global context?

Given above, Section 2 illustrates the complex situation arising due to COVID-19 and constituting a new global order. ASEAN-India relation in the post-pandemic period is discussed in Section 3. Finally, the conclusion is drawn in Section 4.

COVID-19 and the New Global Order

COVID-19 has brought the world in a complex situation testing our globalised world. The virus spreads across geopolitical boundaries and mankind is facing the most serious global public health emergency. The pandemic came with an unexpected bang which had a profound influence on human life and brought much introspection. The vulnerability of people across all nations in the face of the rampaging COVID-19 not only challenges the traditional conception of national security but also the non-traditional security field of human security. The pandemic has accelerated the urgency of building a community of a shared future for mankind which is the imperative of our time.

The world is realising the need to adapt fast to new ways of living, new ways of work and a new kind of normal. It has become common place to say that the COVID-19 virus leads to a "new normal" in international affairs. With all the uncertainties of the COVID-19 virus, scholars and researchers are assessing what the new normal will be, what normal has been in recent years and what will the new normal look like in the future.

The world is affected by the pandemic which has stirred global diplomacy into a new direction that paved the way for a strengthened digital governance space. We witness the way diplomacy is conducted from conference rooms to online space. Diplomacy cannot be stopped in times of crisis and international cooperation is essential. As the COVID-19 goes viral, diplomacy goes virtual, with new ways of work and new normal while effectively fusing them with our traditional practices.

Pandemics has destroyed everything and produced nothing, causing massive economic, social, political and military impacts on human activities. No one could foresee that the new decade of the 21st century would begin with a rapidly unfolding pandemic that indiscriminately attacks countries, both rich and poor.

The COVID-19 pandemic has also changed the geopolitical landscape and the pandemic has far-reaching implications for the world. The strategic dimension has undergone a major change in both Southeast Asia and India with China's belligerent actions and the US-China Cold War. Professor Amitav Acharya said that the US-China issue was not a Cold War in the region and beyond, but seems more like extreme super power relations. We learnt that China may have been a factor in Southeast Asia's security calculus from time to time and also India's Act East Policy. In recent months, the Chinese actions have met with strong protests from ASEAN. At the ASEAN Virtual Summit in June, ASEAN leaders called for strict adherence by all parties to the maritime laws and order as enunciated in the UNCLOS marks a shift, albeit small, in ASEAN's stand. ASEAN countries also subscribe to the principle of open and free navigation in the region.

Scholars and analysts assess US-China to activate and open all channels of dialogue to prevent miscalculation, put all the issues on the table and address the difference, review and agree on the interactions specifying all areas, identifying the tough issues that need proper management that US-China have little chance to agree on in the near future.

ASEAN and ASEAN-India Relations in the Post-COVID-19

Unsettled regional hotspot issues and emerging tensions and competition among major players are also destabilising the regional landscape. In the year 2020, ASEAN chairmanship's theme of "Cohesive and Responsive ASEAN Community" was of great relevance to the needs of today and appropriate as ASEAN has been faced with unprecedented challenges posed by the COVID-19. The leaders in the joint statement have pledged to strengthen mechanisms to create a region "capable of dealing with the current global challenges" and "reduce the impacts of COVID-19 through comprehensive recovery plans". In the statement, the leaders also acknowledged the growing uncertainties of the changing geopolitical dynamics in the regional and global landscape which may have detrimental ramifications for the region. Amidst the growth of geopolitical and major power rivalries, ASEAN positions itself to be neutral while reassuring its unity cohesiveness and resilience. With the changing landscape of global order, there are queries on how do ASEAN and its regional collaborations contribute towards the regional and international peace, security, stability and prosperity?

How will ASEAN connect and lead the world? How can ASEAN and its dialogue partners mutually fulfil each other's needs and interests? The Agenda of ASEAN should not merely be the priorities of ASEAN, but by being relevant to the rest of the world and benefitting from the emerging global trend. ASEAN should voluntarily be the main contributor to the world at large by setting up stronger and broader visions, and likewise, remaining resilient and relevant to the shift of global landscape. Fostering ASEAN Unity, ASEAN Centrality and its role as a primary driving force in the evolving regional architecture is vital. There is a need for ASEAN to continue fostering closer cooperation with dialogue partners, to strengthen its engagement with external parties who can contribute positively to ASEAN Unity, ASEAN Solidarity and ASEAN Community building efforts.

ASEAN is also collaborating with their development and dialogue partners. ASEAN is open to trans-regional multilateral cooperation on the COVID-19. The pandemic offers India an opportunity to ramp up its public diplomacy in Southeast Asia and show its willingness and wherewithal to undertake mutually beneficial collaborations. Ultimately, this would help India broaden and deepen the scope of Act East Policy and secure greater legitimacy for future regional projects.

Within the existing ASEAN-India dialogue mechanism, ASEAN and India will enable two-way knowledge sharing, exchange of technical expertise, and transfer of best practice norms to mutual benefit. The India-ASEAN Plan of Action (2016-2020) had an embedded component of "Health and Pandemic Preparedness and Response". A major provision within this is working together "to enhance ASEAN's preparedness and capacity in responding to communicable and emerging infectious diseases including pandemics" through "preparedness planning preventive efforts, and capacity building". It also includes "the strengthening of area on surveillance, laboratory networking, human resource capacities, and information networking". The health component is also present in the India-ASEAN Dialogue Relations Agenda, as updated in July 2019.

A long-term impact of sustained Indian collaboration with ASEAN over pandemics is that a stronger, more effective and more outcome-oriented Act East Policy would automatically entail greater engagement, including smoother physical connectivity and higher people-to-people contact. To keep the policy's momentum going, crisis-time collaboration is critical.

In the midst of the extraordinary challenge and uncertainty of the pandemic, we need to consider whether there is space for regional cooperation in crisis management and recovery, how might ASEAN and India use this moment to build a more prosperous, equitable and sustainable world. Regional cooperation offers critical opportunities for learning from others and to achieve collectively what would not be possible at the individual country level.

Global problems are best solved with global leadership, which has been lacking during the COVID-19 pandemic. The long-term geopolitical lesson from COVID-19 is not that nationalism must win out over globalism but that we can no longer assume a single country will take on that responsibility. Other countries need to think about how to facilitate international cooperation to deal with global threats in an environment in which great powers fail to lead and may become increasingly fractious. Leaders across the world must cooperate to fight against the virus, collectively eliminating it without being distracted by political differences but by focusing on the extraordinary challenges that lie within their own borders.

In the post-COVID-19 period, India should focus on adopting mutual best practices in the area of health security for the people. We have noted how India's support in the form of medical equipment and medicines to Southeast Asian countries during the pandemic has shown its commitment to work together with the neighbours during the hour of their need. Collaboration in pharmaceutical and vaccine research can be an area of considerable significance in India's Act East Policy. The way Indian Prime Minister is handling the situation is being appreciated by the world assuring India will play a greater role in the new world order post-COVID-19.

Conclusion

We learnt that the pandemic is temporary, but cooperation is everlasting. We have witnessed how fragile the international community's solidarity and cooperation is in the face of this pandemic. The pandemic is not over yet and there remain challenges but turn the crisis into opportunity and make the best use of it. It is too early to forecast what the global order may look like once the pandemic has moved past its worst stage. There are many challenges and conflicts that could face the world as the next disaster looms beyond the COVID-19 pandemic. In the midst of world order in flux, uncertainties underscore the need for global cooperation more than ever. At present, it is difficult to discern the shape, form or substance of the post-COVID-19 world order.

Our world will be transformed by this COVID-19 pandemic. Our responses, nationally, regionally and internationally, will determine whether we are able to learn from this crisis in order to forge a more resilient and sustainable approach to globalisation. There is no "one-size-fits-all" approach to managing the virus. Countries take the challenge seriously with timely steps to mitigate the impact. We need to emphasize dialogue as a bridge to realise concrete cooperation. Communication is a prerequisite for improved relations as well as a way to mitigate miscalculations. Various factors have contributed to South and Southeast Asian countries and beyond for their success, including definitive government actions, experience with pandemics like SARS, MERS, and cultural norms, resulting in better timeliness, preparedness, and ability to adapt as circumstances changed. ASEAN and India have deployed efficient testing and contact tracing systems, tailored technological solutions and community measures. Opportunities like think tank roundtable and other virtual dialogues to exchange experiences and to learn from each other are important and can be very helpful for ASEAN-India to get a better understanding and further strengthen our cooperation.

References

ASEAN Secretariat (2016). "India-ASEAN Plan of Action to Implement the ASEAN-India Partnership for Peace, Progress and Shared Prosperity (2016-2020)", Jakarta.

Aye Thandar Soe (2020). "ASEAN: at 53rd and Beyond-Remaining Resilient and Relevant to the shift of Global Landscape", *The Global Newlight of Myanmar*, August 15, 2020.

Choudhury, A. and Nagda, A. (2020). "India's Covid-19 opportunity in Southeast Asia", *The Diplomat*, June 4, 2020.

Kurbalija, J (2020). "Diplomacy goes virtual as the coronavirus goes viral", *DiPLO*, March 6, 2020.

Miyake, K. (2020). "The Post Covid-19 International Order", *The Japan Times*, April 6, 2020.

Sood, R. (2020). "The Trends shaping the post-Covid-19 World", *The Hindu*, May 11, 2020.

Tirkey, A. (2020). "Uncharted Territory: Emerging World Order Post Covid-19", *ORF, Global Policy*, June 25, 2020.

SECTION II: Emerging Value Chains: Opportunities for ASEAN and India in the Post-COVID-19 Period

6. Emerging Value Chains
Opportunities for ASEAN and India in Post-COVID-19 Period

Ramesh Kodammal

Introduction

Strengthening economic ties with India has been discussed for long, and, in continuation, ASEAN-India Business Council (AIBC) had put forward various recommendations to the annual consultations of the ASEAN Economic Ministers and India. These recommendations are, among others, enhancing participation of MSMEs in the expansion of ASEAN-India trade and investment, including supporting digitalisation of MSMEs, empowering and increasing participation of youth and women entrepreneurship, expanding Fintech and desire by both sides to increase imports and exports towards a more balanced trade.

In today's trade architecture, Global Value Chains (GVC) are important factors that can move forward trade engagements in the post-COVID-19 environment (Kodammal, 2016, 2021). The potentials to expand participation in the GVCs remain high in electrical and electronics, machinery, automotive, agriculture, agro-food, pharmaceuticals and medical equipment sectors.

Currently, despite the huge potentials of an integrated market through the ASEAN-India FTA and growing global importance, trade and industrial linkages are still low, and dominated by exports and imports of few products (MEA, 2017). Participation of ASEAN in the GVCs is higher than India. And, this has got to do with the success of ASEAN attracting Foreign Direct Investments (FDIs) from the US, the EU, China, Japan, Taiwan and Hong Kong to set up manufacturing units in the region in order to take advantage of the ASEAN Economic Community (AEC) as well as ASEAN's Free Trade Agreements with major partners.

The rest of the chapter is designed as follows: Section 2 describes ASEAN-India trade and potential areas of GVC. Section 3 presents the importance of GVC in post-pandemic period. Section 4 mentions that India needs to rethink the decision of withdrawal from RCEP. Concluding remarks are drawn in Section 5.

Outlook of ASEAN-India Trade and GVC

As both ASEAN and India are vying for increasing their participation in the GVCs, it is imperative that ASEAN-India trade and industrial linkages are strengthened. An analysis of the pattern of trade over the last 10 years shows that trade has not been growing exponentially as envisaged at the time of the signing of the ASEAN-India free trade agreement. In absolute terms, trade between ASEAN and India has increased from US$ 56.7 billion in 2010 to US$ 81.0 billion in 2018. However, this is still short of the target of US$ 100 billion by 2015, set at the 10th ASEAN India Summit in November 2012.

Notwithstanding the low trade, it is very encouraging to note that in recent years trade between ASEAN and India has begun to diversify and include electrical and electronics and automotive products. For example, the total value of trade in automotive vehicles and parts in 2019 was US$ 2.13 billion. ASEAN exports US$ 697.9 billion worth of auto products but imports USS 1.43 billion. This shows that India is a supplier of auto parts and components to the automotive manufacturers based in ASEAN. Similarly, ASEAN's trade with India in electrical and electronics products totalled US$ 9.6 billion in 2019 (ASEAN's exports US$ 8.44 billion to India and imports US$ 1.2 billion from India).

In order to increase participation of ASEAN and India in the GVCs, the following two sectors having huge potentials for trade and industrial linkages could be explored. These two sectors are

(i) agriculture and Agro-food Products, and (ii) pharmaceutical and medical equipment.

There are huge potentials for raising the participation of ASEAN and India in the GVCs by enhancing trade in agricultural and agro-food products (MoCI, 2021; Kodammal, 2021). The cooperation in agriculture and forestry must be taken to a much higher level. Apart from focusing on food security, the COVID-19 provides ASEAN and India with an opportunity to relook at facilitation and promotion of trade in agriculture and food, and facilitating private sector investments in large scale food production in the region to serve both the regional and global markets. ASEAN and India could develop strong partnerships to ensure a sustainable supply of sufficient, affordable, safe and nutritious foods that meet the dietary requirements of its populations as well as supplying to the global market and building and becoming part of the GVCs.

GVCs in Post-Pandemic

The COVID-19 pandemic has opened the potential for ASEAN and India to also enhance cooperation on increasing trade in pharmaceuticals and medical equipment. Like the agriculture and agro-food sector, the pharmaceuticals and medical equipment sectors could be developed with the view of ASEAN and India becoming major players in the GVCs.

India can gain by further integrating with ASEAN and increasing participation in the GVCs by building on ASEAN's potentials (De, 2021). According to the available data, ASEAN is much more integrated with the other East Asian countries such as China, Japan, Korea, Taiwan and Hong Kong. The volume of trade with these countries is substantial. For example, China's trade with ASEAN in 2018 was US\$ 482 billion, US\$ 231 billion with Japan, US\$ 161 billion with Korea, US\$ 119 billion with Taiwan and US\$110 billion with Hong Kong. The huge investments by these countries in manufacturing and services related activities have led to ASEAN's participation in the global value chains. Trade is diversified and more than half of the products traded include intermediate goods such as electrical and electronics, machinery, automotive, etc.

As these countries now try and diversify investment locations and reconfigure production processes in the post-COVID-19 period, it is believed that ASEAN is much better placed to attract more knowledge-based and high-value investments. Japan and the US are likely to consider diverting some of their investments into ASEAN, away from China.

At the same time, there is also an opportunity for India to enhance the trade and industrial linkages with ASEAN. With increasing production facilities and services in the region, ASEAN will also be in a better place to look at sourcing intermediate products and services for the GVCs from India, especially partnering SMEs in India to produce intermediate products for companies operating out of ASEAN. This also requires SMEs in India to be more responsive in terms of price competitiveness and quality (Kodammal, 2021).

Regional Comprehensive Economic Partnership: India Need to Relook

India's withdrawal from the Regional Comprehensive Economic Partnership (RCEP) will see ASEAN becoming more and more integrated with the five partner countries, namely, China, Japan, Korea, Australia and New Zealand. Thus, it will not be surprising if ASEAN's participation in the GVCs will become more intensified. It is expected that over the next few years if ASEAN and India can build on enhancing industrial linkages, the trade pattern could be more broad-based and diversified.

From a businessman's view, if India re-joins RCEP, the potentials of increasing India's participation in the GVCs could be substantially increased. From a geopolitical point of view, ASEAN also needs to diversify its market and trading partners beyond the East Asian countries. India offers that alternative for ASEAN.

RCEP has already been signed in 2020 comprising ASEAN 10 and its five major trading partners, namely, Australia, China, Japan, Korea and New Zealand. After almost seven years of negotiations,

India decided to withdraw from the pact that is likely to transform the economic landscape of Asia. So, perhaps India could rethink its decision to withdraw from the RCEP.

Finally, as AIBC representative, I would like to recommend to the governments of ASEAN and India to review the ASEAN-India FTA in Goods, signed in 2010. ASEAN and India must be able to identify the gaps and make further commitments to open trade opportunities through the review. There are still over 20 per cent of the products subject to various levels of import duty.

Concluding Remarks

It is strongly urged that ASEAN and India should re-engage and re-intensify and build trust to forge closer economic relations. Harping on continued trade deficit that India has with ASEAN will not take us forward, but rather ASEAN and India should work to increase trade. Important to take note that ASEAN is a huge and open market and trade (exports and imports) is around US$ 3 trillion or ASEAN imports close to US$ 1.4 trillion worth of goods.

Indian companies should not continue to demand for protection and depend on only the Indian market. India needs to get its companies to be competitive and export to other regional and global markets. While India may have its reasons for not joining RCEP, but in the long run, it is not to India's advantage as the other RCEP countries will take advantage of the absence of India to increase trade with ASEAN. ASEAN-India trade may not grow significantly if this happens.

References

De, Prabir (2021). "Patience please: India's ASEAN journey has much further to go", *The Mint*, 24 February 2021, https://www.livemint.com/opinion/online-views/patience-please-india-s-asean-journey-has-much-further-to-go-11614184689235.html

Kodammal, Ramesh (2021). "Strengthening ASEAN-India MSMEs", Speech Delivered at the 18th ASEAN-India Economic Ministers Meeting, 14 September 2021, https://www.bernama.com/en/world/news.php?id=2003817

Kodammal, Ramesh (2016). "Co–Manufacturing: Creating Manufacturing Value Chains", Speech Delivered at the Delhi Dialogue, New Delhi.

Ministry of Commerce and Industry (MoCI) (2021). Press Release, https://pib.gov.in/PressReleaseIframePage.aspx?PRID=1754798

Ministry of External Affairs (MEA) (2017). "ASEAN-India Relations", New Delhi, https://mea.gov.in/Portal/ForeignRelation/ASEAN_India_August_2017.pdf

7. Emerging Value Chain Opportunities Post-COVID-19 and India-ASEAN Relations

Rupa Chanda

Introduction

Recent years have witnessed trade tensions between major nations coupled with growing protectionism, economic nationalism, and challenges posed by the new industrial revolution. These trends and slowing economic growth have caused global trade to stagnate in the last few years and have brought the world economy to an inflection point where countries are rethinking their approach to globalisation. The outbreak of the COVID-19 pandemic in early 2020 has now further tipped the scales by severely disrupting global trade and output and by exposing the vulnerabilities that come with global integration.

According to WTO estimates, global merchandise trade is expected to decline by 13 to 32 per cent in 2020 and global GDP may contract by 2.5 to 8.8 per cent, depending on different scenarios.[1] Most regions of the world are expected to suffer double-digit declines in exports and imports in 2020.[2] Entire sectors of economies have been shut down, affecting production, supply chains, trade and FDI. The effects of this pandemic on world trade are expected to be long lasting, akin to what happened after the global financial crisis of 2009 when global trade never returned to its pre-crisis growth trajectory. However, this time the challenge to globalisation is possibly more serious. This is because the very model of distributed international production, i.e., Global Value Chains (GVCs), which have been based on scale, supplier networks, and cost arbitrage over the past two decades, is under question today.

Countries have realised how vulnerable they are if they are largely dependent on a few overseas suppliers. The case of the pharmaceutical industry where 80 per cent of active components are based on global sourcing from one or two supplier countries or the case of electronic equipment where 40 per cent of the parts are sourced from one single country[3] have brought these vulnerabilities to the fore. Restrictions on transport and travel and social distancing norms have further compounded the challenges associated with such a distributed production model. Thus, in the aftermath of COVID-19, countries and companies will have to increasingly re-examine their strategies for internationalisation, including both trade and FDI policies.[4]

Several dynamics will be at play in this process, building upon recent trends in protectionism and Industry 4.0. These include the forces of automation, digitalisation, re-shoring, near shoring, diversification, regionalisation, localisation, and divestment, among others. As a result, the world is likely to see new configurations of production networks, suppliers, and supply chains which focus much more on building resilience as well as national and regional productive capacity than in the past. Such forces will in turn affect both global and regional trade flows and the positioning of countries in GVCs and Regional Value Chains (RVCs).

Motivation

For a country like India, which has till date not been a major player in GVCs but which is seeing a renewed thrust on developing manufacturing capacity and incentivising FDI, these shifts present new opportunities. As countries and Multinational Enterprises (MNEs) increasingly look to diversify their sourcing and strategically evaluate critical components of their value chains, and as global demand increases in certain sectors such as healthcare, pharmaceuticals, and digitally delivered services post the pandemic,

India could potentially gain from the production and demand shifts. Post the pandemic, around 1,000 foreign firms have been involved in discussions with Indian authorities and around 300 of these companies are pursuing production plans in India in various sectors such as medical devices, textiles, electronics and mobiles. Such realignments in production bases and value segments could not only help India augment its manufacturing capacity but could also create new opportunities for India to participate in regional and global value chains, particularly with partners such as ASEAN which are well integrated in distributed production networks, and with whom India has a free trade agreement. Furthermore, the likely acceleration of digitisation, AI, and IoT, in a post-COVID-19 world, could also provide a boost to India's MSMEs, startups and digitally based industries to enter into global digital supply chains.

Outline

This article explores the sectors and particular niches where India may have potential opportunities to enter and expand its role in GVCs in the world and specifically in its relations with ASEAN, in a post-COVID-19 scenario. Section 2 outlines existing GVC participation trends and patterns for India and ASEAN to identify areas of strength on both sides and complementarities between the two. Section 3 focuses on possibilities for services linkages and for servicification between India and ASEAN, i.e., how India could leverage its services capabilities to enter the manufacturing value chain in the ASEAN countries. Section 4 concludes by highlighting the domestic policies and strategies needed in India as well as the issues that would need to be addressed in bilateral negotiations to realise the linkages between India and ASEAN.

GVC Trends in Manufacturing in India and ASEAN

A common concern voiced about India's integration with the world market is its low levels of GVC participation, especially when compared to countries in Southeast and East Asia. This is well highlighted in Figures 1 and 2. India's backward as well as forward participation rates[5] in manufacturing remain below that of most ASEAN countries and of ASEAN as a whole. The declining forward participation rates over the 2005-2015 period reflect the inability of Indian manufacturing to compete and enter value chains overseas.

Table 7.1 illustrates the industry-wise decomposition of this participation to highlight how India fares in individual industries in its linkages with the world and with ASEAN. Several salient features can be observed. First, India's backward participation rates in manufacturing are much higher than its forward participation rates, indicating that integration through imported intermediates is greater than integration through supply of intermediates and value-added content to partner's exports. Second, backward participation is much higher in certain manufacturing industries such as electronics, transport equipment, and chemicals and pharmaceutical products, reflecting India's dependence on imported intermediates in these industries. Third, the dependence on ASEAN as a source for most industries is at par with that from the world, indicating the presence of sourcing linkages with Asian suppliers in Indian manufacturing. Fourth, India's forward participation rates, although low in general, are higher with ASEAN than with the world for manufacturing as a whole and in several industries, indicating the potential to integrate with the ASEAN production network in manufacturing. Finally, we observe that for both ASEAN and India, backward linkages are stronger than forwarding linkages, indicating that sourcing for meeting domestic capacity requirements prevails over sourcing for further processing and exports by the other.

Figure 7.3 further shows that while there is significant sourcing among ASEAN countries in certain industries, India is not an important contributor to this regional network.[6] Its value-added contribution to ASEAN's exports has remained low and stagnant across all industries while that of most ASEAN member countries has increased over the 2005-15 period, such as for Vietnam in case of textiles and apparel, Singapore in chemicals and pharmaceutical products, and Thailand in transport equipment. This is also in contrast to China's contribution to ASEAN's exports, indicating that

Figure 7.1: Backward GVC Participation in Manufacturing for India, Selected ASEAN Countries and China, Selected Years (%)

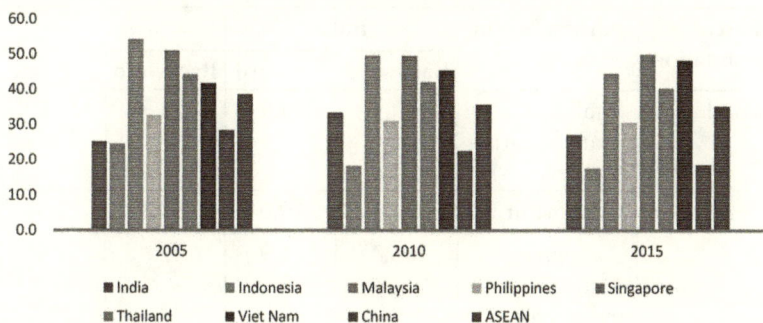

Source: OECD, Stats.

Figure 7.2: Forward GVC Participation in Manufacturing for India, Selected ASEAN Countries and China, Selected Years (%)

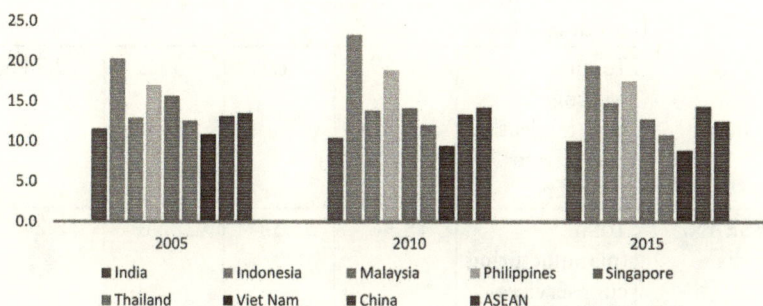

Source: OECD, Stats.

India is at a relative disadvantage compared to China in the ASEAN market. This may again point to the lack of FDI based export networks in sectors such as electronics, transport, and textiles, which are present in case of ASEAN-China relations but not in case of India.

Figure 7.4 shows the share of value-added contributed by ASEAN countries in India's exports. Although this share is low, unlike the stagnant shares exhibited earlier for India in ASEAN's exports, we find that there is an increase in the case of some ASEAN member countries, such as Thailand and Malaysia and for ASEAN as a whole, in India's exports. Thus, there is asymmetry in the

Table 7.1: Industry-wise Breakdown of Backward and Forward Participation Rates for India, ASEAN and China, 2015 (%)

Source/ Destination	Industry/Sector	India		ASEAN	
		Backward	Forward	Backward	Forward
World	Total (manufacturing cum services)	19.09	14.9	28.9	17.02
	Manufacturing	27.26	10.0	35.3	12.53
	Computers, electronic and electrical equipment	36.24	1.9	42.6	4.69
	Transport equipment	26.36	1.6	38.8	1.57
	Chemicals and pharmaceutical products	24.69	1.4	33.7	1.26
	Textiles, wearing apparel, leather and related products	16.39	1.1	33.2	0.94
ASEAN/ India	Total (manufacturing cum services)	18.96	27.54	22.96	12.21
	Manufacturing	29.34	17.81	29.14	9.42
	Computers, electronic and electrical equipment	36.22	5.96	42.45	0.68
	Transport equipment	25.26	1.11	37.92	0.72
	Chemicals and pharmaceutical products	24.69	2.38	33.72	1.37
	Textiles, wearing apparel, leather and related products	16.39	1.58	32.82	1.00

Source: OECD Stats.

relative importance of India in ASEAN's exports versus that of ASEAN in India's exports, indicative of the growing asymmetry in India-ASEAN gross trade relations which has led to India's rising bilateral trade deficit with ASEAN. Figures 7.3 and 7.4 also highlight China's growing importance as a source country in both India's and ASEAN's exports, thus pointing to India's lack of competitiveness relative to China in the ASEAN market.

An examination of India-ASEAN relations in intermediate product exports, which is another way of understanding value chain linkage, reveals the potential for India to enter the ASEAN market through intermediate exports in industries such as electrical equipment and transport equipment. The latter have exhibited rising shares over the 2005-2015 period. It is also interesting to note that India's penetration of ASEAN's intermediates market in other industries such as chemicals and pharmaceuticals, and in textiles and apparel has been poor, while that of China has increased significantly, suggestive of India's relative disadvantage compared to China in these manufacturing industries.

Figure 7.3: Value-Added Content of Countries as a Share of Value-Added Content of the World in ASEAN's Exports for Selected Industries

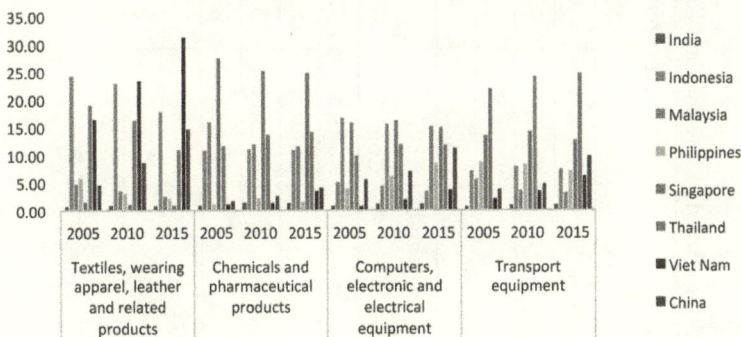

Source: OECD Stats.

Thus, the overall evidence on GVC linkages, as measured by different indicators, suggests that there are untapped opportunities and areas where India-ASEAN relations can be increased in the manufacturing sector. From the Indian perspective, sectors such as

Table 7.2: Domestic Value-Added in Intermediate Exports of India, ASEAN, China to Selected Partners (%)

Industry/Sector	Exporter- India			Exporter- ASEAN			Exporter-China		
	Partner	2005	2015	Partner	2005	2015	Partner	2005	2015
Total (manufacturing cum services)	ASEAN	9.2	10.82	India	4.72	5.97	ASEAN	8.25	11.71
	China	9.86	8.72	China	15.12	24.55	India	2.26	3.97
Manufacturing	ASEAN	8.21	8.58	India	3.35	4.61	ASEAN	7.96	11.57
	China	7.1	10.75	China	19.42	31.32	India	2.21	4.14
Textiles, wearing apparel, leather and related products	ASEAN	2.35	3.6	India	1.6	1.35	ASEAN	4.84	11.08
	China	3.61	18.37	China	6.42	20.22	India	1.83	1.95
Chemicals and pharmaceutical products	ASEAN	9.65	8.39	India	7.85	10.58	ASEAN	10.05	13.64
	China	11.78	10.03	China	24.78	37.3	India	7.35	14.96
Computers, electronic and electrical equipment	ASEAN	6.62	10.72	India	1.85	1.91	ASEAN	8.86	10.21
	China	3.99	7.55	China	28.71	48.26	India	1.52	2.76
Transport equipment	ASEAN	5.6	9.33	India	2.38	1.75	ASEAN	4.76	7.69
	China	0.41	1.18	China	1.58	4.64	India	0.7	1.45

Source: OECD Stats.

Figure 7.4: Value-Added Content of Countries in India's Exports as a Share of Value-Added Content of the World in India's Exports for Selected Industries

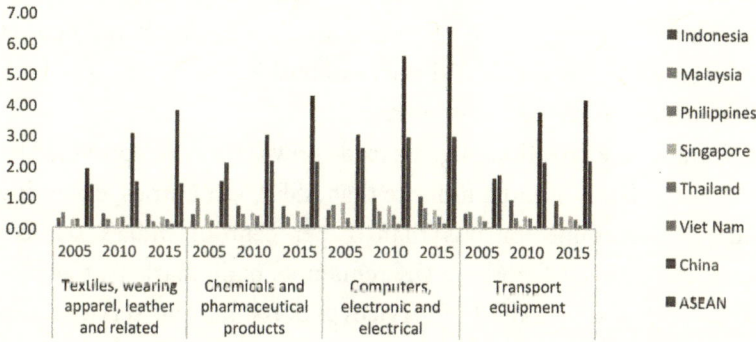

Source: OECD Stats.

transport equipment and electrical equipment show most potential for strengthening linkages with ASEAN, while in sectors such as textiles and apparel and chemicals, India's position appears to be weaker compared to other partners such as China.

These trends are pertinent against the backdrop of the government's "Make in India" initiative to increase manufacturing capacity and competitiveness, recent announcements following the pandemic, to increase self-reliance in several of these industries, and shifting strategies of some MNEs to relocate and diversify their investments from China to other countries. India and ASEAN nations could potentially leverage these developments by positioning themselves within different segments of these industries. This would require an understanding of the specific segments and parts of the value chain within each industry to identify where their strengths lie and in the bilateral context to identify areas of overlap and complementarity between India and ASEAN where value chain linkages, backward and forward, could be created and enhanced.

GVC Opportunities in Services for India and ASEAN

Most of the focus in India-ASEAN relations has been on manufacturing sector linkages. However, GVC opportunities in services warrant a closer look given the fact that India is relatively more competitive in services than in goods, as indicated by its higher penetration of global services compared to goods exports. Moreover, services are a sector where India has consistently sought market access under comprehensive agreements as a trade-off for market access conceded in goods and thus establishing GVC linkages with FTA partners in services is important.

Data on the direction of gross trade flows in services provided by the Reserve Bank of India indicate that ASEAN countries, excepting Singapore, account for less than 1 per cent of India's services exports while the US and the UK remain its main markets, together accounting for over half of its services exports. In some services such as computer and information services, the US and the UK account for over 80 per cent of India's exports while ASEAN's share stands at less than 5 per cent. Similarly, this region accounts for a very small share in India's services imports, except for Singapore whose significance in India's services import basket has grown over time and spans a variety of subsectors.

Figure 7.5: Backward GVC Participation in Services for India, Selected ASEAN Countries and China (%)

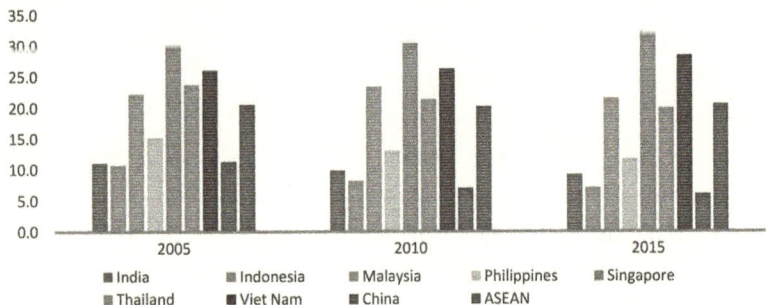

| 2005 | 2010 | 2015 |

■ India   ■ Indonesia   ■ Malaysia   ■ Philippines   ■ Singapore
■ Thailand   ■ Viet Nam   ■ China   ■ ASEAN

Source: OECD Stats.

An examination of GVC participation by India and ASEAN in services also reflects this low level of integration. Both backward and forward participation rates with the world are much lower for both India and ASEAN (excepting Singapore) in the service sector. These low participation levels are likely to reflect the many border and behind-the-border restrictions which impede services trade.

Figure 7.6: Forward GVC Participation for India, Selected ASEAN Member Countries and China (%)

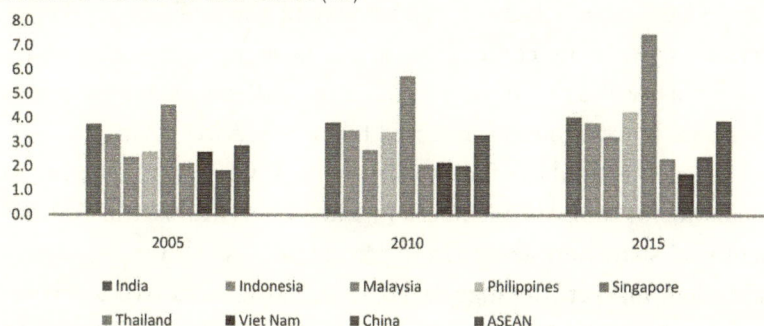

■ India   ■ Indonesia   ■ Malaysia   ■ Philippines   ■ Singapore
■ Thailand   ■ Viet Nam   ■ China   ■ ASEAN

Source: OECD Stats.

A similar picture emerges if one considers bilateral value chain linkages between India and ASEAN in services. India's value-added contribution to services exports of ASEAN members is extremely low and has not shown any increase over the 2005-2015 period, not even in subsectors such as IT and other business services where India is known to be competitive. This is in stark contrast to ASEAN member countries such as the Philippines in the case of IT and information services, Singapore in financial services (with very high shares), Malaysia and Singapore in transport services, and Singapore and the Philippines in other business services. The contribution of ASEAN countries in the region's services exports has also grown

Figure 7.7: Value Added Content of Countries as a Share of Value-Added Content of the World in ASEAN's Exports in Selected Services Subsectors (%)

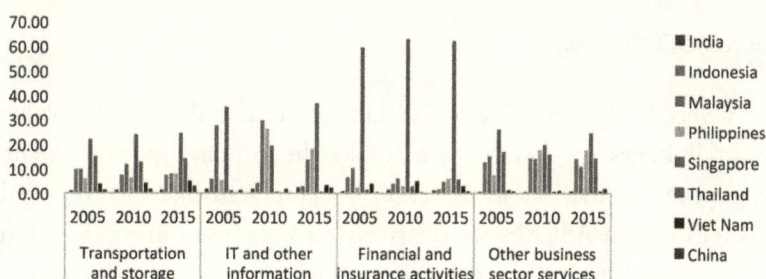

■ India
■ Indonesia
■ Malaysia
■ Philippines
■ Singapore
■ Thailand
■ Viet Nam
■ China

Source: OECD Stats.

over this time period, indicating increased intraregional dependence on services. India's lack of penetration in the ASEAN market in services, even in its competitive areas, is suggestive of regulatory barriers as well as cultural and linguistic differences with ASEAN which are known to have hindered bilateral services relations.

Figure 7.8 similarly indicates that the low levels of penetration also hold for ASEAN members in India's services sector. ASEAN members' shares are less than 2 per cent across all the services in the Indian market, the highest being in the subsector of transport services. Further ASEAN's value-added contribution in Indian services exports has either stagnated or declined over the time period, while that of China, albeit with low shares, shows a much greater increase. These trends indicate India's lack of diversification in its trade relations in the service sector with the Asia-Pacific region, as well as the restrictions that prevail in India's services sector which impede entry of foreign services providers.

Figure 7.8: Value-Added Content of Countries as a Share of the World in India's Exports of Selected Services (%)

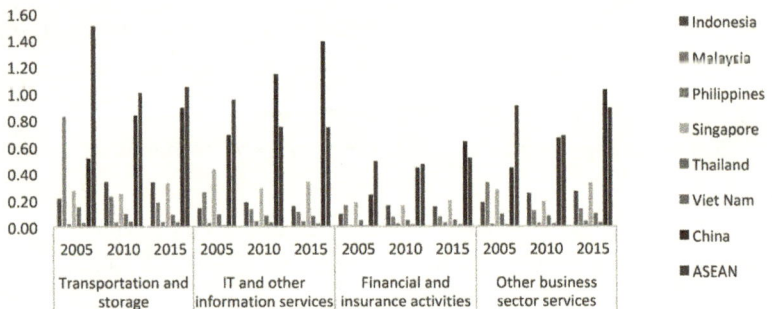

Source: OECD Stats.

Overall, Figures 7.7 and 7.8 indicate that India-ASEAN value chain linkages in services are weak, the primary partner being Singapore. Further, as in the case of manufacturing, intraregional linkages within ASEAN are relatively stronger even in services and India has not been able to participate in this regional value chain. Hence, only if bilateral constraints and regulatory barriers in services on both sides are addressed, can services linkages be strengthened between India and ASEAN.

Servicification Opportunities in Manufacturing

Another important aspect of the India-ASEAN services relationship is the possibility for India to provide services content in ASEAN's manufacturing value chains, complementing ASEAN's relative strength in manufacturing with its strength in services. With growing servicification possibilities in many manufacturing industries, such as transport equipment, electronics, and even traditional ones such as textiles, India may be in a position to enter the ASEAN manufacturing network through services value-added content. Figures 7.9 and 7.10, respectively, illustrate the degree of servicification by India and ASEAN in each other's manufacturing exports.

Figure 7.9: Servicification of Manufacturing Exports from ASEAN by Country VAD Shares (%)

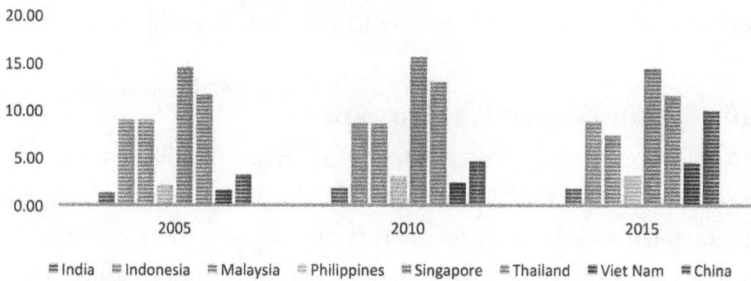

Source: OECD Stats.
Note: This is measured by taking the services value-added by a country in ASEAN's manufacturing exports relative to that contributed by the world.

As seen, the bilateral servicification linkage is very low. However, it is much higher among ASEAN members, particularly Singapore, followed by Thailand. India's services VAD contribution in ASEAN manufacturing remains stagnant at around 2 per cent while that of China has increased from a little over 2 per cent to around 10 per cent over the 2005-2015 period. Likewise, ASEAN's services value-added share is only around 2 per cent in India's manufacturing exports, although China's has increased significantly (though still at low levels). In short, while India and ASEAN exhibit low services contribution to each other's manufacturing sectors, this is not the case within ASEAN and in ASEAN's relations with China.

Figure 7.10: Servicification of India's Manufacturing Exports by Country VAD Shares (%)

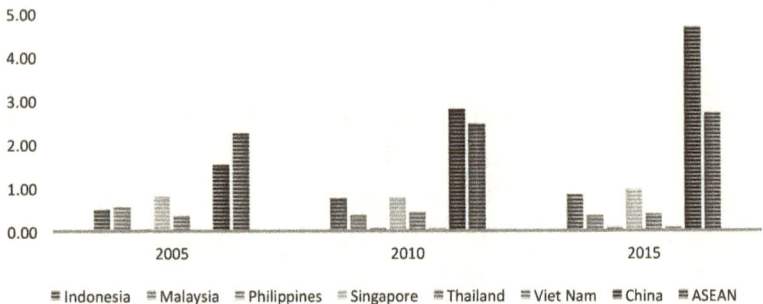

Source: OECD Stats.
Note: This is measured by taking the services value-added by a country in India's manufacturing exports relative to that contributed by the world.

Future Strategies and Way Forward

The main insight that emerges from the preceding discussion is the presence of untapped opportunities for both India and ASEAN to integrate with each other in manufacturing as well as services. To summarise, from India's perspective, within manufacturing, there are opportunities to increase forward linkages in the transport equipment, electrical and electronics, while in services there are prospects in segments like IT and information services and other business services, including through VAD linkages to ASEAN manufacturing. However, for these potential opportunities to be realised, many barriers and bilateral constraints need to be addressed.

Domestic Measures

The overarching constraint stems from structural and policy-related factors in India[7] which have led to India's low GVC participation rates, not only with ASEAN but also with the world. These factors include the low share of manufacturing in India's economy, especially India's lack of manufacturing capacity in network products such as electronics and telecom where there is greater scope for intra-industry trade; India's relatively higher import tariffs; its inability to emerge as a manufacturing hub for foreign investors; and its high logistics costs, among other factors. Thus, the realisation of value chain opportunities between India and ASEAN would in large part depend on domestic reform measures and initiatives taken by India to address these inadequacies and inefficiencies in its economy. Improving India's competitiveness in manufacturing will be the key to any GVC opportunities that can be created with partners like ASEAN.

For this purpose, one of the most important steps would be to attract more FDI in Indian manufacturing. This would enable the creation of both global and regional value chain linkages in the production process given the already strong MNE presence in several ASEAN countries and the production networks within ASEAN in several manufacturing industries. As the above evidence has highlighted, lack of FDI-linked intra-industry manufacturing trade appears to be a limiting factor in India-ASEAN GVC relations. In this regard, recent steps by the Indian government to incentivise foreign companies to establish manufacturing units in segments such as electronics can provide the required fillip. However, integration through FDI-linked intermediate exports and imports with ASEAN would, in turn, require continued unilateral efforts to improve the business environment, in particular on dimensions such as contract enforcement, payment of taxes, logistics efficiency, and trade enabling infrastructure and introduction of WTO compliant incentives.

Bilateral Efforts

Beyond these unilateral measures, steps will also be needed at the bilateral level through dialogue, cooperation, and the ASEAN-India FTA negotiations, as many of the constraints arising from market access and behind-the-border barriers on both sides. From the Indian perspective, this is particularly relevant in services where access for Indian service providers in key modes and subsectors is subject to restrictions arising from lack of mutual recognition, commercial presence conditions, and visa requirements. However, overlapping and competing interests between India and some ASEAN member countries could make progress difficult on certain issues, some of which have been difficult to address even among ASEAN members.

A way forward in this regard would be to focus bilateral discussions on an issue of mutual interest, which is investment facilitation, both by third parties and by each other's companies. In the post-COVID-19 period, investment and associated employment and value creation in the domestic market will become even more important. Focus on investment facilitation would be well-aligned with India's thrust on boosting manufacturing, developing Champion Services and undertaking ease of doing business related reforms. It would also be consistent with ASEAN's thrust on attracting FDI to the region and on creating a strong regional production network. Stronger FDI relations between India and ASEAN, due to the presence of third-country MNEs or of each other's companies, would enable greater backwards and forward integration between the two sides by promoting trade in intermediates and harmonisation of standards and could provide a push to reducing NTMs and trade facilitation measures on both sides. Outward FDI by Indian services companies in the ASEAN region could enable exploitation of synergies between manufacturing industries like IT hardware, electronics, automotive on one hand and IT and IT-enabled services on the other, between overseas commercial presence and movement of its professional services. Going forward, a detailed examination of individual industries and services and segments within each is needed to identify opportunities and constraints that can be addressed through a combination of domestic measures and bilateral discussions.

Need for Coherence

While bilateral and unilateral measures could help India improve its GVC linkages with the world and with the ASEAN region, there needs to be a coherent approach in India's trade and industrial policies. Increasingly, there appears to be dissonance between the two which does not bode well for seizing new GVC opportunities.

In recent years, India has become protectionist. Its last three budgets have increased customs duties across a range of products. According to the WTO, trade-restrictive measures implemented during the October 2018-19 period affected 3.84 per cent of world merchandise imports, of which India alone accounted for 22 per cent of the total impact, second only to the US. Even though the tariff hikes thus far affect only a small share of India's overall imports, these are not consistent with India's goal of increasing GVC participation. Even small tariffs can disrupt such integration by reducing import competition and making imports of intermediate goods more costly, thus raising input costs for exporters and rendering them uncompetitive. Thus, alongside addressing domestic distortions, India must continue to liberalise imports and exports.

Recent calls for self-reliance, what could be termed the "New Import Substitution" and measures to reduce imports from China in segments such as electronics, similarly pose a challenge to India's objectives of GVC integration and of becoming a manufacturing hub. Such steps could put India at a competitive disadvantage, particularly with ASEAN countries which have strong sourcing linkages with China. While the introduction of production-linked incentive and cluster schemes are welcome, the approach taken should be coherent with the objective of ensuring competitiveness and GVC integration rather than creating inward-looking, high-cost and inefficient entities which are shielded by tariff protection and cushioned by incentives. Thus, trade liberalisation undertaken by India in the past three decades and benefits there from should not get undone.

Notes

1. Refer, for example, WTO (2021).
2. Ibid.
3. Refer, for example, Cordon, C. (2020).

4. According to a UBS report in early 2020, over 63 per cent of global executives are considering moving at least 40 per cent of their production in China to another country.

5. Backward GVC participation is defined as foreign value added as a share of gross domestic exports. Forward GVC participation is defined as domestic value added in foreign exports as a share of gross domestic exports. It is to be noted that as these participation measures are as a share of gross domestic exports, they get scaled down for countries which have very high levels of gross domestic exports. Alternative measures are also used for forward participation in this article.

6. Figure 7.3 provides an alternative measure of linkages by taking the value-added content of a supplier country in a country's exports in total value-added content sourced from the world in a country's exports. This shows the significance of a country in total sourcing for the purpose of exports. This measure overcomes the problem that arises in the standard GVC participation index where the domestic or foreign value added content is taken as a share of a country's gross exports, which can skew the shares downwards if gross exports are very large.

7. See, Kowalski et al. (2015).

References

Baschuk, B. (2020). "WTO Says Global Trade Collapse may be worst in a Generation", Bloomberg, April 8, 2020, https://www.bloomberg.com/news/articles/2020-04-08/wto-says-2020-global-trade-collapse-may-be-worst in-a-generation#

Cordon, C. and Buatois, E (2020). "A post COVID-19 outlook: the future of the supply chain", IMD, May 2020, https://www.imd.org/research-knowledge/articles/A-post-COVID-19-outlook-The-future-of-the-supply-chain/

Kowalski, P. et al. (2015). "Participation of Developing Countries in Global Value Chains: Implications for Trade and Trade-Related Policies", OECD. Trade Policy Papers, No. 179, OECD Publishing, Paris, http://dx.doi.org/10.1787/5js33lfw0xxn-en

OECD (2020). "OECD Stats", https://stats.oecd.org/index.aspx?queryid=75537#

UBS Investment (2020). "Supply chains are shifting: how much and where?", https://www.ubs.com/global/en/investment-bank/in-focus/covid-19/2020/supply-chains-are-shifting.htm

8. Emerging Value Chains for ASEAN and India

The Role of RCEP

Tham Siew Yean

Introduction

The emergence of the Coronavirus pandemic this year has raised the possibility of re-configurations in global value chains (GVCs) as firms seek to reduce the risks of input shortages by diversifying the sources of inputs in their production process. Participation in the on-going re-configurations provides an opportunity for each country to resuscitate their respective economies which are weakened by the enforced lockdowns in the race to curb the spread of the devastating disease. Employment opportunities are in particular crucial due to the sharp falls in employment with the lockdown and plummeting demand in sectors such as travel and its associated sectors. According to OECD (2014), developing economies with the fastest growing GVC participation have GDP per capita growth rates of around two per cent above the average. Moreover, wider GVC participation can help countries reduce wage disparities between the rich and the poor.

In the following Section, this chapter discusses the emerging architecture of value chain in ASEAN and India and how far RCEP plays an important role towards building this value chain. Section 2 presents the value chain scenario in ASEAN and India. The importance of trade agreements with special emphasis on RCEP has been discussed in Section 3. Section 4 draws the concluding remarks.

Emerging Value Chains of ASEAN and India

Both India and ASEAN member states (AMS) vie for a place in the new configurations of GVCs. But, ASEAN has an early mover advantage as it is already ahead of India in GVC participation. Figure 8.1 shows the GVC participation index of India and ASEAN. The index provides an estimation of how much an economy is connected to GVCs for its foreign trade. It is composed of two components reflecting the upstream (or forward participation) and downstream (or backward participation) links in international production chains.

India's backward participation, which is measured as the ratio of foreign value-added content in exports to the economy's total gross exports, is lower than that found in developing countries and Cambodia, Malaysia, the Philippines, Thailand and Vietnam. India's backward participation is, however, higher than Brunei and Indonesia. Brunei is an exception because it is an oil dependent economy with limited manufacturing activities. Oil and natural gas account for almost 90 per cent of Brunei's exports, making its forward participation, which is ratio of the domestic value-added sent to third economies to the economy's total gross exports considerably higher than its backward participation in GVCs.

Likewise, Indonesia is relatively more dependent on natural resources. The top exports of Indonesia are coal briquettes (US$ 22.1billion), palm oil (US$ 16.7 billion), petroleum gas (US$ 10.8 billion), crude petroleum (US$ 5.52 billion), and rubber (US$ 4.41 billion), which together account for over 30 per cent of Indonesia's total exports in 2018. The higher share of natural resources in Indonesia's total exports also leads to higher forward participation. The lower backward participation indicates Indonesia's less developed manufacturing sector, which only contributed to about 20 per cent of the country's Gross Domestic Product in 2018.

Based on WTO data, the sectors where GVC participation is highest varies across AMS, though some common sectors can be found. WTO's data indicates among the top three export industries in AMS, computer and electronic products have the highest foreign value-added in Malaysia, the Philippines, Thailand and Vietnam,

Figure 8.1: GVC Participation as Percentage of Total Gross Exports, 2015

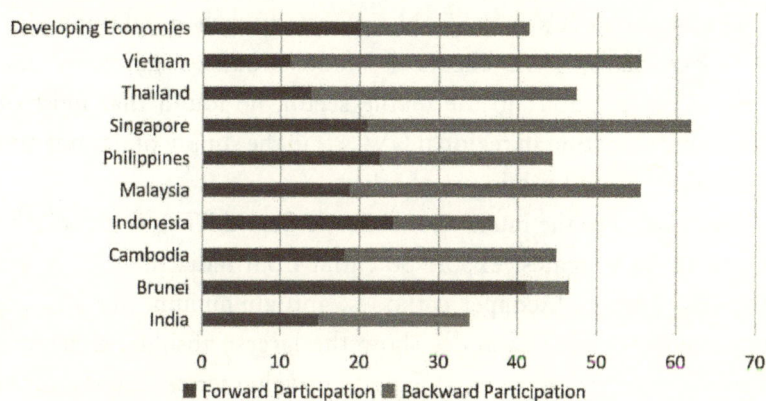

Source: World Trade Organization (WTO).
Note: Data is not available for Laos and Myanmar.

while it has the second-highest foreign value-added for Singapore. Intermediate trade in this sector is prevalent and links the AMS together in their GVC participation. This sector is also among the top three GVC-importing industries in these countries.

For Cambodia and Vietnam, the textile and clothing sector is a sector where the foreign value-added value of exports is high, 39 per cent and 46 per cent, respectively. It is also among the top three GVC-importing industries for these two countries, as well as Indonesia. Indonesia's top export industry however is in mining (energy products) which is tied to its natural resource endowments.

Other studies (Prajongkarn et al., 2015; ASEAN-Japan Study Centre, 2020), Thailand and Indonesia are linked together in the automotive GVC which are headed by Japanese multinational car manufacturers manufacturing in ASEAN, such as Toyota, Honda, and Nissan.

In the case of India, the top export industries are IT services, textiles and clothing and chemical products (WTO undated). The foreign value-added content is highest for chemical products (25 per cent), while it is 16 per cent and 8 per cent respectively for textiles and clothing and IT services. Likewise, the top three GVC-importing industries are IT services, textiles and clothing and chemical products.

Palit (2014) outlined several areas where India has a presence in the major GVCs in ASEAN, in sectors such as automobiles, pharmaceuticals, basic chemicals, food products, garments and metals. For example, in the textile sector, he found that most of India's participation in regional GVCs is in the supply of natural and synthetic fibre and producers of fabric.

According to the International Trade Centre (ITC, undated), the products with greatest export potential from India to ASEAN are diamonds, worked, copper cathodes, and aluminium, not alloyed, unwrought. Copper cathodes show the largest absolute difference between potential and actual exports in value terms, leaving room to realise additional exports worth US\$ 1.1 billion. India has the highest supply capacity in semi-finished products of iron or steel. Other machinery is the product that faces the strongest demand potential in ASEAN. India's best options for export diversification in ASEAN are data processing machines, parts of telephone sets & other transmission apparatus and liquid crystal devices. There are also food products such as dried jelly fungi, whole, cut or in powder. Parts of telephone sets and other transmission apparatus is the product that faces the strongest demand potential in ASEAN.

Thus, apart from the traditional GVCs such as electronics, textiles and clothing, and automotive, there are other potential sectors for connecting with ASEAN through GVCs such as chemicals, jewellery and food products. Palit (2014) also noted the possibilities in the jewellery value chain, whereby India can utilise the semi-precious stones imported from Myanmar and Cambodia. Services such as IT services have a huge potential in view of its important role in the emerging e-commerce markets of ASEAN and increasing pressures to digitalise in the region, especially post-pandemic.

A key driver of GVC participation is trade liberalisation since trade barriers add to the cost of importing inputs which are needed for enhancing GVC participation (World Bank 2020). Tariff barriers are thus an important deterrent for GVC participation.

Figure 8.2 shows the trade-weighted Most-Favoured-Nation (MFN) (or non-discriminatory) tariffs or for India (11.7 per cent) is more than three times the average for the four AMS (3.6 per cent) which are the most active in GVC participation, namely, Malaysia, Thailand, Singapore and Vietnam.

Figure 8.2: Trade Weighted Average MFN Tariffs, 2017

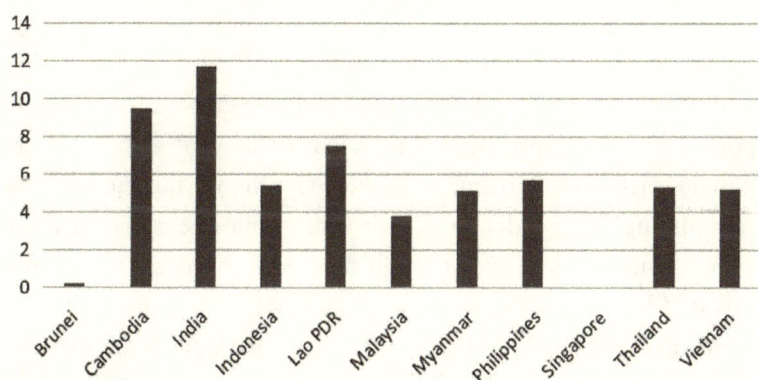

Source: WTO.

Importance of Trade Agreements in Value Chain: Focusing RCEP

Given the importance of trade liberalisation in GVC participation, preferential trade agreements can facilitate GVC participation. Although there is an ASEAN-India Free Trade Agreement (AIFTA), whereby a Trade in Goods Agreement was signed and entered into force in 2010, the scheduled tariff liberalisation in the agreement is clearly not enough as it covered about 76.4 per cent of the goods traded. The remaining 20 per cent of the goods in the sensitive and highly sensitive lists face tariffs ranging from 5-45 per cent. There is also an exclusion list, including 302 tariff lines in agriculture; 81 tariff lines in textile; 32 tariff lines in machinery and auto; and 22 tariff lines in chemicals and plastics, although these products are subject to annual tariff review.

In contrast, tariff liberalisation under the ASEAN Trade in Goods Agreement (ATIGA), ASEAN, the ASEAN-6 (namely, Brunei Darussalam, Indonesia, Malaysia, the Philippines, Singapore, and Thailand) have eliminated 99.3 per cent of all tariffs by 2019, while the corresponding figure for Cambodia, Lao PDR, Myanmar, and Viet Nam (CLMV) is 97.7 per cent. Collectively, ASEAN has eliminated 98.6 per cent of the total number of tariff lines in 2019. By 2017, ASEAN's weighted average effective applied tariff rate has reached 2.0 per cent, with average tariff rates of 1.8 per cent for the ASEAN-6, and 2.7 per cent for the CLMV countries.

The study of Agusin and Schröder (2014) on the Indian automotive industry and its links with ASEAN supply chains reported that it is precisely this disparity in tariffs that led the Japanese carmaker, Nissan, to lower its original targeted 80 per cent sourcing from India to 40 per cent, while the remainder was sourced from ASEAN, even though the initial sourcing targets were motivated by the AIFTA.

More importantly, the top three foreign input providers for Indonesia, Malaysia, the Philippines, Singapore and Thailand are China, Japan and the United States, though not necessarily in the same order of importance. For Cambodia, it is China, Thailand and Japan, while it is China, Korea, and Japan for Vietnam due to the large presence of Samsung in the latter country. This implies a free trade agreement with ASEAN is not enough since the source country for the multinationals heading the GVCs are from outside the region, namely China, Japan and the United States.

While India also has bilateral trade agreements with Singapore, Korea, Japan and Malaysia, Indian exporters and importers navigating through these different bilateral agreements will have to deal with different rules of origin to ascertain their eligibility to utilise the preferential tariffs in each of these agreements. This is both cumbersome and costly to comply.

The incoming Regional Comprehensive Partnership Agreement (RCEP), which was signed in 2020, is the first regional free trade agreement encompassing all of ASEAN with its five-plus partners, namely, China, Japan, Korea, Australia and New Zealand. The agreement, with 20 chapters, is considered to be rather modest compared to the Comprehensive and Progressive Agreement for Trans-Pacific Partnership (CPTPP) (or, TPP-1), which is a trade agreement between Australia, Brunei, Canada, Chile, Japan, Malaysia, Mexico, New Zealand, Peru, Singapore, and Vietnam as the latter has 30 chapters and deeper provisions.

Nevertheless, the RCEP is still a landmark agreement as it bears a special significance in the current rising anti-globalisation and protectionist sentiments. It further shows that this part of Asia is pressing on with trade liberalisation and globalisation.

Although India was part of the protracted negotiations which stretched from 2013 to 2019, it decided to withdraw from the agreement at the last minute due in part to fears that it will be flooded with imports due to its higher initial tariffs compared to the other participating countries. This in turn contributed to a trade deficit with partner countries. However, the Economic Survey of India (2020, p. 125), found that "when the impact of India's trade agreements on overall trade balance is made by accounting for all confounding factors, India's exports have increased by 13.4 per cent for manufactured products and 10.9 per cent for total merchandise while imports increased by 12.7 per cent for manufactured products and 8.6 per cent for total merchandise. Thus, India has clearly gained 0.7 per cent increase in trade surplus per year for manufactured products and 2.3 per cent per year for total merchandise". It, therefore, has recommended a strategy whereby "Assembling in India" can be part of the "Make in India" strategy. Participating in GVCs is a key component of "Assembling in India".

The agreement will have a single, consistent, and cohesive set of trade rules, thereby lowering considerably the compliance costs for accessing the preferential tariffs in the agreement with all partner countries. Consequently, the agreement will reduce the transaction costs for businesses by removing the famously spaghetti-bowl effect of different rules of origin in the 28 bilateral FTAs between the RCEP partners. It will, therefore, reduce the complexities that Indian businesses would have to deal with when trading with the RCEP partners. Indian businesses that plan and or wish to export to the participating RCEP countries will definitely suffer from the lost prospect of an easier access into the partner countries.

Apart from tariff liberalisation, non-tariff measures (NTMs) are also addressed. RCEP has rules in areas such as customs procedures; quarantine and technical standards will address these non-tariff barriers by promoting greater transparency and cooperation among RCEP countries, while reaffirming existing WTO rights and obligations (Australia Government, Regional Comprehensive Economic Partnership undated). RCEP will also establish procedures for technical consultations on non-tariff measures that adversely affect trade, and provide for possible future work on sector-specific initiatives to facilitate trade. This is important in view of the increase in NTMs as tariffs fall globally.

Concluding Remarks

Trade liberalisation under the RCEP can serve to propel India's participation in the reconfiguration of GVCs by connecting India with the old and new GVCs that are emerging in member countries, including especially ASEAN. Given the importance of trade liberalisation in GVC participation, India, therefore, needs to reconsider its exit from the RCEP, especially while the door to re-join the RCEP is still kept open.

References

Agusin, T.L.D. and Schröder, M. (2014). "The Indian Automotive Industry and the ASEAN Supply Chain Relations", https://www.eria.org/RPR_FY2013_No.7_Chapter_5.pdf (accessed on 15 August 2020).

ASEAN-Japan Study Centre (2020). *Global Value Chains in ASEAN: Automobiles*. Paper 12, January 2020, https://www.asean.or.jp/ja/wp-content/uploads/sites/2/GVC_Automobiles_Paper-12_J anuary-24-2020-web-_edited.pdf (accessed on 16 August 2020).

Australia Government (2020). "Regional Comprehensive Economic Partnership", https://www.dfat.gov.au/trade/agreements/negotiations/rcep (accessed on 15 August 2020).

Government of India (2020). "Ministry of Finance, 2020", *Economic Survey 2019-2020*. https://www.indiabudget.gov.in/economicsurvey/doc/echapter.pdf (accessed on 15 August 2020).

International Trade Center (ITC). https://exportpotential.intracen.org/en/products/tree-map?fromMarker=i&exporter=699&toMarker=r&market=1&whatMarker=k (accessed on 15 August 2020).

OECD (2014). "India Policy Brief: Enhancing Global Value Chain Participation", https://www.oecd.org/policy-briefs/India-Enhancing-Global-Value-Chain-Participation.pdf (accessed on 15 August 2020).

Palit, A. (2015). Regional Value Chains, RCEP and India's Priorities. In *ASEAN-India Economic Relations: Opportunities and Challenges. Proceedings of the Third Roundtable on ASEAN-India Network of Think Tanks (AINTT)*, Hanoi.

World Bank (2020). *World Bank Report 2020: Trading for Development in the Age of Global Value Chains.* https://www.worldbank.org/en/publication/wdr2020 (accessed on 15 August 2020).

WTO (undated). *Global Value Chains*, https://www.wto.org/english/res_e/statis_e/miwi_e/miwi_e.htm (accessed on 15 August 2020).

9. GVCs: Opportunities for India and ASEAN Post-COVID-19

Saon Ray

Introduction

The world trade collapse that followed the onset of lockdown in many countries in April and May 2020 was almost as severe as the collapse in world trade volume in January 2009. The global financial crisis in late 2008 and early 2009 saw the volume of exports of emerging economies dip even more than in 2020. However, the important difference with the global financial crisis was that developed countries were hit more badly this time, and the emerging countries, particularly China, are showing signs of a recovery in their exports. Part of the reason for this difference has to do with global supply chains. The East Asian region was the first to be hit by the pandemic, and was also the first to recover from it. The impact of the pandemic on the global demand has been widespread and the disruption in world trade following the pandemic was consistent throughout the different regions of the world. Exports volume declined 8.8 per cent while imports volume 8.5 per cent in 2020 (based on data from January to May of a year, over the previous year) (UNCTAD, 2020). The Euro area showed the largest decline in the volume of its exports and imports (UNCTAD, 2020).

The Coronavirus pandemic hit the world when India and many other Asian economies were making efforts to streamline and integrate their supply and value chains both domestically as well as internationally. The value and share of exports that depend on GVCs can come from either upstream links (foreign value-added in exports) or downstream links (exports that are incorporated in other products and are re-exported). The smallest share of foreign value-added in exports is found in South Asia, mainly because of the importance of service exports, which typically use fewer foreign inputs. Member states of the ASEAN have embraced GVCs, their participation has grown and the region has positioned itself as a key global production hub (Lopez Gonzalez, 2016).

This article examines the extent of GVC integration of India with reference to the ASEAN and the opportunities that exist for both. The rest of chapter is organised as follows: Section 2 illustrates India and ASEAN trade relations. Section 3 discusses way of measuring GVC integration and GVC in automobile industry is discussed in Section 4. Lastly, concluding remarks is made in Section 5.

India's Trade with ASEAN

India and the Association of South East Nations (ASEAN) signed a Free Trade Agreement (FTA) which came into force on 1 January 2010. From India's point of view, ASEAN is an important trading partner with increased imports coming to India from the ASEAN countries. From the ASEAN perspective, India's importance in its imports is small but increasing. Both partners would be interested in increasing their share in each other's market and there are implications of tariff reduction that have been committed under the agreement.

The top exports of India to the ASEAN region in 2009-10 were in the category residues food (HS 23), mineral fuels (27), organic chemicals (HS 29), natural and cultured pearls (HS 71), iron and steel (HS 72), nuclear reactors (HS 84), electrical machinery (HS 85), ships and boats (HS 89), and miscellaneous goods (HS 99). India's imports from ASEAN are highest in the mineral fuels category (HS 27) in 2009-10. The top items of imports of India from the ASEAN region were animal fats (HS 15), mineral fuels (HS 27), organic chemicals (HS 29), wood and wood products (HS 44), nuclear reactors (HS 84), and electrical machinery (HS 85) in 2009-10. Of these, except for the wood and the animal fat category each of the other items are being exported too.

In 2016-17, Coke, Refined Petroleum Products and Nuclear fuel, Basic Metals and Fabricated Metal Products, Transport Equipment, Food Products, Beverages and Tobacco accounted for 60 per cent of India's total exports to ASEAN; and Coke, Refined Petroleum Products and Nuclear fuel, Food Products, Beverages and Tobacco, Electrical and Optical Equipment and Basic Metals and Fabricated Metal Products accounted for 60 per cent of India's imports from ASEAN (Jena and Saini, 2020).

Several elements of policy determine participation in GVCs such as regional trade agreements; investment barriers to multinational corporations; infrastructure development; speed and flexibility of movement of physical goods and information; effectiveness of legal and regulatory systems; efficiency of services; developing a skilled workforce; friendliness of the business climate; and capacity of domestic firms (often SMEs) to contribute to the supply chain (OECD, 2013). Other factors include border administration, market access barriers, and transport logistics (WEF, 2013).

In Asia, regional trade agreements followed GVC creation rather than preceding it, which was the case in the European Union and North America (UNIDO, 2018). Most East Asian countries have also successfully integrated with global and regional value chains. Singapore, which has the maximum trade agreements in place, is acted as a hub to Malaysia and Indonesia. India has been a late starter in signing trade agreements and has recently withdrawn from the RCEP.

Examining India's exports in terms of intermediate goods, capital goods and final goods for the years 2008, 2012 and 2017 (based on UN Comtrade data), the following emerges: in 2008 and 2012 and 2017, Singapore is among the top ten countries to which India exported intermediate goods. In 2012, Indonesia joins the list. Indonesia is also among the top 10 countries from which India imports intermediates in 2012 and 2017.

In the exports of final goods, Vietnam is among the top 10 countries to which India exported final goods in 2012 and 2017. The imports of final goods in 2008 and 2012 include Myanmar, while the top 10 imports of final goods come from Malaysia, Thailand in 2012 and Malaysia, Thailand and Vietnam in 2017.

In the capital goods category, Singapore is at number 1 position of countries of India's exports of capital goods in 2012. In 2017, both Singapore and Indonesia are among the top10 countries. The imports of capital goods from the ASEAN region include Singapore in 2008, Singapore, Malaysia and Thailand in 2012 and 2017, respectively.

To put this in perspective, imports of intermediate goods accounted for 83 per cent of total merchandise imports in 2017, while imports of final and capital goods made up 6 per cent and 11 per cent, respectively, in 2017. Also, 60 per cent of export value in 2017 was in exports of intermediate goods. By comparison, the share of final and capital goods reached 33 per cent and 6 per cent, respectively, in 2017. India has consistently been a net importer of intermediate goods over the period 2008-2017. It is also a net exporter of final goods and net importer of capital goods for the period of 2008-2017.

Measuring GVC Integration

A large share of the exports of developed countries comprises value-added exports, which, in turn, depend upon imports. Much of this share in value-added trade of developed countries can be attributed to the highly integrated the EU economy, which accounts for over 70 per cent of exports originating in the EU. Japan and the United States have a smaller share of foreign value-added content in their exports. Developing countries have a still lower share of foreign value-added content with countries in East and Southeast Asia and Central America (including Mexico) having the largest share among developing countries. India, on the other hand, is not well integrated in global value chains (Ray and Miglani, 2018).

Stöllinger (2018) derived a comprehensive GVC participation measure, by summing the backward and forward integration measures from the OECD Inter-Country Input-Output tables. According to his classification, two broad groups of economies can be identified according to the intensification of GVC integration in Asia. The first group, which saw their comprehensive GVC integration increase between 1995 and 2011, includes Japan, the Republic of Korea, Taiwan, China and Thailand. The second group, consisting of many ASEAN countries including Malaysia, Indonesia, the Philippines and Viet Nam, GVC participation peaked between 2000 and 2005. According to the OECD-TIVA, India's foreign content of exports increased from 18.8 per cent in 2005 to 25.1 per cent in 2011 and 2012, thereafter declining to 16.1 per cent in 2016.

Athukorala (2011a) looks into the global production sharing and network trade in East Asia and how it has grown recently. Asia has been divided into NIE (newly industrialised economies), PRC (People's Republic of China) and ASEAN. The study observes a large rise in non-oil export share of East Asia from 11 per cent in 1969-70 to 33 per cent in 2006-07 and attributes the structural shift mainly to the rise of PRC. Further, the export structure has shifted away from primary commodities to manufacturing. The concentration of trade in electronics is much larger in the ASEAN Free Trade Area (AFTA). The paper explores the reasons behind East Asia's emergence as a centre for global production sharing and narrows three factors: First, a diverse range of labour supply: Japan and four NIEs which offer relatively skilled labour compared to the second-tier countries in South Asia like Vietnam. Second, favourable trade and investment policy regimes have been adopted in the region along with better communication and transport, thus lowering transaction costs, which has attracted more investors. Third, PRCs emergence as a low-cost assembly centre is leading to more production activities being undertaken by other countries in the region.

Athukorala (2011b) uses the case of Penang export hub in order to take policy implications and shows through this case study how a region can be integrated into the global production networks and benefit from it. The state government took steps such as developing Free Trade Zones (FTZs) and took necessary steps towards making the government machinery conducive for foreign investment. The first FTZ in 1972 aimed at attracting clean industries that required air transport such as electronics, medical equipment, etc. Land acquisition was streamlined and fairness was ensured. The government also undertook investment promotion campaigns portraying the picture of skilled Penang workers who could complement the needs of high-tech industries. The government undertook various vocational training programs. It later even included the benefits offered to foreign firms in FTZs to local contractors so that they could be sub-contracted by the MNEs.

Athukorala (2013) explores the reasons for India's failure to fit into global production networks. It looks into India's overall export share, to begin with, and observes that India's contribution to world exports has been very small especially compared to developing countries emerging as the export hubs and participating extensively in production sharing. Moreover, the pattern of trade observed for India is quite different to rest of developing nations or Asian countries. Indian export expansion has been expanding mainly in resource-based products and miscellaneous products (clothing, footwear and other such labour-intensive products). India again stands out against other East Asian countries, in road vehicles and other transport equipment in which it accounted for 28 per cent of total network exports in 2010-11 (compared to 13.2 per cent average for East Asia). Various automakers have established assembly plants in India and even started using India as export platform for the global production networks. Two reasons for expansion of this sector are the low value-to-weight nature of products of the automobile industry. This makes air transport rather non-feasible which leads to location of industries in regions of high demand. Second, there are a handful of auto makers that purchase components from number of manufacturers, which makes it feasible to locate the parts and component manufacturing close to assemblers in order to secure position.

A country's value addition in a GVC depends on its location in the value chain OECD (2013). Countries upstream produce raw materials or the knowledge (e.g. research and design) at the beginning of the process while countries downstream assemble processed products and specialise in customer services. Most upstream activities such as research and development (R&D) and design, and certain services create more value than assembly functions.

The Automobile Industry: Scope for Greater Integration with ASEAN?

The Indian Prime Minister stated that India, with the right blend of the physical and the virtual, can emerge as the global nerve centre (supplier of crucial products) of complex modern multinational supply chains in the post-COVID-19 world.[1] WTO (2020a) has estimated, as a result of COVID-19, trade will most likely fall more in sectors with complex value chains, particularly electronics and automotive products. Even before the pandemic, merchandise trade volume already fell by 0.1 per cent in 2019, weighed down by trade tensions and slowing economic growth.

India has restricted the imports of goods from China after the recent tension between the two countries. A recent study from RIS has shown that 327 products comprise of 3/4th of the imports of India from China. These products ranging from mobile phones and telecom equipment, could be sourced from elsewhere.[2] Some other items including certain auto components are ones where China is the sole supplier. The question that we posit here is, can these be sourced from the ASEAN?

In the FTA between India and ASEAN, India reduced tariffs on goods for all ASEAN member states except the Philippines from 2011 until 2016. At the same time, Brunei, Indonesia, Malaysia, Singapore, and Thailand are going to lower their tariffs for India. The CLMV countries, Cambodia, Lao PDR, Myanmar, and Vietnam reduced tariffs for Indian goods from 2016. From 2016, India and the Philippines agreed to lower tariffs on a reciprocal basis. Simply put, while India reduced its tariffs for all ASEAN members except the Philippines from 2011, only the more advanced ASEAN members are opening up for exports from India in that year. CLMV countries enjoyed a special status during a transition period until 2016 and got more liberal access to the Indian market without opening their markets for Indian products in a similar fashion. The review of the agreement between India and the ASEAN countries, has the potential to double trade.[3] In recent times, India has increased its integration with Southeast Asia in the automobile industry. In this context, Augustin and Schröder (2015) discuss the various strategies followed by firms, namely, Toyota, Tata, TVS and Mitsubishi.

In the context of automotive parts, the tariff reduction schedule for India does not reveal signs of strong protection for certain products. However, tariffs on certain products (clutches, flywheels and gaskets) are only mildly reduced from 7.5 to 5 per cent by 2020. However, this lowered level of protection might still be high enough to make exports from India to ASEAN less attractive than sourcing within ASEAN.

Concluding Remarks

The economic shocks associated with COVID-19 are shutdowns, layoffs, firm exits and supply shocks (Guerrieri et al., 2020). The pandemic has disrupted global value chains, and manufacturing is affected by non-availability of imported parts and postponement of demand (Baldwin and Weder di Mauro, 2020). The risks inherent in global supply chains are becoming clearer and have implications for developing countries from where the manufacturing activity is being shifted. Will the pandemic force the auto industry to change the way it operates? The disruptions caused by COVID-19 revealed the problem with the 'just in time' model of operation. Resilience in supply chains could be the key to surviving the pandemic. How can countries increase their resilience (WTO, 2020b)? Some analysts feel that greater regionalism may be the way the chains will be organised in future. The auto industry has in the past, recovered from several crises, including the Japan earthquake and tsunami of 2011 (Olcott and Oliver, 2014).[4] According to Holweg and Oliver (2016), the ability to design, develop, and scale have been key to the resilience of auto firms. To survive in the automotive industry, technology is a key element and therefore, companies, with government support, need to acquire skills and know-how in order to secure a place in either global or regional supply chains (Augustin and Schröder, 2015).

Notes

1. India has introduced the Production Linked Incentive (PLI) Scheme which includes the automobile and auto components. https://pib.gov.in/PressReleasePage.aspx?PRID=1671912. See also Ray (2021): https://saonray.com/will-the-pli-scheme-help-achieve-scale-in-indian-manufacturing/ and https://www.livemint.com/companies/news/govt-may-set-a-high-pli-bar-for-auto-cos-11606262604693.html

2. http://timesofindia.indiatimes.com/articleshow/77453001.cms?utm_source=contentofinterest&utm_medium=text&utm_campaign=cppst

3. https://economictimes.indiatimes.com/news/economy/foreign-trade/india-asean-free-trade-agreement-review-can-double-bilateral-trade-hardeep-puri/articleshow/77353430.cms; https://www.business-standard.com/article/economy-policy/review-of-india-asean-goods-agreement-to-help-realise-trade-potential-puri-120080401562_1.html and https://thewire.in/trade/asean-goods-fta-india-rcep

4. Another issue confronting the auto industry is electric vehicles. The supply chain considerations for batteries are quite different from internal combustion engines.

References

Agustin, T. L.D., and Schröder, M. (2015). "The Indian Automotive Industry and the ASEAN Supply Chain Relations The Indian Automotive Industry and the ASEAN Supply Chain Relations", in ERIA (eds.), *Automobile And Auto Components Industries In ASEAN: Current State And Issues*. Research Institute Auto Parts Industries Waseda University, Jakarta: Economic Research Institute For ASEAN and East Asia and Waseda University, pp. 51-114.

Athukorala, P.C. (2011a). "'Production Networks and Trade Patterns in East Asia': Regionalization or Globalisation?", *Asian Economic Papers*, 10(1), 65-95.

Athukorala, P.C. (2011b). 'Growing with global production sharing: The tale of Penang export hub'. Working papers in Trade and Development No. 2011-13, Arndt-Corden Department of Economics, Australian National University.

Athukorala, P. C. (2013). "How India Fits into Global Production Sharing: Experience, Prospects, and Policy Options", India Policy Forum 2013-14, NCAER.

Baldwin, R. and B. Weder di Mauro (2020). *Economics in the Time of COVID-19*, VoxEU CEPR Press.

Guerrieri, V., Lorenzoni, G., Straub, L., and Werning, I. (2020). "Macroeconomic Implications of COVID-19". NBER working paper 26934.

Holweg, M. and Oliver, N. (2016). *Crisis, Resilience and Survival: Lessons from the Global Auto Industry.* Cambridge: Cambridge University Press.

Jena, D. and Saini, S. (2020). "Impact of Trade with ASEAN on India's Employment in Industrial Sector", Working paper, Madras School of Economics.

Jenny, F. (2020). "Economic resilience, globalisation and market governance: Facing the Covid-19 test", Vox EU.org.

Jorda, O., Singh, S. S. and Taylor, A. M. (2020). "Longer-run economic consequences of pandemics," in Baldwin, R. and B. Weder di Mauro, *Economics in the Time of COVID-19*, VoxEU CEPR Press.

Lopez Gonzalez, J. (2016). "Using Foreign Factors to Enhance Domestic Export Performance: A Focus on Southeast Asia". Working Party of the Trade Committee, TAD/TC/WP(2015)25/REV1/PART1. Paris: Organisation for Economic Co-operation and Development.

Marin, D. (2020). "How COVID-19 is transforming manufacturing? Project Syndicate", April 3, 2020, https://www.project-syndicate.org/commentary/covid19-and-robots-drive-manufacturing-reshoring-by-dalia-marin-2020-04.

Olcott, G. and Oliver, N. (2014). "Social Capital, Sense-Making and Recovery from Disaster: Japanese Companies and the March 2011 Earthquake", *California Management Review*, vol. 56, no. 2, pp. 5-22.

Ray, S. and Miglani, S. (2018). *Global Value Chains and the Missing links: Cases from Indian Industry*, Routledge.

Stöllinger, R. (2018). "Asian Experiences with Global and Regional Value Chain Integration and Structural Change", Research Report 436, WIIW.

UNCTAD (2020). Trade and Development Review 2020.

UNIDO (2018). "Global Value Chains and Industrial Development Lessons From China, South-East And South Asia", https://www.unido.org/sites/default/files/files/2018-06/EBOOK_GVC.pdf

WTO (2020a). "COVID-19 and world trade", https://www.wto.org/english/tratop_e/covid19_e/covid19_e.htm#collapse0

WTO (2020b). "Ensuring Resilience of Global Supply of Essential Services in Combating COVID-19" 1 April 2020, https://www.wto.org/english/tratop_e/covid19_e/gsc_statement_e.pdf

SECTION III: New Normal and Significance
of 4IR on ASEAN-India Partnership and
Future Collaborations

10. ASEAN-India Cooperation and the Pandemic's Push towards a Digital Economy

Impact and Policy Response

Jayant Menon

Introduction

Although ASEAN-India economic relations have a long history that dates back several centuries, more recent engagement started to strengthen only following the 'Look East' policy of Prime Minister Narasimha Rao in the early nineteen nineties. Following this policy, various bilateral, sub-regional and regional initiatives were pursued. The ASEAN-India Trade in Goods Agreement was signed in 2009 and entered into force a year later, while the negotiations for a free trade agreement (FTA) in services and investment were concluded in 2012. The next step in consolidating the relationship within the broader regional context was to take place through the Regional Comprehensive Economic Partnership (RCEP), but India had opted out of this agreement before it was signed in late 2020. Nevertheless, there has been rapid growth in trade and investment, with bilateral trade surpassing US$ 90 billion before the Coronavirus (COVID-19) pandemic hit in 2020.

The pandemic hit investment harder than trade in 2020, but both have fallen sharply, as has economic growth. Although there are signs of the bottom having been reached in the second quarter of 2020, the shape and strength of the economic recovery varies across the countries of ASEAN and India. New waves of community transmission associated with new variants have affected recovery in India in particular, but also several ASEAN countries, as many have been forced to tighten social distancing measures.

One of the supposed and oft-cited silver linings associated with the pandemic has been the acceleration towards embracing the Fourth Industrial Revolution (4IR). Although there is optimism that all aspects of the 4IR such as artificial intelligence, robotics, blockchain and 3D printing may have sped up, it is the transition towards a digital economy that has captured our attention. Lockdowns and other social distancing measures have accelerated the creation and adoption of new technologies that enable work from home and remote learning. Looking forward, firms are already starting to restructure their operations to better adapt to a new normal that will involve less human interaction and be restricted by other risk mitigation regulations (see APEC, 2020).

In this article, we consider the likely impacts of the COVID-19 induced acceleration towards the 4IR, focusing on its distributional consequences. Although a lot has been written about how the 4IR may worsen existing inequalities between and within countries (see, for instance, UN, 2017), we look more closely to see if there might be offsetting effects that may reduce or even reverse this apparent trend. The paper aims to contribute to the discussion of the impacts of the 4IR by synthesizing the often neglected, potentially inclusive or inequality-offsetting effects, and examining national and regional policy choices in the short and long run that can contribute to their realisation.

The chapter begins with a brief overview of what is meant by the 4IR, and the role that regional and cross-regional institutional arrangements can play in responding to the challenges that it poses. This is discussed in Section 2. We then examine the distributional impacts of the move towards a digital economy, both positive and negative. Section 4 then considers how policy should respond, both in the short run and in the long run. The final section concludes.

The Fourth Industrial Revolution: An Overview

The 4IR is the fusion of technologies across physical, digital and biological realms which will transform our way of life. It builds on the technological advancements of previous industrial revolutions, particularly those of the Third Industrial Revolution (3IR) such as computers, the Internet and digital technologies. However, the 4IR is unlike other revolutions due to the breadth, depth and speed of change.

Technologies of the 4IR and the interaction between them, offer new ways to create and consume, will transform how we deliver and access public services, and open new ways to communicate and govern (see Shwab 2016; 2018).

With the 4IR, new technologies are emerging faster, being adopted more quickly and delivering greater impact. For instance, while landline telephones took more than 75 years to reach 100 million users, mobile phones took less than 15 years. More recently, the internet reached 100 million users in about 6 years, Facebook in about 4 years, WhatsApp in about 3 years, and Instagram in about 2.

Machine learning and big data analytics mean the process of discovery and analysis no longer requires human agency. Digital networks allow products and services to scale more quickly. The processing power of computer chips (from the 3IR) has increased by one quadrillion times over the past 50 years but quantum computing has the potential to perform tasks which would not even be possible today.

The consequence of all this is that change in the 4IR will be hard to predict. The technology itself is difficult to map because its growth rate could be exponential, factorial or higher. It is this unpredictability that is making impact assessments difficult, but not impossible.

Equally, it heralds a new brand of 'superstar' economics (Rosen, 1981; Nuesch, 2007). Returns to knowledge and skills are exponential which – if not equally shared – can lead to increasing inequality. This in turn could lead to social exclusion and political instability. The 4IR provides transformative technologies but it will be the job of our social and political institutions to ensure the technologies are used for the benefit of all humankind and not just a few.

Importantly, however, some of the greatest impacts of the 4IR will play out not at a national scale, but at a regional scale. The nature of cross-border relations and economic interaction will be revolutionised. It will not be enough to think only about a national response. In the years ahead, regional organisations like ASEAN will be called upon ever more heavily to help steer and shape these historic transformations.

Other institutional arrangements and regional and cross-regional trade and economic cooperation agreements will also have to play a role in guiding the process, in accommodating its requirements, and dealing with its consequences. And yet, given the accelerating speed and breadth of technological change, shaping regional policy is growing ever harder. It means that ASEAN and organisations like it will need to re-imagine and re-design the way they manage regional governance (see ADB and WEF, 2017). It will also mean that the agenda of regional economic cooperation agreements will have to evolve and respond to changing needs and impacts in a timely fashion.

The Distributional Impacts of the 4IR

As noted earlier, the impetus that the pandemic has provided in accelerating the move towards a digital economy is often hailed as one of the few positive things to come out of this crisis. Even as lockdowns were lifted, various social distancing measures remained in place, necessitating the use of technology to continue working and learning.

The adoption rate of these technologies has varied across countries, however, with the more developed economies are better able to respond to this need than less developed ones. The level of preparedness of countries is negatively correlated to their level of development, and this may widen development gaps if left unaddressed. In a cruel twist, there is concern that even this supposed silver lining of the pandemic may end up exacerbating inequality between countries, further increasing the digital divide.

Apart from the digital infrastructure being limited in poor countries, access to what is available can vary by income class within society. The poor in developing countries are less likely to have the means to access this infrastructure, and hence be further marginalised as a result. The 4IR may also lead to a further concentration of the gains from trade in the hands of the few (see, for instance, Bacchetta et al., 2021). Therefore, not only is inequality between countries likely to increase, there could also be a rise in income and wealth disparities within them.

The poor may also be disadvantaged by the fact that the sectors within which they tend to be employed are usually less amenable to the adoption of such technologies. Physical contact may represent a critical aspect of work for low-skilled employees in the manufacturing or construction sectors, for instance. The introduction of social distancing measures may leave them temporarily unemployed, as a result. More generally, the 4IR may also pose a greater threat to their jobs, as automation and robotics take hold initially in the low-skilled, repetitive tasks before progressing to more complex activities.

Apart from these negative impacts, there are several ways in which the 4IR can either reduce inequality or have offsetting effects that can limit its increase. Although a lot of attention has been focused on how the 4IR can exacerbate inequality, there are various countervailing effects that are often overlooked or ignored.

Increasing Economic Inclusion

The 4IR can be a powerful force for economic inclusion. 4IR technologies will create new ways for citizens to connect to each other, to trade with each other, and to access services that are currently not available. In Indonesia, Myanmar, the Philippines and Vietnam, less than a third of the population have a bank account. The share of the unbanked is even higher in India. Innovations such as

Aadhaar, a digital identification system, is driving financial inclusion and bringing banking services to more than a billion people in India who had previously been excluded. These financial services enabled by technology allow households to save in secure instruments to enlarge their asset base and escape cycles of poverty and inequality.

Under the 4IR, citizens will gain access to new sources of information, such as high-frequency news and market prices that can materially affect incomes and welfare. In a now famous study, Jensen (2007) showed how the adoption of mobile phones by fishermen and wholesalers in South India was associated with a dramatic reduction in price dispersion and the elimination of waste, resulting in increases in consumer and producer welfare. It can also enable new forms of education, such as online courses and virtual classrooms, and new healthcare services, such as telemedicine powered by smartphones linked to diagnostic pills (Menon and Fink, 2018).

These innovations should result in a reduction in all forms of social and economic inequities and drive a much more inclusive form of economic growth.

Opportunities for Leapfrogging

The opportunities for leapfrogging provided by the 4IR are related to the so-called latecomer's advantage hypothesis.[1] This is where late adopters of technology may be better positioned because they can avoid the mistakes of the past and adapt technologies in a way that benefits them more than early adopters.[2] In certain instances, they are even able to leapfrog early movers, further consolidating their advantage.

Technologies of the 4IR create the opportunity for developing countries to bypass traditional aspects of industrial development. A commonly cited example relates to avoiding costly investments in telephone lines and focusing instead on mobile telephone infrastructure. Apart from the savings in public expenditure that can be directed towards other social goods and services, this type of technology can also be used to access other services such as financial transfers and medical advice, as noted earlier. The technologies of the 4IR can also help find alternative solutions to connecting people in isolated regions where physical infrastructure is costly and/or limited.

Localised renewable energy production, such as solar power coupled with new battery storage technology, could reduce the need for investing in expensive power distribution networks. Drones could help to deliver light weight high-value goods such as medical supplies to remote regions with poor transport infrastructure. While drones will not remove the need to build roads for the transport of heavy goods and people, they do offer the opportunity to sequence and design transport infrastructure in new ways and to reduce the need for "last-mile" road connectivity. These alternatives can increase economic inclusion for poor and marginalised communities, leading to lower inequality.

Enhancing Agriculture

Apart from its richest city-state members of Singapore and Brunei Darussalam, agriculture remains a significant source of growth and employment in all the other ASEAN countries, and of course in India. It is the largest employer among the newest members of ASEAN (Cambodia, Lao PDR and Myanmar), and in 2019 it accounted for 43 per cent of employment in India. Both poverty and inequality cannot be addressed without improving the incomes and livelihoods of those employed in agriculture.

The 4IR has the potential to transform agriculture in these countries. In the short run, the impact of connecting farmers to the internet has already brought well-documented improvements to farmer productivity, profitability and sustainability. Smart phones give farmers better access to market prices, weather information, and knowledge about soil, seeds and fertiliser. Smart phones may also enable a "sharing economy" to take hold, whereby farmers who cannot afford to buy expensive mechanical equipment can rent it by the hour from other farmers by accessing online sharing sites. In India, Mahindra & Mahindra, an equipment maker, has set up a platform of this type called Trringo.

The 4IR could improve the traceability of products, reduce logistics costs, and overcome constraints of agricultural finance by enabling suppliers to use new credit scoring technologies. In the longer term, as farming is primarily a biological process, new technology will enable the easier creation of elite genetic material (seeds, plants, and livestock) and the increasing usage of microbiology in farming systems (Menon and Fink, 2019).

These enhancements will allow both poverty and inequality to be addressed at its source. It will also reduce the pressure on densely populated urban centres by limiting the amount of rural-urban migration that might occur in the absence of such enhancements improving returns to agriculture.

Supporting Micro and Small and Medium Enterprises (MSMEs)

More than 90 per cent of enterprises in the formal sector within both ASEAN and India are micro and small and medium enterprises (MSMEs). MSMEs have become almost synonymous with the informal sector. These MSMEs, in the formal and the informal sector, account for the overwhelming majority of employment in ASEAN and in India.

MSMEs are often constrained by lack of access to business and financial services, but blockchain technology has the potential to dramatically increase the security of cross-border financial transactions and logistics even in countries where these services are relatively underdeveloped. Therefore, this technology has the potential to benefit the smallest firms in India, and in the poorest regions of ASEAN. The rise of online marketplaces also provides platforms for MSMEs in India to access markets in ASEAN, and vice-versa.

Although large multinational enterprises have already adopted most of the technologies enabled by the 4IR, it is the MSMEs that stand to gain the most from them. The potential exists for these technologies to revolutionise the ways in which MSMEs operate by creating game-changing opportunities, as opposed to incremental changes in efficiency for the early adopters. As a result of the differences in the magnitude of the potential impacts, the technologies of the 4IR can produce outcomes that reduce various forms of inequality.

Policy Options in the Short-and Long-run

As noted earlier, one of the major challenges of the 4IR will be the impact on the labour market caused by automation and increasingly advanced robotics and artificial intelligence. Many low-skilled, repetitive jobs are being automated, starting in high wage countries but already spreading quickly to the developing world. With two-thirds of the world's robots already in the Indo-Pacific, some expect this region to be particularly susceptible to these changes. Although the net impact on jobs and the labour market, in the long run, remains unclear,[3] there is little doubt that disruptive technologies will result in significant labour churning and job displacement in the short-run (see McKinsey, 2017). These adjustment costs and associated negative employment outcomes will affect some countries more than others. Low-skilled, repetitive jobs, such as assembly line workers, are most at risk, and service jobs, such as business process outsourcing, will be increasingly under threat.

As an immediate response, enabling greater mobility of unskilled workers would curtail unemployment in net labour-sending countries and help sustain growth in net labour-receiving ones while also helping counter growing economic inequality within and between these countries.

Apart from the challenges posed by the 4IR, India and ASEAN also have to deal with another long-term factor in the form of divergent demographics. While India and the newest members of ASEAN have relatively young populations, the rest of ASEAN is ageing rapidly.

For the younger and less developed economies, the biggest challenge lies in adopting policies that will allow them to utilise the demographic window to achieve rapid economic growth, increase per capita incomes, and build up human capital. Central to meeting this challenge is providing productive employment and enhancing the skills of the growing labour force. This is particularly critical considering the negative impact that 4IR technologies can have on industries and jobs in the short run.

Regional cooperation initiatives that promote greater capital and labour mobility can help mitigate many of the negative impacts that demographic and technological trends may have at the domestic level. Ageing countries could get around labour shortages by allowing greater migration or immigration, or continuing to export capital to countries with a youth bulge (Menon and Nakamura, 2009). In the short run, greater capital and labour mobility can help equalise capital-labour ratios and normalise differences in labour and capital productivity to promote more inclusive growth. In the immediate future, greater capital rather than labour mobility may prove to be the easier alternative given continuing border restrictions on people movement during the pandemic. Countries in the region have made considerable progress in removing restrictions to capital flows, whereas liberalising labour flows continues to be fraught with controversy, even before the pandemic hit.

Support for greater labour mobility will have to play a complementary role in overcoming remaining bottlenecks, however. In ASEAN, for instance, harmonisation and streamlining of employment visas have been an important initiative in reducing barriers to labour mobility. ASEAN economies have signed a number of mutual recognition agreements (MRAs) for skilled jobs, but implementation has been stymied by domestic rules and regulations on employment and licensing requirements. Furthermore, these MRAs will have to be more responsive to the rapidly changing skill and labour market conditions as a result of the 4IR.

But removing the barriers to labour mobility will involve more difficult and politically-sensitive policy reforms. Pursuing behind-the-border policy reforms and policy harmonisation has proven the most difficult. But it is in the region's best interest to continue to seek uniformity in regulatory rules that facilitate freer movement of skilled and unskilled labour.

Given these sensitivities, bilateral agreements may end up being more feasible than regional ones. In fact, the India–Singapore Comprehensive Economic Cooperation Agreement (CECA) is one such bilateral deal that has enabled short and long-term employment visas, ranging from 2 months to 3 years, to nationals of both countries. Similar agreements involving other ASEAN countries would be of mutual benefit.

While importing skills can help countries catch-up and address the challenges posed by the 4IR in the short run, the long-term challenges of 4IR will require a fundamental transformation in systems of education and learning. Governments must pursue education reform and promote lifelong learning. Augmenting cognitive skills such as math's and sciences will be critical for the transition to a more innovative, knowledge-based economy. There will also be a need to strengthen regional education networks and connect innovation incubators in the region. New and innovative approaches to public-private collaboration are also needed, particularly in areas such as research and development.

To help offset the impacts that the 4IR could have on the lower-income classes, the existing, fundamental challenges facing the education system and skills development should not be ignored either. Increasing retention rates in secondary education and improving post-secondary vocational training will be necessary to build a foundation upon which other innovations can succeed. Addressing the skills issue may also need to address underlying problems that may begin much earlier in the schooling life of students, starting with primary education, if we are to ensure that the post-secondary education system has the rooting and basis to succeed.

Once these improvements are set in train, we can expect a ratcheting effect to kick in, whereby the enhancements of the system affecting the first generation of students is compounded as some of them go on to become the providers of training, or the teachers, for the next generation. This is a virtuous circle that creates its own inertia, and results in an inter-generational augmentation of skills and human capital at an increasingly rapid pace. The sooner this change is made to the system of basic education, the earlier can this positive cycle be set in motion, in preparation for the demands of the 4IR.

Conclusion

ASEAN-India economic relations have come a long way since the advent of the 'Look East' policy of almost three decades ago. The COVID-19 pandemic has created new challenges, as well as new opportunities for collaboration between India and ASEAN. The pandemic has sped up the move towards a digital economy, as well as other aspects of the 4IR. There are fears that this accelerated transition will result in a rise in inter- and intra-country inequality. Often overlooked are the various ways in which the 4IR can produce offsetting effects, by increasing social, financial and economic inclusion, increasing connectivity, improving agriculture, and supporting MSMEs. To enable this, however, policy changes need to be made.

In the short run, greater factor mobility can help equalise capital-labour ratios and normalise differences in labour and capital productivity to promote more inclusive growth. Greater labour mobility, while politically sensitive, can reduce skill deficits in poorer countries in the short run, and help in preparing the workforce for the 4IR. Given the sensitivities involved, however, bilateral agreements may end up being more feasible than regional ones. The India-Singapore Comprehensive Economic Cooperation Agreement (CECA) provides a useful model that other ASEAN countries could consider, adapting it to suit their specific needs after accounting for differences in skills requirements and demographic trends.

In the longer term, changes in education and learning systems will be necessary, in moving towards an innovative society. This will need to be done while concurrently addressing basic challenges in improving retention rates in secondary schooling, for instance. Overcoming these fundamental challenges is necessary to provide a strong base to build upon in order to exploit the opportunities presented by the 4IR and mitigate its negative impacts, including limiting the rise in inequality.

Notes
1. This was noted as far back as Veblen (1915), although modernized by Gershenkron (1952) as "the advantage of relative backwardness".
2. This assumes that the technology is available for purchase or is easily diffused, which may not be unreasonable given that intellectual property rights are poorly protected or enforced in developing countries.
3. Far a discussion on how the long run impacts are likely to be net positive, see OECD (2016) and Menon (2019).

References

ADB and WEF. (2017). "ASEAN 4.0: What does the Fourth Industrial Revolution mean for regional economic integration?", Asian Development Bank and World Economic Forum (ADB and WEF), Manila.

APEC. (2020). "COVID-19, 4IR and the Future of Work". Report #220-SE-01.9, Asia-Pacific Economic Cooperation (APEC), APEC Secretariat, Singapore.

Bacchetta, V.C., Piermartini, R. and Smeets, M. (2021). "Trade and Inclusive Growth". IMF Working Paper 21/74, International Monetary Fund (IMF), Washington, DC.

Gerschenkron, A. (1952). "Economic Backwardness in Historical Perspective", in M. Granovetter and R. Swedberg (eds.), *The Sociology of Economic Life*, Westview Press, Boulder, CO.

Jensen, R. (2007). "The Digital Provide: Information (Technology), Market Performance, and Welfare in the South Indian Fisheries Sector". *The Quarterly Journal of Economics,* 122(3), 879-924.

McKinsey & Company. (2017). *Jobs Lost, Jobs Gained: Workforce Transitions in a Time of Automation.* McKinsey Global Institute.

Menon, J. (2019). "Why the Fourth Industrial Revolution could spell more jobs – not fewer", *Agenda,* World Economic Forum.

Menon, J. and Nakamura, A. (2009). "Ageing in Asia: Trends, Impacts and Responses", *ASEAN Economic Bulletin* 26 (3), pp. 293-305.

Menon, J. and Fink A. (2018). "ASEAN4.0: What does the Fourth Industrial Revolution mean for regional economic integration?", *Journal of Asian Economic Integration,* 1(1), pp. 2-18.

Nuesch, S. 2007. *The Economics of Superstars and Celebrities*. Springer, Frankfurt.

OECD. (2016). "Automation and independent work in a digital economy: Policy brief on the future of work". Organisation for Economic Cooperation and Development (OECD), Paris.

Rosen, Sherwin. (1981). "The Economics of Superstars". *The American Economic Review*, 71(5), pp. 845-858.

Schwab, K. (2018). "Shaping the Fourth Industrial Revolution: A Handbook for Citizens, Policy-Maker, Business Leaders and Social Influences". World Economic Forum.

Schwab, K. (2016). *The Fourth Industrial Revolution*. New York: Crown Business.

UN. (2017). *The impact of the technological revolution on labour markets and income distribution*, United Nations (UN), New York.

Veblen, T. (1915). *Imperial Germany and the Industrial Revolution*. Macmillan, New York and London.

11. 4IR and the Digital Platform Economy

Opportunities and Policy Challenges for the ASEAN and India

Balaji Parthasarathy

Introduction

The term "Fourth Industrial Revolution" (4IR) became part of the popular imagination after the theme of the World Economic Forum (WEF) Annual Meeting in 2016: "Mastering the Fourth Industrial Revolution". According to Schwab (2016), the Executive Chairman of the WEF, 4IR is led by "emerging technology breakthroughs in fields such as artificial intelligence, robotics, the Internet of Things, autonomous vehicles, 3-D printing, nanotechnology, biotechnology, materials science, energy storage, and quantum computing." The revolutionary impact of a technology like artificial intelligence (AI), and its branches such as machine learning (ML), comes from it being a general purpose technology (Brynjolfsson and Mitchell, 2017) i.e., besides emerging as an important sector in its own right but also has the potential "to transform an economy by finding new applications and fusing with existing technologies to rejuvenate other, pre-existing sectors of the economy" (David, 2000). Thus, the 4IR, like the earlier industrial revolution, has the potential to raise income levels and improve the quality of life globally by making possible new products and services, while it also likely to lead to greater inequality, especially by disrupting labour markets.

Economics rejects the claim that advances in technology will reduce employment (the so-called "lump of labour argument"), on the grounds that emerging technologies will offer new opportunities for labour to serve the infinite range of needs that humans have (Brynjolfsson and McAfee, 2015). However, adjusting to new opportunities is not frictionless, as short-term pain is inflicted when new technologies render many skills obsolete (Frey, 2019). Indeed, a study of 702 occupations in the US by Frey and Osborne (2013) estimated that 47 per cent of those occupations were susceptible to automation by the mid-2030s, thanks to machine learning and robotics. But Castells (2010: 280) emphatically states that there are no "systematic links" between ICTs and employment, as specific outcomes depend on "macro-economic factors, economic strategies, and socio-political context". The relationship between technology and work can only be understood as a "complex interaction within a social system" comprising "management decisions, systems of industrial relations, cultural and institutional environments and government policies" (ibid.: 256).

Thus, Frey (2019: 13) writes, "The Industrial Revolution was the beginning of an unprecedented transformation that benefited everyone in the long-run. AI systems have the potential to do the same, but the future of AI depends on how we manage the short run." Brynjolfsson and Mitchell (2017) further highlight that, since ML systems do not excel at all tasks in all jobs, there is little agreement on the specifics of the impacts on the labour market and the "effects on employment are more complex than the simple replacement and substitution story emphasized by some".

The rest of the chapter is classified as follows: Section 2 discusses 4IR in context to digital platforms. The growth of these platforms is narrated in Section 3. Some drawbacks are highlighted in Section 4. Finally, the outlook of 'New Normal' in post-pandemic situation is mentioned in Way Forward.

4IR and Digital Technology Platforms

A manifestation of the 4IR are digital-technology platforms that "combine both demand and supply to disrupt existing industry structures, such as those we see within the "sharing" or "on demand" economy" (Schwab, 2016). A category of such platforms offer "work on-demand via apps" including "activities such as transport, cleaning and running errands" and "forms of clerical work … channelled through apps managed by firms" (De Stefano, 2016:1). Srnicek (2017) also refers to these platforms as lean platforms, as they provide services with a minimal ownership of assets. It is the growth of such platforms, and the characteristics of the work they offer in India and ASEAN, that this paper will discuss to highlight certain shared areas policy concerns in the post-COVID-19 era.

The paper will limit itself to India and Indonesia, which is the single largest market for platforms in the ASEAN (*Economist*, 2018). Of the many platforms in operation, it will also focus on four platforms whose services many in this workshop have likely used: Ola and Uber in India, Gojek and Grab in Indonesia. Ola was founded in Mumbai in 2010, but is now Bangalore-based, while Uber arrived from California to the Indian market in 2014, as provider of car taxi services. Since then, they have expanded to offer two-wheeler and autorickshaw taxi services, while Uber also offers business to customer, and customer to customer deliveries (Salman, 2020). Gojek, which was started in Indonesia in 2011, as a provider of motor-bike taxi services, now offers a suite of 18 products, including car taxis, food delivery, logistics, electronic payments, and beauty services, such as massage and makeup (Colgrave, 2019). Grab, which was founded in Malaysia in 2010, is now Singapore-based, entered the Indonesian market in 2014 and now offers transportation and food delivery services, and electronic payments through its Ovo application.

These platforms provide employment opportunities that are not insignificant. In India, Ola and Uber accounted for 2.2 million jobs of the 14.62 million added between 2014 and 2018 (Pradhan, 2019). In Indonesia, Gojek says that it has more than 2 million motor-bike taxi driver-partners, and "hundreds of thousands" of car taxi driver-partners.[1,2] The third section will examine the reasons for the growth of platforms in the two countries, while the fourth will highlight the concerns raised by the work opportunities offered by platforms.

The final section will discuss the adverse impacts of the COVID-19 pandemic on platforms and especially their workers. However, since growth is expected to pick up after the pandemic subsides, the paper will conclude with an overview of the policy directions that must be pursued to encourage the growth of platforms while ensuring socially acceptable work conditions.

The Growth of Platforms in India and ASEAN

Platforms such as Ola, Uber, Gojek or Grab aggregate demand and supply. More specifically, they are transaction platforms or "marketplaces that make it possible for participants to exchange goods and services or information. The more participants and functions available on a transaction platform, the more useful it becomes. These platforms create value by enabling exchanges that would not otherwise occur without the platform as an intermediary" (Cusumano, 2020). As intermediaries that coordinate the interaction of two sets of agents, each of whose actions affect outcomes for the other, typically through network externalities, platforms lie at the heart of two-sided markets (Rysman, 2009). Such markets exhibit two types of network effects: "a same-side effect, in which increasing the number of users on one side of the network makes it either more or less valuable on the same side; and a cross-side effect, in which increasing the number of users on one side of the network makes it either more or less valuable to the users on the other side" (Eisenmann et al., 2006: 95).

In addition to the network externalities they generate, there are at least other three reasons why transaction platforms have grown to provide significant employment opportunities in India and in Indonesia. First, employment opportunities in both countries are limited, as a result of which the share of non-agricultural informal employment in non-agricultural employment in 2018, in India, was 78.1 per cent, and 80.2 per cent in Indonesia (ILO, 2018).[3] For those who are informally employed, platforms become an attractive employment opportunity when one could connect to them.

Facilitating this connection was the growth of mobile broadband internet access: by 2019, in India, the mobile phone density (per 100 inhabitants) was 88.45, and 46.9 per cent of mobile phones had broadband internet access, while in Indonesia the corresponding figures were 133 and 84 per cent.[4] The physical means of last-mile service delivery comes from the growing ownership of motorcycles and scooters. According to a Pew Survey conducted in April-May 2014, 47 per cent of households in India, and 85 per cent of households in Indonesia, reported owning one (Poushter, 2015). On the supply side, these platforms have attracted substantial venture capital to support their growth. Ola has, thus far, attracted US$ 3.78 billion, Uber US$ 24.8 billion, Gojek US$ 4.8 billion and Grab US$ 10.1 billion.[5] As of August 2020, with the exception of Uber (a public listed company), the others were valued as "unicorns".[6]

The Concerns with Digital Platforms

Despite the growth of the platforms, there are concerns. One is the nature of the employment relationship. Although they offer a "workforce" to customers, the platforms do not recognise workers as employees; instead, workers are euphemistically classified as independent contractors or partners, which allow the platforms to minimise their legal and social responsibilities, such as providing minimum wages or other employment benefits. The platforms are not entirely to blame for taking advantage of loopholes in the law. For instance, in Indonesia, the 2003 Manpower Law fails to recognise these workers as employees.[7] In other words, most workers perform digital gig work, or a "non-standard form of employment", a term that designates all employment that is definite, and neither full time nor part of a subordinate and bilateral employment relationship (ILO, 2016).

Indeed, even before the COVID-19 pandemic affected the business of platforms acutely, the number they employed, with social security and benefits, in areas such as customer support, business development, legal, finance, policy and marketing, was but a small fraction of their workforce. Approximate figures for Ola were 4500,[8] 2400 for Uber,[9] 4750 for Gojek,[10] and 7200 for Grab.[11] While workers are lured by the "flexibility" of being an entrepreneur, in reality, they are squeezed between paying commissions to the platforms (25-35 per cent of earnings for Ola and Uber), covering the mortgage/rental payment of their vehicles, besides meeting the operational expenses and overheads such as fuel and maintenance cost. The squeeze is because much of worker earnings comes from incentives, chasing which means being "flexible" about working up to 16 hours, especially as incentives declined by ~50 per cent in India between 2015 and by late 2019 (Ray, 2019). Like in India, "GoJek and Grab drivers have the freedom of independent contractors but do not get to negotiate their contract and are instead reined in by company regulations akin to formal employment.... Furthermore, Go-Jek and Grab can terminate a driver's contract anytime, often citing a list of regulations, and once laid off, there are cases of owed money being withheld from drivers" (Colgrave, 2019: 9).

A second concern has to do with the mechanism of control over workers. Platforms embody "an architecture – a design for products, services, and infrastructure facilitating network users' interactions – plus set of rules; that is, the protocols, rights, and pricing terms that govern transactions" (Eisenmann et al., 2006: 95, original emphasis). As the implementation of the architecture and rules of digital platforms increasingly relies on advances in AI, worries have surfaced about "algorithmic management", defined as work settings where "human jobs are assigned, optimized, and evaluated through algorithms and tracked data" (Lee et al., 2015:1603).

Algorithmic management continuously tracks workers' behaviour; constantly evaluates the performance of workers from client reviews, and the client's acceptance or rejection of their work; automatically implements decisions, without human intervention; and, requires workers to interact with a "system" rather than humans, thus depriving them of opportunities for feedback or discussion and negotiation with their supervisor, as would be typical in offline jobs (Möhlmann and Zalmanson, 2017). Worse, there is low transparency. The low transparency, or what Burrell

(2016) terms opacity, renders algorithmic management particularly problematic as it implies that workers have no access to the logic or criteria behind key decisions being made about their performance evaluation and, consequently, future opportunities.

Indeed, as Uber's Head of Engineering in Bangalore describes, "the algorithm learns from patterns of behaviour, rider preferences, the timing of the day and kind of ride preferences. We work along with both individual rider perspectives and a broad preference understanding.... On the driver's side, the algorithms work on the number of trips each driver takes during the day, hours that are spent, which areas they work out of and then there is the angle of mapping and routing. The timings are then given depending on the driver's location and customer location.... Since our algorithms are constantly learning, with time we want to be able to show what the top rides from your history are, prompt destinations based on your preferences and make the process faster and seamless" (cited in Mallya and Kashyap, 2017, emphasis added).

The COVID-19 Pandemic and Looking Ahead to a "New Normal"

Worldwide, the COVID-19 pandemic has hit the platform economy hard. It has led to a decline in demand for platforms' services, and trapped workers in a vicious cycle of having to work harder amidst growing income and job insecurity (Moulds, 2020). For instance, in Indonesia, social distancing requirements made it impossible for motor-bike taxis to board passengers (Adjie and Prawira, 2020). To deal with such challenges, in India, as elsewhere, workers have received support that is negligible at best, whether from the government or the platforms they work for.[12] However, there are signs that demand for ride-hailing could bounce back after the pandemic ends, with demand for freight/logistics services growing even faster.

In India, an online survey by Thakur et al. (2020), showed that 35 per cent of 438 respondents between 7 and 26 April in 51 cities, indicated that they would change their mode of transport after the pandemic, mostly from public transport (metro, buses and local trains) to private vehicles (cars and motorcycles/scooters), and also to intermediate public transport (cabs, auto-rickshaws and carpooling) or to non-motorised transport (bicycling or walking). Of the respondents, 45 per cent of the 46 per cent were used to ordering groceries online even before the pandemic, said they would increase online purchases. Of the 54 per cent who had never relied on online grocery shopping, 24 per cent said that they would begin to do so. The findings in India are corroborated in Indonesia where, as the "virus has battered the gig economy", Gojek's Chief Operating Officer was quoted as saying that "transport has fallen off a cliff, food has held steady, while logistics went through the roof and online payments are high … so having a portfolio of products helps" (*The Straits Times*, 2020).

Although the extent to which food delivery and logistics can compensate for the loss of ride-hailing is unclear, it is evident that platforms, and the work they offer, are not going to disappear after the pandemic ebbs. Thus, the challenge for India and Indonesia, with their levels of informal employment, is to consider how best to harness the potential of digital platforms instead of merely replacing one form of worker precarity (Standing, 2011), with another. In other words, it is to determine how to ensure that platforms generate what Berg et al. (2018: 1) term decent work, or "work that is productive; ensures equality of opportunity and treatment for all women and men; delivers a fair income, security in the workplace and social protection for families; provides prospects for personal development; and gives workers the freedom to express their concerns, organize and participate in decisions that affect their working lives."

Critical to ensuring the growth of platforms while offering decent work in India and Indonesia (and much of the ASEAN) is creating a supportive regulatory framework. This article provides a couple of examples of promising initiatives, and limits, by India to overcome the regulatory vacuum and change the opportunities and experience of platform work.

The first is the law pertaining to motorbike taxis whose deployment has been encouraged by the Government of India since 2016. In a report, the Ministry of Road Transport and Highways (2016: 22) recommended that, "the State Transport Department may allow two-wheeler taxi permit on the lines similar to those for city taxi…. It is highly recommended that existing private bikes may be allowed for such transportation in order to facilitate utilisation of idle assets and state governments may also consider online option to allow private bikes to convert to taxis." Further reinforcing this message was the Motor Vehicles (Amendment) Act, 2019, which explicitly recognizes motorbike taxis.[13] However, implementation of this policy, which has the potential to expand opportunities for platform work, has been lax. In 2020, only 14 states and union territories had notified motorbike taxi policies, while in the rest, the lack of clear policies has resulted in penalties, license cancellations of operators and bans (Raman, 2020).

The second example is India's recent reform to consolidate 44 labour laws under 4 categories of Codes. The Code on Social Security, 2020, introduces the terms "platform workers" ("a person engaged in or undertaking platform work") and "gig worker" ("a person who performs work or participates in a work arrangement and earns from such activities outside of traditional employer-employee relationship") for the first time.[14] Section 114(1) of the Code goes on to state that "The Central Government may formulate and notify, from time to time, suitable social security schemes for gig workers and platform worker on matters relating to (a) life and disability cover; (b) health and maternity benefits; (c) old age protection; and (d) any other benefit as may be determined by the Central Government", to pay for which platforms will be required to contribute between 1 and 2 per cent of their annual turnover.

While the reference to gig and platform workers may be considered a conceptual departure, it is not reinforced in other codes. The Code on Wages, 2019, for example, fails to make a reference to these categories and only mentions that all workers will be covered by a national floor wage below which no regional minimum wage can be set. However, it is unclear if workers on India's platforms will have a right to the legal minimum wage like their UK counterparts have been entitled to following a recent ruling by the Supreme Court in that country (Sarkar, 2021).

Another approach to ensuring decent work is adopted by the Fairwork Foundation in its studies in India and Indonesia, amongst other countries.[15] The Foundation scores platforms between 1 and 10 on the basis of five Fairwork principles, which are structured to capture various aspects of work conditions. The advantage of this approach is that the variation in scores across platforms shows there is nothing inevitable about the conditions of platform work. It allows platforms to also note where they stand vis-à-vis competitors, and regulators to not paint all platforms with the same brush. Workers too have an opportunity to determine which platform may be preferable to work on. Finally, it gives customers an opportunity to seek their services from platforms that score better, thereby encouraging a bias toward more socially acceptable work conditions.

Notes

1. https://www.gojek.com/
2. Although neither Gojek nor Grab provide services in India, they have a presence. Gojek established a development centre by acquiring Bangalore based C42 Engineering and CodeIgnition in 2016, followed by the acquisition of the Bangalore-based AI recruiting platform air CTO in 2019. It also opened an engineering and product development centre in Gurgaon. It aimed to have 500 employees in India by the end of 2019. Grab has more than 200 employees in its Indian engineering team in Bangalore working on building payment systems, geomapping and data science (Whye, 2020).
3. The ILO (2018:10), defines informal employment in terms of the employment relationship. "… for a job held by an employee to be considered as informal, the employment relationship should not be, in law or in practice, subject to national labour legislation, income taxation, social protection or entitlement to certain employment benefits (advance notice of dismissal, severance pay, paid annual or sick leave, etc.). The underpinning reasons may be the non-declaration of the jobs of the employees, casual jobs or jobs of a short duration, jobs with hours of work or wages below a specified threshold (e.g. for social security contributions) or lack of application of law and regulation in practice. Employers and own-account workers are considered to be

informal when their economic units belong to the informal sector. In practice, the formal or informal nature of a job held by an employee is determined on the basis of operational criteria such as social security contributions by the employer (on behalf of the employee), and entitlement to paid sick leave and paid annual leave."

4. Data for India from Telecom Statistics India – 2019, accessed at: https://dot.gov.in/sites/default/files/Telecom%20Statistics%20India-2019.pdf?download=1; data for Indonesia from https://datareportal.com/reports/digital-2019-indonesia
5. 5 Venture capital data from https://www.crunchbase.com/
6. https://www.cbinsights.com/research-unicorn-companies
7. https://www.ilo.org/dyn/travail/docs/760/Indonesian+Labour+Law+-+Act+13+of+2003.pdf
8. https://www.livemint.com/companies/start-ups/ola-to-fire-1-400-employees-as-revenue-down-by-95-in-2-months-11589961627720.html
9. https://www..com/news/india/uber-india-fires-600-employees-a-quarter-of-its-workforce-in-country-11590465019010.html livemint
10. https://www.thejakartapost.com/news/2020/06/24/gojek-lays-off-430-employees-amid-pandemic-impact.html
11. https://www.bloomberg.com/news/articles/2020-06-16/grab-to-cut-5-of-employees-in-another-setback-for-softbank
12. https://tandemresearch.org/blog/covid19-and-relief-measures-for-gig-workers-in-india
13. http://egazette.nic.in/WriteReadData/2019/210413.pdf
14. labour.gov.in/sites/default/files/SS_Code_Gazette.pdf
15. https://fair.work/en/fw/homepage/

References

Adjie, M. and Prawira, F. (2020). "App-based 'ojek' drivers demand compensation as new social restrictions bar them from taking passengers". *The Jakarta Post*. 8 April.

Berg, J., Furrer, M., Harmon, E., Rani, U. and Silberman, M.S. (2018). "Digital Labour Platforms and the Future of Work: Towards Decent Work in the Online World". International Labour Organization, Geneva.

Brynjolfsson, E. and McAfee, A. (2015). "Will humans go the way of horses? Labour in the second machine age". *Foreign Affairs*. 94(4): 8-14.

Brynjolfsson, E. and T. Mitchell. (2017). "What can machine learning do? Workforce implications". *Science* 358(6370):1530-1534.

Burrell, J. (2016). "How the machine 'thinks': Understanding opacity in machine learning algorithms". Big Data and Society. January-June, 1-12.

Castells, M. (2010) *The Rise of the Network Society. Volume 1 of The Information Age: Economy, Society and Culture,* (2nd edition). Wiley-Blackwell, Chichester, Wiley-Blackwell, UK.

Colgrave, L. (2019). "Ride-Hailing in Indonesia and Australia Gig Economies: The Case of Go-Jek, Grab, and Uber. Case Stud #59", Center for Digital Society, Universitas Gadjah Mada.

Cusumano, M.A., Yoffie, D.B., and Gawer, A. (2020). "The future of platforms". *Sloan Management Review.* Spring, https://sloanreview.mit.edu/article/the-future-of-platforms/

David, P.A. (2000). "Understanding digital technology's evolution and the path of measured productivity growth", in E. Brynjolfsson and B. Kahin (eds.) *Understanding the Digital Economy: Data, Tools and Research,* pp. 49-98, Cambridge, MA: MIT Press.

De Stefano, V. (2016). "The Rise of the 'Just-In-Time Workforce': On-demand Work, Crowdwork and Labour Protection in the 'Gig-Economy'", Conditions of Work and Employment Series No. 71, International Labour Organization (ILO). Geneva.

Eisenmann, T., Parker, G., and Van Alstyne, M.W. (2006). "Strategies for two-sided markets". *Harvard Business Review.* 84(10): 92-101.

Frey, C.B. (2019). *The Technology Trap: Capital, Labor, and Power in the Age of Automation.* Princeton, NJ: Princeton University Press.

Frey, C.B. and Osborne, M.A. (2013). "The future of employment: How susceptible are jobs to computerisation?", *Technological Forecasting and Social Change.* 114: 254-280.

ILO. (2016). "Non-Standard Employment around the World: Understanding Challenges, Shaping Prospects". International Labour Organization (ILO), Geneva.

ILO. (2018). "Women and Men in the Informal Economy: A Statistical Profile". Third Edition. International Labour Organization (ILO), Geneva.

Kumar, R.P. (2020). "Uber India lays off 600 employees, a quarter of its workforce in the country". *The Mint,* 26 May, https://www.livemint.com/news/india/uber-india-fires-600-employees-a-quarter-of-its-workforce-in-country-11590465019010.html

Lee, K., Kusbit, D., Metsky, E. and Dabbish, L. (2015). "Working with machines: The algorithmic and data-driven management on human workers". Proceedings of the 33rd Annual ACM Conference on Human Factors in Computing Systems. pp. 1603-1612, 18-23 April, Seoul.

Mallya, H. and Kashyap. S. (2017). "What happens inside Uber after you book a cab?", *Yourstory*. 31 May, https://yourstory.com/2017/05/inside-uber-cab

Ministry of Road Transport and Highways. (2016). "Report of the Committee Constituted to Propose Taxi Policy Guideline to Promote Urban Mobility", https://smartnet.niua.org/sites/default/files/resources/Taxi%20Policy%20Guidelines.pdf

Möhlmann, M. and Zalmanson, L. (2017). "Hands on the wheel: Navigating algorithmic management and Uber drivers' autonomy". Proceedings of the Eighth International Conference on Information Systems (ICIS 2017), 10-13 December, Seoul.

Moulds, J. (2020). "Gig workers among the hardest hit by coronavirus pandemic". World Economic Forum, 21 April.

Poushter, J. (2015). "Car, bike or motorcycle? Depends on where you live", https://www.pewresearch.org/fact-tank/2015/04/16/car-bike-or-motorcycle-depends-on-where-you-live/

Pradhan, D. (2019). "Jobs are being created, Ola and Uber added 2.2 mn jobs: NITI Aayog CEO Kant". Inc42, 2 February, https://inc42.com/buzz/jobs-are-being-created-ola-uber-added-2-2-mn-jobs-niti-aayog-ceo-kant/

Raman, A. (2020). "The Power of Two Wheels. Bike-Taxi: India's New Shared Mobility Frontier". Ola Mobility Institute, https://olawebcdn.com/ola-institute/bike-taxi-report.pdf

Ray, A. (2019). "Unrest in India's gig economy: Ola-Uber drivers' strikes and worker organisation". Futures of Work. 9 December. https://futuresofwork.co.uk/2019/12/09/unrest-in-indias-gig-economy-ola-uber-drivers-strikes-and-worker-organisation/

Rysman, M. 2009. "The economics of two-sided markets", *Journal of Economic Perspectives*, 23(3): 125-143.

Salman, S.H. (2020). "As demand falls, Uber to focus on B2C logistics services in India", https://www.livemint.com/companies/news/as-demand-falls-uber-to-focus-on-b2c-logistics-services-in-india-11595853544996.html

Sarkar, K. (2021). "Why UK Supreme Court's Uber driver verdict can impact Indian gig workers". *The Leaflet*, 10 March, https://www.theleaflet.in/why-uk-supreme-courts-uber-driver-verdict-can-impact-indian-gig-workers/

Schwab, K. (2016). "The Fourth Industrial Revolution: what it means, how to respond", https://www.weforum.org/agenda/2016/01/the-fourth-industrial-revolution-what-it-means-and-how-to-respond/

Srnicek, N. (2017). *Platform Capitalism*. Cambridge, Polity Press, UK.

Standing, G. (2011). *The Precariat: The New Dangerous Class*. London, Bloomsbury Academic, UK.

Thakur, P., Mookerjee, P., Jain, A. and Harikumar, A. (2020). "Impact of COVID-19 on Urban Mobility in India: Evidence from a Perception Study". The Energy and Resources Institute (TERI), New Delhi.

The Economist. 2018. "After Uber: A ride-hailing battle in South-East Asia". 29 September, https://www.economist.com/business/2018/09/29/a-ride-hailing-battle-in-south-east-asia

The Hindu. (2020). "HC rejects plea to direct govt. to enact law to protect gig workers". *The Hindu*, 14 May, https://www.thehindu.com/news/national/karnataka/hc-rejects-plea-to-direct-govt-to-enact-law-to-protect-gig-workers/article31584316.ece

The Straits Times. (2020). "Fifty drivers fight for one order: South-east Asia's gig economy battered by virus", 11 June, https://www.straitstimes.com/business/economy/fifty-drivers-fight-for-one-order-southeast-asias-gig-economy-slammed-by-virus

Whye, L. K. (2020). "Southeast Asia's most valuable startups shed staff due to COVID-19". *Business World*, 29 June, http://www.businessworld.in/article/Southeast-Asia-s-most-valuable-startups-shed-staff-due-to-COVID-19/29-06

SECTION IV: **ASEAN Outlook on Indo-Pacific (AOIP) and Indo-Pacific Oceans Initiative (IPOI): Complementarities and Cooperation**

12. Indo-Pacific Oceans Initiative (IPOI) and ASEAN Outlook on the Indo-Pacific (AOIP)

Views on Complementarities

Pradeep Chauhan

Introduction

India's Prime Minister enunciated a new "Indo-Pacific Oceans Initiative" (IPOI) at the 14th East Asia Summit (EAS) in Bangkok, on 4 November 2020.[1] The IPOI has been conceptually positioned so as to be in consonance with the UN's Sustainable Development Goals (SDG) – specifically with 'SDG 14': Life Below Water.[2] The IPOI is designed to further the endeavour of countries of the Indo-Pacific, stretching from the east coast of Africa to the west coast of the Americas,[3] "to create a safe, secure and stable maritime domain" within which collective and collaborative mechanisms could be created to "conserve and sustainably use" this domain and "safeguard the oceans, including from plastic litter; build capacity and fairly share resources; reduce disaster risk; enhance science, technology and academic cooperation; and promote free, fair and mutually beneficial trade and maritime transport."[4]

This chapter discussed the emerging concept of Indo-Pacific through the lenses of India and ASEAN. The structure of IPOI is presented in Section 2. Indo-Pacific narrative of ASEAN and other countries are covered in Section 3. Section 4 discussed the Indo-Pacific cooperation framework between ASEAN and India. Africa plays a major role in Indo-Pacific construct. The role of Africa and

India's MAUSAM initiative are briefly covered in Section 5. Lastly, concluding remarks are made in Section 6.

Structure of IPOI

The IPOI builds upon the Indian vision of SAGAR, which apart from being the Hindi word for 'Ocean', is, more pertinently, an acronym for 'Security and Growth for All in the Region'.[5] The vision of SAGAR itself rests upon India's formulation of the Indo-Pacific as a region – and, specifically, the Indian outlook towards it. Abundant specificity in this regard has been provided by India, and clearly articulated at the highest level of the Government of India. Delivering the keynote address at the 2018 edition of the *Shangri La Dialogue*, in Singapore, on 1 July 2018, India's Prime Minister was unequivocal in his presentation of the Indian outlook, as witness the following extract from his address:[6]

India's own engagement in the Indo-Pacific Region – from the shores of Africa to that of the Americas - will be inclusive. We are inheritors of Vedanta philosophy that believes in essential oneness of all, and celebrates unity in diversity एकमसत्यम, विप्रा:बहुदावदंति (Truth is one, the learned speak of it in many ways). That is the foundation of our civilizational ethos – of pluralism, co-existence, open-ness and dialogue. The ideals of democracy that define us as a nation also shape the way we engage the world.

So, it translates into five S in Hindi: सम्मान [Sammaan] (respect); सम्वाद [Samvaad] (dialogue); सहयोग [Saheyog] (cooperation), शांति [Shaanti] (peace), and समृद्धि [Samridhdhi] (prosperity). It's easy to learn these words! So, we will engage with the world in peace, with respect, through dialogue and absolute commitment to international law.

We will promote a democratic and rules-based international order, in which all nations, small and large, thrive as equal and sovereign. We will work with others to keep our seas, space and airways free and open; our nations secure from terrorism; and our cyber space free from disruption and conflict. We will keep our economy open and our engagement transparent. We will share our resources, markets and prosperity with our friends and partners. We will seek a sustainable future for our planet, as through the new International Solar Alliance together with France and other partners.

As may be seen from the foregoing extract, 'inclusivity', and 'transparency' are fundamental to India's Indo-Pacific formulation,[7] as also to the vision of SAGAR, and these, therefore, drive the 'IPOI'.

The 'IPOI' identifies seven basic facets of maritime cooperation and collaboration. These are (i) Maritime Security; (ii) Maritime Ecology; (iii) Maritime Resources; (iv) Capacity Building and Resource Sharing; (v) Disaster Risk Reduction and Management; (vi) Science, Technology and Academic Cooperation; and (vii) Trade, Connectivity and Maritime Transport. These facets of maritime cooperation and collaboration have been described by India's Ministry of External Affairs (MEA) as seven "pillars".[8] The usage of the word 'pillars' is a foundational error and a great pity. This is because such an analogy is fraught with the risk of viewing the 'IPOI' as a set of seven vertical-silos, rather than an intricate web of linkages that connect any one basic facet of the IPOI to the other six. The 'pillar-approach' might well make for administrative convenience, but this notwithstanding, it is very strongly recommended that this approach be consciously abjured at all levels in favour of the more complex but far more advantageous one of considering these to be the seven pillars may consider as the seven spokes of a heptagonal-web of the most intricate inter-linkages that serve to disaggregate the SAGAR-vision into a set of specific programmes and activities.

Indo-Pacific Strategies: Different Countries and ASEAN

It is important to note that both, 'SAGAR' (as a vision) and the 'IPOI' (as an initiative), are synchronous with other recent maritime initiatives and strategies relevant to the Indo-Pacific. Prominent amongst these is Japan's "Free and Open Indo-Pacific" (FOIP). This term, much favoured by Tokyo, actually has two distinct (albeit related) points of reference. The first is as a 'concept' in which the adjectives 'free' and 'open' are envisaged as "international public goods" that can be provided through the leveraging of the dynamism inherent in the combination of two continents (Asia and Africa) across two oceans (the Indian Ocean and the Pacific Ocean). The second point of reference – and here the acronym 'FOIP' is used almost as a common noun – is a key strategy of Japan, by means of which a troika of objectives, namely, 'peace' 'stability', and, 'prosperity', all three of which result from a foundational adherence to a rule-based international maritime order, are sought to be achieved in a comprehensive, inclusive and transparent manner, across the geography defined by the aforementioned combination of the two continents (Asia and Africa) and the two oceans (the Indian Ocean and the Pacific Ocean).[9] As with the FOIP, the IPOI emphasizes 'inclusivity', 'transparency', a 'rules-based international order', and the centrality of ASEAN and ASEAN-led constructs, such as the East Asia Summit (EAS)[10] and the ASEAN Regional Forum (ARF).[11] A similar congruence between the Indian conceptualisation of the Indo-Pacific as a 'strategic-geography' may be seen with France's own concept as enunciated in the 2019-update to the French MoD's policy document, "France and Security in the Indo-Pacific", and, here too, 'peace' 'stability', and, 'prosperity' are enunciated as desired goals. As in the case of India and Japan, France has unequivocally stated that the attainment of these goals requires adherence to a rules-based international order that has been set through multilateral dialogue and comity.[12] While the geography of the Indo-Pacific specified in the Government of Australia's "2017 Foreign Policy White Paper" ("We define the Indo-Pacific as the region ranging from the eastern Indian Ocean to the Pacific Ocean connected by Southeast Asia, including India, North Asia and the United States."),[13] is more limited than that of India, Japan and France, there is very substantial conceptual and geopolitical alignment, particularly where the IPOI is concerned. This congruity is most evident in the India-Australia "Joint Declaration on a Shared Vision for Maritime Cooperation in the Indo-Pacific" of 4 June 2020.[14] Some analysts have tended to club the USA, Japan, India and Australia into something called a 'FOIP bloc', which they have posited is distinct from (and opposed to) China.[15] Considerable significance is provided by these analysts to the potential of the expected initiative from Indonesia by way of an "Indo-Pacific Infrastructure and Connectivity Forum". However, this seems to be a force-fitted difference-of-approach because it is acknowledged by these very scholars that "Several principles of the Jakarta-led Indo-Pacific cooperation concept – namely, openness, transparency, and upholding of international law (rules-based order) – are compatible with those proposed by the United States and its partners within their FOIP vision". In any case, the basic tenet of ASEAN-centrality embodied in this soon-to-be-proposed 'forum' has already been fully embraced by India, Japan, Australia and the USA. Indeed, the very conceptualisation by India of the Indo-Pacific, as also its 'subsets', namely, the vision of SAGAR and the IPOI, is founded precisely upon the centrality of ASEAN. This is equally true of the FOIP and the Australian and US formulations.

At this stage, it would be appropriate to briefly review ASEAN's own formulation, embodied in the "ASEAN Outlook on the Indo-Pacific" (AOIP).

In terms of the geography of the Indo-Pacific, the AOIP makes two main assertions. The first is that ASEAN views the Indo-Pacific as being equal to the wider Asia-Pacific region plus the Indian Ocean region.[16] The second assertion both, modifies and amplifies, the first, in averring that the Indian Ocean region and the Pacific Ocean region are not perceived by ASEAN as being merely "contiguous territorial spaces but as a closely integrated and interconnected region, with ASEAN playing a central and strategic role".[17] There is no doubt that, cartographically, the Indian Ocean region does, indeed, stretch eastward from the east coast of Africa, and that the Pacific Ocean region does, indeed, stretch westward all the way to the western shores of the Americas. It is thus clear that, contrary to the views of some European scholars,[18] there is actually close congruence between ASEAN, Japan, France and India, insofar as the geographic framework of the Indo-Pacific region is concerned.

Framework of Indo-Pacific Cooperation between India and ASEAN

Beyond the strict confines of geography, too, clear congruence is visible in the functional framework of the Indo-Pacific perspectives of both, ASEAN and India. This commonality runs unbroken through the Indian concept of the Indo-Pacific itself, India's own outlook as encapsulated by the acronym of SAGAR, and the programmes envisaged under the rubric of the IPOI. Specific evidence of this congruence is to be found in the following commonalities between the outlooks of ASEAN and India, respectively:

- The centrality of ASEAN, as a foundational principle.
- The predominance of dialogue and cooperation instead of rivalry.
- The pursuit of peace and stability as a prerequisite for prosperity.
- The pursuit of inclusive development and prosperity for all.
- The criticality of the maritime domain.
- The primacy accorded to inclusivity, openness, and transparency.
- The indispensability of a rules-based framework whose structural strength is derived from internationally and consensually derived laws, treaties and conventions such as the UN Charter, the ASEAN Charter, the 1982 UN Convention on the Law of the Sea (UNCLOS 1982), the SOLAS Conventions, the SUA Convention, the 1976 ASEAN Treaty of Amity and Cooperation (TAC, 1976), the 2011 EAS Principles for Mutually Beneficial Relations, etc.
- The essentiality of an abiding respect for sovereignty.
- The importance is given to complementarity with existing ASEAN-led cooperation-frameworks, such as the East Asia Summit (EAS), the ASEAN Regional Forum (ARF), the ASEAN Defence Ministers Meeting 'Plus' (ADMM-Plus), the Expanded ASEAN Maritime Forum (EAMF), etc.

There is, once again, an almost complete commonality in the specific areas of cooperation envisaged by the AOIP and the IPOI, although the former has a more exhaustive listing and the latter, a more consolidated set that encompasses very nearly all the broad areas of cooperation enumerated in the AOIP, as well as their more detailed amplification.[19] The following tabulation offers adequate evidence of this striking commonality:

Table 12.1: Identified Broad-Areas of (Maritime) Cooperation

	ASEAN Outlook on the Indo-Pacific (AOIP)	Indo-Pacific Oceans Initiative (IPOI)
Maritime Cooperation	Freedom of Navigation and Over-flight	Maritime Security Capacity Building and Resource Sharing
	Peaceful Dispute-settlement	
	Promote Maritime Connectivity	
	Maritime Safety & Security	
	Promote Maritime Commerce	
	Address Transnational Crime (e.g., trafficking in persons or illicit drugs, sea-piracy, robbery and armed robbery against ships at sea, etc.)	
	Develop a Blue Economy	Maritime Resources Capacity Building and Resource Sharing
	Sustainable Management of Marine Resources	
	Address Marine Pollution	
	Mitigate impacts of Sea-level Rise	
	Tackle Marine Debris	
	Preserve and Protect the Marine Environment and Biodiversity	Maritime Ecology
	Promote 'Green' Shipping,	Capacity Building and Resource Sharing
	Protect the Livelihood of Coastal Communities	
	Support Small-scale Fishing Communities	
	Technical Cooperation in Marine Science Collaboration (R&D; sharing of experience and best practices, capacity-building, managing marine hazards, raising awareness on marine and ocean-related issues, etc.)	Science, Technology and Academic Cooperation

Connectivity (Connecting the Connectivities)	Reinforce existing MPAC 2025	Trade Connectivity and Maritime Transport Capacity Building and Resource Sharing
	Mobilise resources for connectivity projects via regional public-private partnerships (PPP)	
	Promote regional public-private partnerships (PPP) for infrastructure projects	
	Explore potential synergies with sub-regional frameworks (e.g., IORA, BIMSTEC, BIMP-EAGA, MGC, ACMECS, etc.)	
	People-to-people connectivity (including academia and business communities)	
UN Sustainable Development Goals 2030	Utilisation of the digital economy	IPOI's underpinning as a whole
	Align regional development with the SDGs	
Economic and Other Areas of Cooperation	Trade Facilitation and Logistics Infrastructure and Services	Trade Connectivity and Maritime Transport Capacity Building and Resource Sharing
	Climate Change and Disaster Risk Reduction and Management	Disaster Risk Reduction and Management
	Maritime Implications of Industrial Revolution 4.0	

Source: Author's own.

Special mention must be made of 'Connectivity' and, as the AOIP puts it – "connecting the connectivities". It is a central theme along which maritime cooperation and collaboration between ASEAN and India can and should be progressed. In August 2017, Dr S. Jaishankar, who was then Foreign Secretary in the Government of India, had unequivocally stated, "Growth and connectivity are, today, very central to India's foreign policy thinking. The approach of 'sabka saath, sabka vikas' (collective action, inclusive growth) is as much a belief in international relations as it is in the domestic development... Across South Asia, one can see today transformational initiatives in energy, road and rail connectivity and infrastructure building... As these initiatives are realised, their contribution to the emergence of a larger regional cooperative architecture would be increasingly appreciated. Significantly, we are today working closely with a number of other international players whose approach is similar in this regard".[20]

Role of Africa and India's MAUSAM Initiative

From India's perspective, two major connectivity initiatives into which ASEAN can seamlessly blend and greatly enhance are the Asia-Africa Growth Corridor, which provides for predominantly-economic connectivity, and, the MAUSAM Initiative, which provides for cultural and people-to-people connectivity.

In 2016, a study at the Chulalongkorn University (Bangkok) indicated that amongst ASEAN nations, the biggest traders with Africa were Thailand (US$ 11.6 billion), Indonesia (US$ 10.7 billion) and Singapore (US$ 9.5 billion), while South Africa, Nigeria and Egypt had the largest import markets in Africa for ASEAN goods. Additionally, the Asian Development Bank (ADB) is understood to be keen to develop trade agreements between Asia and Africa, which may, in the not-too-distant future, see ASEAN reaching out to one of the African trade blocs. Indeed, 7 ASEAN nations have already formed an ASEAN-Pretoria Committee to boost trade with South Africa.[21] However, the fruit of this labour must, of necessity, lie somewhat farther in the future, since the South African economy is currently in shambles with Government Debt having reached 87 per cent of GDP. Moreover, the economic impact of the ongoing COVID-19 pandemic is very likely to remain severe and adverse for at least another year.

That said, Africa's exports to Indonesia increased by 147 per cent between 2006 and 2016, while imports grew by 107 per cent.[22] In August of 2019, Indonesia hosted the second annual Indonesia-Africa Infrastructure Dialogue (IAID), "attended by Indonesian officials, vice president of Equatorial Guinea and ministers from Zanzibar, Tanzania as well as senior officials from 53 African countries." The inaugural (April 2018) edition of the IAID "resulted in US$ 586.56 million worth of cooperation transactions between Indonesian and African companies in infrastructure, financing, mining, aircraft maintenance service and commodity trade sectors... The 2019 IAID is expected to expand the cooperation transactions to US$ 822 million."[23] Likewise, Viet Nam, Cambodia and Laos have seen sharp increases in trade since the Organisation Internationale de la Francophonie strengthened economic ties with French-speaking African countries.[24] Clearly, there appears to be no shortage of infrastructure projects that could entice ASEAN investors.[25] Moreover, Nigeria and Angola are key suppliers of oil and gas to Indonesia, whose own falling production and increased consumption have (since 2014) made Indonesia a net importer of crude oil. Nigeria accounts for 5.4 per cent of Indonesia's total imports of mineral fuels including oils, whereas Angola accounts for 1.6 per cent.[26] Figure 12.1 provides an indicator of the growing trade between some member-countries of ASEAN and Africa.[27]

Figure 12.1: Merchandise Trade with Sub-Saharan Africa

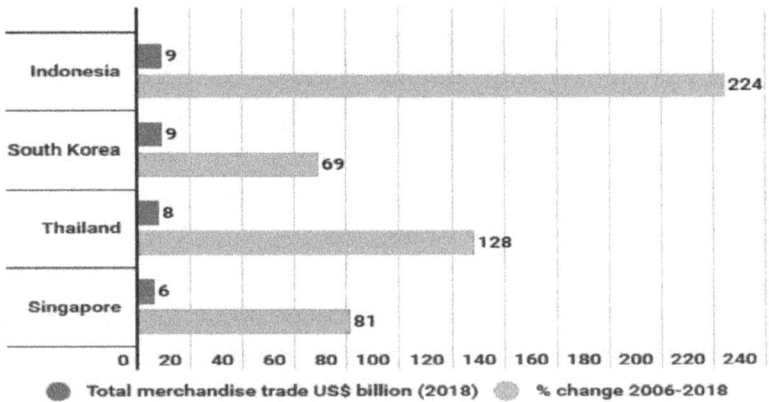

Source: *The Economist.*

With Africa becoming a trade-centric driver for ASEAN, there are several opportunities for India and ASEAN to progress the AAGC, particularly since India brings considerable value to the ASEAN table in terms of the 5.4 million-strong Indian diaspora in Africa,[28] India's acceptability in Africa as a result of its cultural sensitivity that is guided by ten principles articulated by the Prime Minister of India in 2018, for India's own engagement with Africa.[29]

Insofar as the MAUSAM Initiative is concerned, this offers enormous opportunities for India and ASEAN to engage under the AOIP-IPOI joint rubric to advance cultural and people-to-people connectivity. It is, as this author has penned elsewhere:[30]

> a historical fact that the great cultural contribution of at least four major religions – Hinduism, Buddhism, Christianity and Islam – have, over history, quite literally sailed eastward with the monsoon winds holds out the promise of enormous potential that surely needs to be realised.... These maritime journeys, and the journeymen – both, religious and secular – that have undertaken them, have connected peoples and geographies, as also the histories of those geographies. Architecture, sculpture, dress, various forms of the performing arts, value-systems, societal structures, civic norms, legal and societal mores, find similarities and commonalities across vast oceanic expanses with a resultant melding of civilizational commonalities that often sit uneasily with the much greater rigidity of the modern Westphalian State system. The question that tantalizes and teases us is whether the former can temper the much more recent and hence much sharper edges of the latter... This is the great challenge to which India's Project MAUSAM, which focuses upon monsoon patterns, cultural routes and maritime landscapes, must be able to rise. It has successfully aroused the interest of several countries including China, UAE, Qatar, Iran, Myanmar, and Vietnam,[31] who are intrigued by the spread of shared knowledge systems, traditions, technologies and ideas along maritime routes. At the macro level, "... the Project aims to re-connect and re-establish communications between countries of the Indian Ocean world, which would lead to an enhanced understanding of cultural values and concerns ...", while "... at the

micro-level, the focus is on understanding national cultures in their regional maritime milieu".[32] It is a truism that there is no boring history – only boring historians. So, how far, how well, and, most important of all, how interestingly can Project MAUSAM capture the imagination of not merely the drones of governments, but also of the actual peoples that the monsoon winds so comprehensively connected?"

Concluding Remarks

Finally, in this examination of complementarities between the AOIP and the IPOI, it is important to avoid undue self-limitation by restricting the geographic scope to the western Pacific alone. The Indo-Pacific maritime expanse offers opportunities for a number of cooperation-mechanisms within the Indian Ocean, too. The willingness of ASEAN member-States such as Singapore, Indonesia, Malaysia and Thailand, to involve themselves in protecting and preserving freedoms in the maritime common in the north-western Arabian Sea within the Indian Ocean, offers a number of exciting pointers for future maritime collaboration that both, India and ASEAN would do very well to explore. An overarching facet of cooperation stipulated in the IPOI is that of "Capacity Building and Resource Sharing". As Table 12.1 shows, this is a recurring facet of complementarity across several, if not all, the areas of cooperation listed in the AOIP document. For instance, the enormous success that India has garnered in addressing water-stress in volcanic islands, such as those in the Lakshadweep, by way of Low-Temperature Thermal Desalination (LTTD), can easily be leveraged and proliferated across several island nations of the Indo-Pacific as a whole. This offers immediate opportunities for several technologically-advanced ASEAN nations to improve the engineering of these LTTD plants and offer them as "public goods" in both, the western pacific as well as the Indian Ocean, under the common rubric of the AOIP and the IPOI.

It may thus be seen from the foregoing arguments, that the complementarities between the AOIP and the IPOI are legion and the opportunities for maritime cooperation between ASEAN and India are limited solely by the collective imagination of the respective policy-makers.

Notes

1. Refer, Prime Minister's Speech at the East Asia Summit, 4 November 2019, MEA, India.
2. Refer, UNDP, SDG, Goal 14 and SDG 14: Life Below Water.
3. Refer, Prime Minister's Keynote Address at Shangri La Dialogue, 1 June 2018, MEA, India.
4. Refer, Prime Minister's Speech at the East Asia Summit, 4 November 2019, MEA, India.
5. Refer, PMO 2015.
6. Refer, Prime Minister's Keynote Address at Shangri La Dialogue, 01 June 2018, MEA, India.
7. Ibid.
8. Refer, Indo-Pacific Division Briefs, MEA, India.
9. Refer, Free and Open Indo-Pacific, MFA, Japan.
10. Refer, East Asia Summit, 2018, MEA, India
11. Refer, http://aseanregionalforum.asean.org/about-arf/
12. Refer, France and Security in the Indo-Pacific, Ministry of Defence, France.
13. Refer, 2017 Foreign Policy White Paper, Department of Foreign Affairs and Trade, Australia.
14. Refer, Joint Declaration on a Shared Vision for Maritime Cooperation in the Indo-Pacific Between the Republic of India and the Government of Australia, 2020.
15. Refer, Leong, K.L.C. (2020).
16. Refer, ASEAN Outlook on the Indo-Pacific, 2019.
17. Ibid.
18. Refer, Heiduk, F. and Wacker, G. (2020).
19. Refer, ASEAN Outlook on the Indo-Pacific, 2019.
20. Refer, The Economic Times, 2017.
21. Refer, http://www.gis-reseau-asie.org/en/asean-africa-toward-renewed-partnership
22. Refer, Tan, K. (2019).
23. Refer, Nugraha, A. (2019).
24. Refer, ASEAN-Africa: Toward a Renewed Partnership, *Contra* 21
25. Refer, The Asia-Africa Nexus, *Contra* 22
26. Refer, ASEAN Today, 21 March 2019.
27. Refer, Economist, Briefing, 7 March, 2019.

28. Refer, Sinha, N. (2019).
29. Refer, Prime Minister's address at Parliament of Uganda during his State Visit to Uganda", 25 July 2018. MEA, India.
30. Refer, Chauhan, P. (2020).
31. Refer, http://www.indiaculture.nic.in/project-mausam
32. Ibid.

References

ARF. About the ARF. ASEAN Regional Forum (ARF), http://aseanregionalforum.asean.org/about-arf/

ASEAN Today. (2019). "Indonesia Strengthens its Presence in Africa through Deeper Economic Ties", 21 March, https://www.aseantoday.com/2019/03/indonesia-strengthens-its-presence-in-africa-through-deepening-economic-ties/

ASEAN. (2019). "ASEAN Outlook on the Indo-Pacific, Background and Rationale", p. 1. Association of Southeast Asian Nations (ASEAN, https://asean.org/storage/2019/06/ASEAN-Outlook-on-the-Indo-Pacific_FINAL_22062019.pdf

Chauhan, P. (2020). "Geopolitics, Maritime Connectivity and Cultural Heritage". Unpublished Paper (Submitted to the Indian Council for World Affairs (ICWA), 5 July 2020.

DFAT. (2017). "2017 Foreign Policy White Paper. Department of Foreign Affairs and Trade (DFAT)", Government of Australia, https://www.fpwhitepaper.gov.au/foreign-policy-white-paper/chapter-three-stable-and-prosperous-indo-pacific/indo-pacific

Government of India, Ministry of Culture, Project MAUSAM, http://www.indiaculture.nic.in/project-mausam (accessed on 5 June 2020).

Heiduk, F. and Wacker, G. (2020). "From Asia-Pacific to Indo-Pacific: Significance, Implementation and Challenges". *Stiftung Wissenschaft und Politik,* German Institute for Security and International Affairs, SWP Research Paper 9, July 2020, Berlin, https://www.swp-berlin.org/fileadmin/contents/products/research_papers/2020RP09_IndoPacific.pdf

Leong, K.L.C. (2020). "What to Expect from Indonesia's Indo-Pacific Push in 2020?". *The Diplomat,* 6 March 2020, https://thediplomat.com/2020/03/what-to-expect-from-indonesias-indo-pacific-push-in-20

MEA (2018a). "Prime Minister's Keynote Address at Shangri La Dialogue", 1 June 2018. Ministry of External Affairs (MEA), Media Center, Government of India, https://

mea.gov.in/Speeches-Statements.htm?dtl/29943/Prime+
Ministers+Keynote+Address+at+Shangri+La+Dialogue+
June+01+2018#:~:text=Center

MEA (2018b). "India at the East Asia Summit, August 2018". East Asia
Summit, Ministry of External Affairs (MEA), Government of India,
https://mea.gov.in/aseanindia/about-eas.htm

———— (2018c). "Prime Minister's address at Parliament of Uganda
during his State Visit to Uganda", 25 July 2018.

———— (2019a). "Prime Minister's Speech at the East Asia Summit", 4
November 2019. Ministry of External Affairs (MEA), Government of
India, https://mea.gov.in/Speeches-Statements.htm?dtl/ 30152/Prime_
Ministers_address_at_Parliament_of_Uganda_during_his_State_Visit_
to_Uganda

———— (2019b). "Prime Minister's Speech at the East Asia Summit", 4
November 2019. Ministry of External Affairs (MEA), Media Center,
Government of India, https://www.mea.gov.in/Speeches-Statements.
htm?dtl/32171/Prime_Ministers_Speech_at_the_East_Asia_
Summit_04_November_2019

———— (2020a). "Joint Declaration on a Shared Vision for Maritime
Cooperation in the Indo-Pacific Between the Republic of India and
the Government of Australia". Ministry of External Affairs (MEA),
Media Centre, Government of India, https://www.mea.gov.in/
bilateral-documents.htm?dtl/32730/ Joint_Declaration_on_a_Shared_
Vision_for_Maritime_Cooperation_in_the_IndoPacific_Between_the_
Republic_of_India_and_the_Government_of_Australia

———— (2020b). "Indo-Pacific Division Briefs". Ministry of External
Affairs (MEA), Government of India, https://mea.gov.in/Portal/
ForeignRelation/Indo_Feb_07_2020.pdf

MFA (undated). "Free and Open Indo-Pacific". Ministry of Foreign
Affairs (MFA), Government of Japan, https://www.mofa.go.jp/
files/000430632.pdf

Ministry of Defence (2019). "France and Security in the Indo-Pacific".
Ministry of Defence, Government of France, https://www.defense.
gouv.fr/layout/set/print/content/download/532754/9176250/version/3/
file/France+and+Security+in+the+Indo-Pacific+-+2019.pdf

Nugraha, A. (2019). "Bali Hosts 2019 Indonesia-Africa Infrastructure
Dialogue". Asia-Pacific Daily (APD), https://www.apdnews.com/news/
962160.html

PMO (2015). "Text of the PM's remarks on the Commissioning of Coast Ship Barracuda", 12 March 2015. Prime Minister's Office (PM India) (PMO), Government of India. https://www.pmindia.gov.in/en/news_updates/text-of-the-pms-remarks-on-the-commissioning-of-coast-ship-barracuda/

Sinha, N. (2019). "An Overview of Indian Diaspora in Africa: Implications for India", Vivekanand International Foundation (VIF), VIF Paper, https://www.vifindia.org/sites/default/files/final-an-overview-of-indian-diaspora-in-africa.pdf

Tan, K. (2019). "The Asia-Africa Nexus". Orbit, https://orbitt.capital/the-asia-africa-nexus/

The Economic Times. (2017). "Growth, Connectivity Key to India's Foreign Policy Thinking: S Jaishankar". Address by Dr S Jaishankar at the Consultation on Asia-Africa Growth Corridor: The Way Forward event hosted by the Research and Information System for Developing Countries, New Delhi, https://economictimes.indiatimes.com/news/economy/policy/growth-connectivity-key-to-indias-foreign-policy-thinking-s-jaishankar/ articleshow/60224892.cms

The Economist. (2019). "Africa is Attracting ever more Interest from Powers Elsewhere". Briefing, 7 March 2019, https://www.economist.com/briefing/2019/03/07/africa-is-attracting-ever-more-interest-from-powers-elsewhere

UNDP. "Sustainable Development Goals, Goal 14: Life Below Water". United Nations Development Programme (UNDP), https://www.undp.org/content/undp/en/home/sustainable-development-goals/goal-14-life-below-water.html

13. ASEAN-India

Strengthening Partnership in the Post-COVID-19 Era

Fukunari Kimura

Introduction

Indo-Pacific idea is so far dominated by politics and national security issues. From an economic perspective, connection between South Asia and East Asia are so far a bit disappointing but has a lot of potentials. Since the 1990s, the Association of Southeast Asian Nations (ASEAN) has established itself as a central figure of international production networks (IPNs) (Ando and Kimura, 2005) or the second unbundling (Baldwin 2016) and has made itself a hub of free trade agreements (FTAs). However, despite its huge potentials, India has not yet participated in Factory Asia extended in ASEAN and East Asia. It is very important to widen and tighten the economic relationship between India and ASEAN in this context (Kimura and Umezaki, 2011).

In the following, three possible economic channels will be discussed between India and ASEAN: manufacturing production networks, Trilateral Highway, and services and information and communications technology (ICT) connection.

Indo-Pacific on Manufacturing Production Networks

Factory Asia extended to the whole East Asia is formed on the basis of IPNs, particularly in machinery industries. However, India is not much connected with them.

IPNs or the second unbundling requires the upgrade of location advantages and the reduction in service link costs (ERIA 2010, 2015). Different from the industry-by-industry international division of labour or the first unbundling, IPNs must be supported by time-sensitive reliable logistics in order to overcome geographical distance. IPNs generate the movement of "ideas," not just the mobility of "goods". Ideas here include technology, managerial know-how, capital, and technicians, which accelerates technology transfer and spillover. In addition, fragmentation of production can go together with the formation of industrial agglomeration. Policies are crucial to taking advantage of this type of international division of labour.

Indian people are worried about flooding over big imports, particularly the light industrial products coming from China. It is true that in international trade some time a country may inure a trade deficit unless the exchange rate is properly adjusted. However, in IPNs, the trade pattern is based on intra-industry trade and has larger room for the international division of labour rather than doing the industry-by-industry division of labour. Following this many countries are doing exports and imports at the same time, or rather, imports are often essential to exports. India has a lot of potential for doing that, but unfortunately, it is not realised. India and South Asia should enhance economic integration and connectivity, rather than protecting industries from trade.

In Indo-Pacific, seawater is not an obstacle but an advantage in manufacturing IPNs. ASEAN has been successful in reducing service link costs by the sea, which is much less costly than ground transportation costs in Europe. Indo-Pacific has advantage of sea linkages, and cost of production networks will be reduced by trade through container transportation, complemented by air transportation.

India and South Asia still need the manufacturing sector though India has more strength in the service sector. Manufacturing and related services generate massive jobs for relatively poor people, helping the region to achieve inclusive growth.

Trilateral Highway

Trilateral Highway is very symbolic for inter-regional cooperation between South Asia and ASEAN. It also addresses stability and inclusiveness by activating economic activities between two regions. Northeastern parts of India and Bangladesh are connected to ASEAN through Myanmar. These areas have been relatively slow in economic growth and politically a bit unstable. We have to give them some economic benefits of globalisation. At the same time, the Bangladesh, Bhutan, India, Nepal (BBIN) Initiative also has a very important economic role in the region.

Some small improvements of institutional connectivity (like border issues) and the provision of medium grade physical connectivity would drastically change the industrial structure and people's welfare in Myanmar, Northeastern parts of India, and others. A relatively small amount of projects will help the region to connect properly. However, we should not expect huge effects at the macroeconomic level because the connectivity enhanced by trilateral highways would be, at least in the short run, traditional rural connection rather than tight and thick connection between industrial agglomerations. See ERIA (2020) for some exercise with the IDE-ERIA Geographical Simulation Model in order to quantify economic effects of trilateral highways on neighbouring countries.

Indo-Pacific on ICT Services

India has the advantage in information and communication technology (ICT) services. Many Indian engineers and technicians are already active in ASEAN, in particular, Singapore, Indonesia, Malaysia, Thailand. So, it is important to nurture a "partnership" between India and ASEAN, and therefore homework for liberalising service industry is essential. It is also important that ASEAN must remove redundant restrictions on various modes of services trade including ICT.

ASEAN must be in the heart to establish an effective and efficient policy regime for the flow of data and data-related businesses as these policies are not properly developed. India also considers the possibility of harmonisation of policy systems. The big issues like personal data, competition, cyber security, and taxation need to be tackled efficiently. India and ASEAN can cooperate relatively easily in areas such as consumer protection, e-government, e-payment areas. Cheng et al. (2019) provide a policy framework for addressing economic and social concerns on the flow of data and data-related businesses.

Way Forward

India is still struggling to contain the disease. Even in ASEAN, some countries are experiencing another wave of infection. So, the region requires emergency responses and prioritizes health policy to contain the pandemics within the capacity of medical services. If we fail to do that, the political and economic costs are going to be very large. On the exit stage, we will have a very slow removal of restrictions on people's movements.

However, we should not forget about the manufacturing sector in this hard time. I think the reshuffling of production networks will come to some extent, particularly with the aggravation of the US-China confrontation. ASEAN and India should attract production blocks and link between ASEAN and South Asia.

ICT services will become more important in terms of medium and short-run points of view. Further, consider how to utilise them for economic development, particularly inclusiveness in this context. Deeper integration in Indo-Pacific must be realised to strengthen the regional ties. Therefore, it is important to do our homework both from the Indian side as well as ASEAN side so as to have a background of a good international relation.

References

Ando, M. and Kimura, F. (2005). "The Formation of International Production and Distribution Networks in East Asia", in Takatoshi Ito and Andrew K. Rose, *International Trade in East Asia*. (NBER-East Asia Seminar on Economics, Volume 14), pp. 177-213. Chicago: The University of Chicago Press.

Baldwin, R. (2016). *The Great Convergence: Information Technology and the New Globalization*. Cambridge, MA: Belknap Harvard University Press.

Chen, L., Chang, W., Ciuriak, D., Kimura, F., Nakagawa, J., Pomfret, R., Rigoni, G., and Schewarzer, J. (2019). "The Digital Economy for Economic Development: Free Flow of Data and Supporting Policies". Policy Brief No. 4, Task Force 8 (Trade, Investment, and Globalization), T20 (Think 20), Tokyo, https://t20japan.org/policy-brief-digital-economy-economic-development/

ERIA. (2010). "The Comprehensive Asia Development Plan". Economic Research Institute for ASEAN and East Asia (ERIA), Jakarta.

————— (2015). "The Comprehensive Asia Development Plan 2.0 (CADP 2.0): Infrastructure for Connectivity and Innovation." Economic Research Institute for ASEAN and East Asia (ERIA), Jakarta.

————— (2020). "The India-Myanmar-Thailand Trilateral Highway and Its Possible Eastward Extension to Lao PDR, Cambodia, and Viet Nam: Challenges and Opportunities: Integrative Report". ERIA Research Project Report 2020, No. 02a. Economic Research Institute for ASEAN and East Asia (ERIA), Jakarta.

Kimura, F and Umezaki, So, (eds.) (2011) "ASEAN-India Connectivity: The Comprehensive Asia Development Plan, Phase II". Economic Research Institute for ASEAN and East Asia (ERIA), Jakarta.

14. ASEAN Outlook on Indo-Pacific (AOIP) and the Indo-Pacific Oceans' Initiative (IPOI)

Complementarities, Challenges and Opportunities

Premesha Saha

Introduction

The Indo-Pacific region is marred by regional uncertainty for the Chinese territorial expansionist policies and concerns for the US's long term commitment to Asia. Therefore, the time seems opportune for stronger cooperation and alignment between India and ASEAN which could boost regional stability and provide strategic benefits for both. With US-China geostrategic competition heating up, ASEAN and India can draw on their middle power status to bolster regional security and economic cooperation to protect their interests from any potential superpower fallout. It is time for the rising and middle powers of the region to start pulling their weight to ensure a stable, rules-based global order. Given the respective sizes of their economies and their military capacities, India and ASEAN can stand to gain from each other. The growth of one can act as a tail-wind to bring growth to the others, through complementary trade and investment. At the same time, the security and economic risk to one will also likely impact the others. The rise of China and the re-focusing of the US's influence in the region has forced India and the ASEAN countries to re-assess their long-term strategic outlook and their role in the changing regional diplomatic geometry. In short, India and ASEAN share a convergence of interests in the Indian and Pacific Oceans and should work to deepen their mutual understanding, strategic conversation and habits of cooperation. Amidst an ambitious China asserting itself and concerns about US' long-term commitment to Asia, both must improve their cooperation to help maintain stability.

In recent years, each country has proposed its own "vision" for the Indo-Pacific. India views the Indo-Pacific as a geographic and strategic expanse, with the ASEAN connecting the two great oceans. "Inclusiveness, openness, and ASEAN centrality and unity" lie at the heart of India's conception of the Indo-Pacific.[1] While the intensifying US-China trade war may have been the main push factor for the adoption of the 'ASEAN Outlook on Indo-Pacific', but in the document, there is hardly any mention of the ongoing US-China trade war or even the other strategic challenges that the region is facing which compelled ASEAN to adopt its own Indo-Pacific outlook. The document does not also provide some measures by which ASEAN will be able to navigate these strategic challenges.[2] Though it has been pointed out in the key elements or principles of the Indo-Pacific outlook that a rules-based order should be maintained and the Indo-Pacific region should be looking at achieving "dialogue and cooperation instead of rivalry"[3], but unlike the policy papers and the strategic documents of other countries like US, Australia and also Japan where the threats and challenges have been clearly outlined, the ASEAN document chose to take the safer or the diplomatic route. This will be a positive factor in boosting India-ASEAN ties as Indian Prime Minister's 2018 Shangri-La Dialogue keynote speech reflected, India too has taken a more subtle attitude towards China and a diplomatic stance in pointing out the "China threat" in global platforms.

The aim of this chapter is to chart out the complementarities in India's IPOI and the ASEAN Outlook on the Indo-Pacific. In doing so, firstly, India's vision of the Indo-Pacific will be looked upon; second, the principles and imperatives underlying the ASEAN Outlook on the Indo-Pacific will be delved into. The following section would map out the progress in the India-ASEAN cooperation in the Indo-Pacific as well as the challenges that lies ahead in making this relationship a more concrete one. The last section will lay out some recommendations, which will primarily centre around the maritime domain, but looks at both bottom-up and top-down initiatives that can be undertaken under the IPOI banner with the ASEAN member countries.

India's Indo-Pacific Vision

For India, the geography of the Indo-Pacific stretches from the eastern coast of Africa to Oceania (from the shores of Africa to those of the Americas), which also includes the Pacific Island countries.[4] Moreover, its "Act East Policy" is similarly geared towards deepening economic engagement with Southeast Asia and broader cooperation with East Asia and the Pacific island countries. India has been an active participant in mechanisms such as the Indian Ocean Rim Association (IORA), the East Asia Summit (EAS), Association of Southeast Asian Nations (ASEAN) Defence Ministers Meeting Plus, ASEAN Regional Forum, the Bay of Bengal Initiative for Multi-Sectoral Technical and Economic Cooperation (BIMSTEC), and Mekong-India Economic Corridor (MIEC), in addition to convening the Indian Ocean Naval Symposium. Through the Forum for India-Pacific Islands Cooperation (FIPIC), India is moving towards engaging with the Pacific Island countries.

India's trade in this region is growing rapidly, with several overseas investments being directed towards the East, e.g. the Comprehensive Economic Partnership Agreements with Japan, South Korea, and Singapore; and the Free Trade Agreements with ASEAN and Thailand. Of late, India has viewed the Western Pacific as falling within the ambit of its maritime security interests. The focus on maritime issues is evident from the increase in maritime exchanges led by the Indian Navy, with countries such as Vietnam, Singapore, Indonesia and Japan.

To promote its strategic interests in the Indian Ocean, India launched the SAGAR (Security and Growth for All in the Region) vision. On 4 November 2019, the Indian Prime Minister launched the Indo-Pacific Oceans' Initiative (IPOI) at the East Asia Summit held in Bangkok, Thailand. The main objective of the IPOI is to ensure the safety, security and stability of the maritime domain. As an open global initiative, the IPOI draws on existing regional cooperation architecture and mechanisms to focus on seven central pillars conceived around Maritime Security; Maritime Ecology; Maritime Resources; Capacity Building and Resource Sharing; Disaster Risk Reduction and Management; Science, Technology and Academic Cooperation; and Trade, Connectivity and Maritime Transport.[5]

ASEAN's Outlook on the Indo-Pacific

The ASEAN has adopted the 'ASEAN Outlook on the Indo-Pacific' after more than a year of negotiations at the ASEAN Senior Officials Meeting (SOM) held in Bangkok, Thailand in June 2019.[6] This document finally outlines the organisation's concept and strategy of the Indo-Pacific, in which the Asia-Pacific and the Indian Ocean regions have been regarded as the most dynamic expanse and centre of economic growth. The centrality of the ASEAN has been emphasized amidst the geopolitical shifts that this region is encountering like the ongoing tussle between the US and China.[7] By ASEAN Centrality, the 'Outlook' denotes that the grouping wants to maintain its central role in the evolving regional architecture in Southeast Asia and its surrounding regions. The aim is not to create new mechanisms or replace existing ones; rather, it is an 'Outlook' intended to enhance ASEAN's Community building process and to strengthen and give new momentum for existing ASEAN-led mechanisms such as the East Asia Summit (EAS), as platforms for dialogue and implementation of the Indo-Pacific cooperation.[8] Besides this, the document impinges upon a rules-based order anchored upon international law, openness, transparency, inclusivity and commitment to advancing economic engagement in the region. In this regard, four areas of cooperation-maritime cooperation; connectivity; UN Sustainable Development

Goals 2030; and economic development have been put forward for engaging with other countries in the Indo-Pacific.[9]

The document does lay out areas of cooperation to engage with other like-minded players in the region. Given that India also champions the need for a free, open, inclusive, rules-based Indo-Pacific, it has warmly welcomed the ASEAN Outlook on the Indo-Pacific.[10]

India-ASEAN Cooperation in the Indo-Pacific: An Assessment

Countries like the US, Japan, Australia and even the ASEAN countries have been calling upon India to play a more active role in the Indo-Pacific region. The ASEAN leaders, during their visit to India to take part in the Republic Day celebrations in 2018, had welcomed "India's positive role in the Indo-Pacific and described it as an important factor for peace and stability".[11] Kentaro Sonoura, the advisor to the Prime Minister of Japan, also reflected on India's role in the region when he underlined that "New Delhi's role in the region is extremely important, given that India is a global power facing the Indian Ocean and has strong historical ties with both Asia and East Africa."[12] This section will look at the recent initiatives to provide an overview of how the relations between India and the ASEAN countries have been evolving. This primarily hints at the fact that the trust and the groundwork for forming a 'like-minded middle power countries partnership' is already in place.

Table 14.1: Select Cooperative Initiative (Focussing on the Maritime Domain) Undertaken between India and the ASEAN Member Countries

ASEAN Member Country	Cooperative Initiatives
The Philippines	Capacity building, training; exchange and visits of delegations; naval and coast guard ship visits.
	Two Indian naval ships, INS Sahyadri and INS Kitan visited the Philippines from October 23-26, 2019.

Malaysia	Defence cooperation included regular exchanges and visits of Indian Naval Ships. Indian Coast Guard ships made port calls at Port Klang in April 2019 and August 2019. Samudra Laksmana 2019 (joint naval exercise)
Indonesia	Joint Task Force set up for strengthening physical, economic and people to people connectivity between Andaman and Nicobar islands and Aceh province, and to develop port related infrastructure in Sabang. The first meeting was held on December 2019 in Aceh. Regular engagements at the operational level between the three services. Joint naval exercises Samudra Shakti have been initiated.
Singapore	Navy Staff talks Naval exercises (SIMBEX) The 10th edition of Air Force Joint Military Training conducted between October to December 2019 included a naval component for the first time. INS Sagardhwani visited Singapore in August 2019 to promote scientific collaboration between DRDO and Singaporean agencies.
Vietnam	Navy to navy staff talks Port calls Good will visits
Singapore and Thailand	India-Singapore-Thailand Trilateral maritime exercise was successfully conducted at Port Blair from September 16-20 2019.
Thailand	Three MOUs were signed between Ranong Port and Indian ports of Vizag, Chennai and Kolkata during BIMSTEC Ports Conclave held from November 7-9, 2019 in Vizag.

Source: Compiled by author from various sources.

India-ASEAN Cooperation in the Indo-Pacific: Challenges Ahead

The potential and the will for further boosting of India-ASEAN relations in the Indo-Pacific is undoubtedly present, but at the same time, there are certain challenges which also need to be factored in. For instance, as mentioned above, when the Indian Prime Minister laid out India's vision of the Indo-Pacific, it did appear that India has opted the safer route whereby it is seen to hedge and balance its relations with the US and China. But after the Galwan valley clash of June 2020, a shift in India's approach towards China has been clearly visible. Additionally, though countries like India, Japan, Australia, US have always harped on 'ASEAN centrality' in their Indo-Pacific visions and strategies, but there is profound anxiety over broader implications for ASEAN and its "centrality" in shaping the regional security architecture. Managing the strategic challenge from China has become the topmost foreign policy priority for India. Given the structural constraints shaping New Delhi-Beijing ties, the need to step up its engagements in the Indo-Pacific region is well recognised in India.[13] With growing concerns in India about China's expansionist tendencies, India is ready to embark on a more proactive role in the region. Even if, India's China policy is going through a change, which may not bode very well with some ASEAN countries who have always been resisted from being looped in great power competition, but still it cannot be denied that there are several areas where India can work with ASEAN for enhancing cooperation in the Indo-Pacific, especially on the pillars of India's IPOI.

While the FOIP concept was welcomed by countries like Vietnam, Singapore, Indonesia and possibly Thailand, though with some amount of apprehension, nations like Malaysia, the Philippines (initially), Cambodia and Laos had largely remained silent on the same. There are fears that the change in and widening of geostrategic focus will diminish the diplomatic centrality and relevance of ASEAN, even though ASEAN-led meetings such as the EAS includes India and is increasingly taking on an Indo-Pacific perspective. Initiatives such as the Quad, other minilateral platforms heighten the fears of a "post-ASEAN future within which ASEAN's standing and ability to set the regional agenda and lead discussion is diminished".[14] The fact that the newfound interest in the Indo-Pacific was an initiative by non-ASEAN countries heightens ASEAN's apprehension that diplomatic events and discussion may well transcend ASEAN centrality.[15]

How Can India and ASEAN Countries Cooperate under the IPOI Framework: Policy Proposals

The IPOI seeks to promote a forum under which countries deliberate cooperative ways to secure maritime boundaries, promote free trade and sustainable use of marine resources. The IPOI echoes India's plurilateral approach of engagement and focuses not only on ASEAN centrality, but also on Indo-Pacific connectivity, sustainable infrastructure and economic cooperation leading to regional integration.[16]

Though the adoption and implementation of the 'ASEAN Outlook on the Indo-Pacific' did pacify the thinking of many that 'ASEAN centrality and unity' have been fading away, but still, there are lingering doubts on the notion of 'ASEAN centrality and unity' and sometimes sceptics have even questioned the necessity of making 'ASEAN centrality' the fulcrum in most country's Indo-Pacific visions and strategies. India does have the option to engage with ASEAN as a whole, or enter into plurilateral arrangements with a few ASEAN member states, who have been strong advocates of the Indo-Pacific construct and have also voiced their support for India's IPOI. It is true, that the existing plurilateral arrangements in the Indo-Pacific like the Quad have raised apprehensions in the minds of the ASEAN countries, that these are leading to the hindrance of ASEAN centrality and the ASEAN countries do prefer that the existing platforms like the East Asia Summit (EAS) should be perceived as the regional organisation of the Indo-Pacific, but at the same time, some countries have been open to the idea of plurilateral arrangements, provided these are issue-based partnerships like the Malacca Straits Patrol involving Malaysia, Singapore and Indonesia, recently the revamping of the India-Australia-Indonesia Trilateral partnership. India, on the other hand, is also seen to be engaging in issue-based partnerships with like-minded countries in the Indo-Pacific- this move, according to scholars and policy makers signifies a shift from India's pro-longed non-alignment stand to now an 'issue-based alignment' posture in policy making.

This section will provide some policy recommendations on how the IPOI's pillars could work around such "cooperative, consultative, inclusive" framework involving the ASEAN member countries. These policies are sufficiently broad to accommodate a wide range of activities and engagements, from highly informal conversations to institutionalised cooperation – both bottom-up and top-down initiatives.

Maritime Security

- Track-1 maritime security dialogues and workshops over regional issues such as piracy, IUU fishing, humanitarian assistance, and disaster relief. The naval heads of Indonesia, Malaysia, Thailand, Singapore, Vietnam, Philippines can participate in these events.
- An exercise involving the coast guards of the ASEAN countries. Considering that BAKAMLA (the Indonesian Coast Guard) is a new establishment, it is possible to provide training at the Indian naval war colleges.
- The ASEAN countries could invite India to the ASEAN Coast Guard and Law Enforcement Forum, or India can initiate an India-ASEAN Coast Guard Forum where regular exercises and interactions between the Indian and the coast guards of the ASEAN countries can take place. Capacity building and training, exchange visits of delegations under this forum can be organised.
- Deals can be entered into with the Indian shipyards like Mazagon Dock Limited in Mumbai, Cochin Shipyard Limited in Chennai, or Garden Reach Shipbuilders and Engineers in Kolkata to supply patrol vessels and coast guard ships to the Indonesian, Filipino, Vietnamese coast guards.[17]

- Coordinated patrols conducted with the Indonesian Navy in the Sunda and Lombok straits, since these straits are strategically important for all three countries, for their interests in the Indian Ocean. These straits are being increasingly used for human trafficking. Additionally, there is a growing presence of Chinese vessels and submarines in these straits.[18]

Disaster Management and Risk Reduction

- The naval exercises between countries with India and/or ASEAN Multilateral Naval exercise can introduce disaster preparedness, response, mitigation, and recovery.
- India's National Disaster Management Authority (NDMA) can organise workshops and joint research programmes on awareness and best practices with Asian Disaster Preparedness Centre (ADPC) located in Bangkok, Thailand, Asian Disaster Preparedness Centre in Yangon, Myanmar and ASEAN Coordinating Centre for Humanitarian Assistance on Disaster Management in Jakarta, Indonesia.
- Countries like Indonesia, Thailand, Malaysia, and Singapore are members of PM Modi's recently launched Coalition for Disaster Resilient Infrastructure (CDRI). Other countries should also be encouraged to become members of this initiative, as they face challenges in building and/or retrofitting infrastructure to withstand disasters.

Academic Collaboration and Enhancing Civil Society Linkages

- Education exchanges and training exercises must be expanded to include all levels – from the academy to the senior staff colleges. Broader joint research on maritime studies involving think tanks and universities from India, and the ASEAN countries could strengthen bottom-up approaches to maritime security architecture-building.
- Workshops on both maritime domain awareness and UNCLOS familiarity amongst the maritime security practitioners of India, ASEAN. Given the ongoing SCS dispute, the importance of

understanding and interpreting different regional views on how "freedom of navigation" applies to foreign military activity in exclusive economic zones cannot be ignored.

- Future collaborations can happen between Indian Institute of Technology, Madras (IITM) and the Department of Aquatic Resources Management of Institut Pertanian Bogor, Indonesia for short-term courses on Aquatic resource management.

Maritime Ecology and Safeguarding of Marine Resources

- Indonesia, Malaysia, Thailand can be potential partners for India to work along with on many aspects of Blue Economy, primarily on sustainable use of ocean resources: reducing marine plastic debris, and curbing illegal, unreported, and unregulated fishing. Given that the dumping of marine plastic debris is one of the focus areas in India's IPOI, India and Indonesia can form a working group along with other littorals like Malaysia and Thailand to deal with issues in the eastern Indian Ocean.[19]
- The ASEAN Working Group on Coastal and Marine Environment work as a forum for coordinating ASEAN initiatives on sustainable marine resource management. By consistently bringing together member states for project collaboration, ASEAN creates an environment of mutual understanding and solidarity in Southeast Asia. India's National Fisheries Development Board can partner with this working group and host conferences on sustainable use of marine resources in the eastern Indian Ocean. Further work can happen between India's National Fisheries Development Board and the ASEAN Working Group on Coastal and Marine Environment on synchronizing mandates that govern best practices in the blue economy and fisheries sectors.[20]

Connectivity and Maritime Transport

- The ports of Thailand, Singapore, Malaysia, and Indonesia are more advanced than those on the eastern coast of India. Therefore, India-ASEAN Connectivity Summits can be organized by India where the port authorities of these countries like the

Port Authority of Thailand, PELINDO of Indonesia along with the private players like Port of Singapore Authority (PSA) can be invited. India can also draw lessons from their experience.

- India's Sagarmala project should aim at collaborating with other regional connectivity initiatives like the Eastern Economic Corridor (EEC) of Thailand, the Sea Toll Highway of Indonesia, the 'Build Build Build' of the Philippines; and the ASEAN Master Plan on Connectivity 2025.

- Prospects for greater connectivity with other ports in Western Sumatra besides Aceh and Sabang, like Sibolga, Teluk Bayar, Bengkulu, Bandar Lampung, Cilacap, Belawan, Kota Cina in west Sumatra and Malahayati, Kuala Tanjung, Belawan in Northern Sumatra with the ports in eastern India like Kolkata-Haldia, Paradip, Visakhapatnam, Kattupalli, Chennai and Port Blair, along with the Krishnapatnam, Kamarajar and Tuticorin ports should be explored. The development of India's eastern ports and the creation of new ones in Enayam, Paradip, Sirkhadi and Sagar Island should provide greater opportunities for ports in Sumatra.[21]

- The Government of Thailand is putting emphasis on stepping up the infrastructure on the Ranong port, which is near South Asia. Thailand plans to develop Ranong as an international port, increase its connectivity with the Andaman coast, and link it with the multimodal transport of the BIMSTEC and Greater Mekong Subregion (GMS). The Trilateral Highway Project with India and Myanmar will be an important development for Ranong in terms of multimodal links with Myanmar and the Kolkata Port in India and India's northeast.[22]

- India can initiate talks on coastal shipping, cruise tourism with Thailand, Indonesia, and Malaysia under the Expanded ASEAN Maritime Forum.

Conclusion

The IPOI was launched by India in 2019 with the aim to manage, conserve, sustain, and secure the maritime domain. Since then, India has been working to strengthen practical cooperation with its like-minded partner countries to provide solutions to global challenges. Some challenges are likely to remain, but it is time for a revival of the 'middle-powers partnership' in the Indo-Pacific region. For one, some ASEAN countries would be unwilling to get caught between great-power rivalries and also hesitant to be part of initiatives that would purposefully exclude any particular country and compromises 'ASEAN centrality'. In this regard, the bottom-up approaches and the initiatives involving the various agencies of the ASEAN suggested under the pillars listed can be a good starting point for the short term. In the medium and long term, other more formal measures can be embarked upon.

The scholarly community in some ASEAN countries have been advocating that, "ASEAN can more proactively adopt "minilateralism," whereby core, likeminded Southeast Asian countries can adopt more expedient and robust responses to shared threats, including in cooperation with external powers."[23] It has also been pointed out by scholars like Evan Laksmana that, "in general, policymakers find minilateralism appealing because of its inherent flexibility, relatively low transaction costs, and voluntary, rather than mandatory, commitments. In the Indo-Pacific, minilateral cooperation does not negate or eliminate pre-existing multilateral commitments (like ASEAN) or bilateral alliances (with the US for example)."[24] For ensuring security, stability, peace, and prosperity of the vast Indo-Pacific region, India has been forming issue-based partnerships with like-minded countries of the Indo-Pacific and this plurilateral/minilateral form of engagement will continue to form the core tenet of India's IPOI.

Notes

1. Refer, Prime Minister's Keynote Address at Shangri La Dialogue, 1 June 2018, MEA, India.
2. Refer, Saha, P. (2019).
3. Refer, "ASEAN Outlook on the Indo-Pacific", ASEAN (2019).
4. Refer, Minister's Keynote Address at Shangri La Dialogue, 1 June 2018, MEA, India.

5. Refer, Indo-Pacific Division Briefs, MEA. (2020).
6. Refer, Sepitiari, D. (2019).
7. Refer, Ibid.
8. Refer, 'ASEAN Outlook on the Indo-Pacific', ASEAN (2019).
9. Refer, Ibid.
10. Refer, Business Standard. (2019).
11. Refer, Jain, A. (2018).
12. Refer, Ibid.
13. Refer, Kaura, V. (2020).
14. Refer, Lee, J. (2018).
15. Refer, Ibid.
16. Refer, Panda, J. (2020).
17. Refer, Saha, P. and Mishra, A. (2020).
18. India has been conducting coordinated patrol with the TNI-AL (Indonesian Navy) from 2002 onwards, but these patrols take place at Port Blair under the aegis of Andaman and Nicobar Command. The closing ceremony of this patrol is usually hosted at Belawan, Indonesia (see, https://www.indiannavy.nic.in/content/27thindia-indonesia-coordinated-patrol-corpat).
19. Refer, Ibid.
20. Refer, Ibid.
21. Refer, Rusdi, S. (2019).
22. Refer, Basu Ray Chaudhury, A., Basu, P. and Bose, S. (2019).
23. Refer, Heydarian, R. H. (2020).
24. Refer, Saha, P., Bland, B. and Laksmana, E. (2020).

References

ASEAN (2019). "ASEAN Outlook on the Indo-Pacific. ASEAN Statement & Communiques", Association of Southeast Asian Nations (ASEAN), https://asean.org/asean-outlook-indo-pacific/

Basu Ray Chaudhury, A., Basu, P. and Bose, S. (2019). "Exploring India's Maritime Connectivity in the Extended Bay of Bengal". ORF Monograph, November 2019, Observer Research Foundation (ORF), New Delhi, https://www.orfonline.org/ research/exploring-indias-maritime-connectivity-in-the-extendedbay-of-bengal-58190/

Business Standard. (2019). "India welcomes ASEAN's outlook on Indo-Pacific", 27 June, https://www.business-standard.com/article/pti-stories/india-welcomes-asean-s-outlook-on-indo-pacific-119062700020_1.html

Heydarian, R. H. (2020). "At a strategic crossroads: ASEAN centrality amid Sino-American rivalry in the Indo-Pacific". *Brookings*, April

2020, https://www.brookings.edu/research/at-a-strategic-crossroads-asean-centrality-amid-sino-american-rivalry-in-the-indo-pacific/

Jain, A. (2018). "With an assertive China and change in global power axis to Indo-Pacific, can India remain a 'mere spectator'?", *First Post*, 31 January 2018, https://www.firstpost.com/india/with-an-assertive-china-and-change-in-global-power-axis-to-indo-pacific-can-india-remain-a-mere-spectator-4323433.html

Kaura, V. (2020). "Incorporating Indo-Pacific and the Quadrilateral into India's strategic outlook". *Maritime Affairs*, Volume 15, Issue Number 2, https://www.tandfonline.com/doi/full/10.1080/09733159.2020.171 2012?scroll=top&need Access=true

Lee, J. (2018). "The Free and Open Indo-Pacific and Implications for the ASEAN". Institute of Southeast Asian Studies, p. 28, Singapore.

MEA. (2018), "Prime Minister's Keynote Address at Shangri La Dialogue", 1 June 2018. Ministry of External Affairs (MEA), Media Centre, Government of India, https://mea.gov.in/Speeches-Statements.htm?dtl/ 29943/Prime+Ministers+Keynote+Address+at+Shangri+La+Dialogue+ June+01+2018#:~:text=Center

———— (2020). "Indo-Pacific Division Briefs". Ministry of External Affairs (MEA), Government of India, https://mea.gov.in/Portal/ ForeignRelation/Indo_Feb_07_2020.pdf

Panda, J. (2020). "The Strategic Imperatives of Modi's Indo-Pacific Oceans Initiative". Asia Pacific Bulletin, No. 503. East-West Center, Washington, D.C., https://www.eastwestcenter.org/ publications/the-strategic-imperatives-modi%E2%80%99s-indopacific-ocean-initiative

Rusdi, S. (2019). "Connecting India-Indonesia Maritime Domain". *The Economic Times*, 3 May 2019, https://economictimes.indiatimes.com/ blogs/et-commentary/ connecting-india-indonesia-maritime-domain/

Saha, P. (2019). "ASEAN's Indo-Pacific Outlook: An Analysis". Observer Research Foundation (ORF), New Delhi, https://www.orfonline.org/ expert-speak/aseans-indo-pacific-outlook-an-analysis-52542/

Saha, P. and Mishra, A. (2020). "The Indo-Pacific Oceans Initiative: Towards a Coherent Indo-Pacific Policy for India". ORF Occasional Paper, December 2020, Observer Research Foundation (ORF), New Delhi, https://www.orfonline.org/research/indo-pacific-oceans-initiative-towards-coherent-indo-pacific-policy-india/

Saha, P., Bland, B. and Laksmana, E. (2020). "Anchoring the Indo-Pacific: The Case for Deeper Australia-India-Indonesia Trilateral Cooperation".

ORF Policy Report, 15 January 2020, Observer Research Foundation (ORF), New Delhi, https://www.orfonline.org/research/anchoring-the-indo-pacific-60358/

Sepitiari, D. (2019). "ASEAN Leaders adopt Indonesia-led Indo-Pacific Outlook". *The Jakarta Post*, 23 June 2019, https://www.thejakartapost.com/seasia/2019/06/23/asean-leaders-adopt-indonesia-led-indo-pacific-outlook.html

15. Ocean Renewable Energy
A Conflux of AOIP and IPOI

Joefe B. Santarita

Introduction

The Association of Southeast Asian Nations (ASEAN) has introduced the ASEAN Outlook of Indo-Pacific (AOIP) in June 2019. This document officially serves as a guide for ASEAN's engagement in the Asia-Pacific and the Indian Ocean regions. It also recognizes the potential for cooperation with other regional mechanisms in the Asia-Pacific and Indian Ocean region on issues of common interests through innovative, inter-disciplinary and complementary approaches based on the relevant ASEAN-led mechanisms such as the East Asia Summit,[1] Four months after, the Indian Prime Minister introduced the Indo-Pacific Oceans Initiative (IPOI) at the 14th East Asia Summit in November 2019. This is one of India's official pronouncements in calling for a free, open and inclusive order in the Indo-Pacific, based upon respect for sovereignty and territorial integrity of all nations, peaceful resolution of disputes through dialogue and adherence to international rules and laws. As an open global initiative, the IPOI draws on existing regional cooperation architecture and mechanisms to focus on seven central pillars conceived around Maritime Security; Maritime Ecology; Maritime Resources; Capacity Building and Resource Sharing; Disaster Risk Reduction and Management; Science, Technology and Academic Cooperation; and Trade, Connectivity and Maritime Transport.[2]

The launching of the said visions for Indo-Pacific has gained the attention of scholars, policymakers, observers and enthusiasts globally. Thus, it is imperative to examine the visions and explore their confluence. For brevity, Table 15.1 shows three commonalities where India and the Southeast Asian countries could possibly concentrate in their future collaborations.

Table 15.1: Commonalities between AOIP and IPOI

ASEAN Outlook of Indo-Pacific (AOIP)	Indo-Pacific Oceans Initiative (IPOI)
Maritime Cooperation; Connectivity; Sustainable Development; Economy	Freedom of Navigation, Overflight Sustainable Development, Protection of the Ecology Especially the Marine Environment Open, Free, Fair and Mutually-Beneficial Trade and Investment System are Guaranteed to all

Among the elements considered, maritime cooperation and connectivity, sustainable development and economy are prominent in discussing the significance of renewable energy in Indo-Pacific. The demand for a growing economy, especially after the pandemic, will mean an increased industrialization and therefore put more pressure on energy sector. Thus, there is a race to search for sources of fuel to support power-hungry economies. The ocean is the answer to assist countries in Indo-Pacific in realising sustainable development and active connectivity through maritime cooperation. These conditions have undoubtedly allowed the urgency of developing ocean renewable energy (ORE) as a source to sustain the economy in the region in near future. A potential that perfectly fits the bill as the conflux of both outlooks. Hence, this article examines the potential of ORE as collaborative project of India and ASEAN countries in near future.

Indo-Pacific has become a centre of global energy demand growth, driven by continued economic and population growth. In addition to China, whose energy demand is forecast to continue accounting for one-quarter of the global total until 2040, Southeast Asia and South Asia are raising their profiles in the global energy system. For example, Southeast Asia's energy demand is forecast to grow by almost two-thirds by 2040, as the regional economy triples in size. This demand growth, in turn, will make the region more dependent on energy imports, raising its annual net import expenditure to over US$ 300 billion in 2040. Moreover, energy access remains to be a challenge for some time despite ongoing improvements. For example, about one-tenth of Southeast Asia's 640 million people are estimated to remain without electricity. Also, India, whose energy market is expected to overtake that of China by 2030, continues to struggle with delivering universal access to electricity, with an estimated 300 million of its population without access today.[3]

Aside from household electrical and industrial consumptions, India and ASEAN countries are also actively engaged in the fourth industrial revolution to enhance further the digital revolution. ASEAN too is embracing smart cities projects among others recently. The presence of these projects alone requires a lot of energy supply especially renewable ones to sustain the operation. Thus, there is an urgent need to explore energy sources both from fossil-based to renewable energy such as solar and now marine resources. It should be noted that prior to the launch of AOIP and IPOI, India and ASEAN have cooperated on several occasions in generating energy. The bulk of energy cooperation, however, focuses on fossil-based energy extraction and is usually generated from countries that are at least geographically proximate to India such as Cambodia, Lao PDR, Myanmar, and Vietnam. Cooperation between India and the archipelagic countries in Southeast Asia such as the Philippines is said to be negligible when compared to other countries' partnerships.

The rest of the chapter is designed as follows: Section 2 considers the ORE and its potential engagement between India and ASEAN. The prospects of India-ASEAN Ocean energy collaboration are discussed in Section 3. Concluding remarks are mentioned in Section 4.

ORE and Its Potential for India-ASEAN

ORE refers to the form of marine resource energy that pertains specifically to energy drawn from the power potential of the ocean. There are five resources related to ocean water that can be tapped for energy: currents, tides, waves, temperature gradients and salinity gradients.[4] Also known as ocean energy, this form has been declared by the Indian Ministry of New and Renewable Energy as renewable energy. The energy produced using various forms of ocean energy shall be considered as renewable energy and shall be eligible for meeting the non-solar renewable purchase obligations.[5]

The current energy is a type of energy that is very similar to the wind above the oceans. Underwater turbines, large propellers tethered to the seabed, are moved with the marine currents to generate electricity. Tidal Energy, on the other hand, generates energy from power plants that are built on river estuaries and hold back huge amounts of tidal water twice a day which generates electricity when released while wave energy is generated by the movement of a device either floating on the surface of the ocean or moored to the ocean floor. Ocean Thermal Energy, on one hand, is sourced from the steam that is produced from the temperature difference between warm surface waters and the cold deeper layers that can be used to generate steam and then power. Lastly, Osmotic Energy or Salinity Gradient Energy is a technique that produces energy from the movement of water across a membrane between a saltwater reservoir and fresh water reservoir.[6]

India has a long coastline with the estuaries and gulfs, which can be fully used to harness ORE. Tidal streams and ocean currents are huge and almost endless resources which can be used with relatively small environmental interactions for large scale electricity generation. It is estimated that the total identified potential of tidal energy is about 12,455 MW, with potential locations identified at Khambat and Kutch regions, and large backwaters, where barrage technology could be used. The total theoretical potential of wave energy is estimated to be about 40,000 MW. This energy is however less intensive than what is available in more northern and southern latitudes. OTEC has a theoretical potential of 180,000 MW in India subject to suitable technological evolution. Ocean energy has the potential to grow fully, fuelling economic growth, reducing carbon footprint and creating jobs not only along the coasts but also inland along its supply chains.[7] Since 1980s, India has made successful undertakings related to OER and gradually producing electricity from such sources.

Southeast Asia, on the other hand, is generally an archipelagic region with more than 25,000 islands. The power potential of ORE in the region is vast with a total power potential of 1 terawatt (TW) which is the largest among all renewable sources in the region. This means that such supply can already power one-third of the entire America for the whole year. Indonesia is projected to produce 727 GW (tidal, OTEC and wave) followed by the Philippines with 170 GW (tidal, OTEC and wave), then by Myanmar with 135 GW, Malaysia with 1 GW and Singapore with 0.25 GW (tidal).[8]

Although the estimated ORE potential available in India and Southeast Asian countries could be minuscule for now when compared to other energy sources, its future prospects are gargantuan.

Prospects of India-ASEAN Ocean Energy Collaborations

Given the enormous ORE potential in India and ASEAN countries, it is in the best interest of these countries to synergise their efforts in jointly extracting the ocean energy resources. The scope of cooperation includes but is not limited to:

Academic institutions' expertise should be tapped and an alliance of best engineering centres specialising in ocean engineering must be encouraged. Institutions like National Institute of Ocean Technology (NIOT) and Jawaharlal Nehru University (JNU) among others should be part of an organisation to cover related activities and collaborations pertaining to ORE such as India-Southeast Asian Collaboration for Ocean Renewable Energy. Such interaction falls within the purview of people-to-people connectivity which is highlighted in the AOIP through cooperation, collaboration and exchanges between the academe and business, etc.

This kind of connectivity should be consistently followed by collaborative workshops of experts on how to address main bottlenecks: technology development, finance and markets, environmental and administrative issues, and grid availability.[9] In their article, Magagna and Uihlein explain these bottlenecks encountered in Europe that are most likely to be encountered in Indo-Pacific region and should be the focus of workshops. Technology development refers to the preparation of technology with due consideration to the reliability and the performance as well as survivability of the devices during storms and extreme conditions. Technology development should also ensure that increased innovation and research efforts can take place, that best practice sharing is encouraged to spread the risk among stakeholders and that the development of test centres is supported.

The second bottleneck is finance and markets. This covers support mechanisms for emerging technologies and their need to be implemented with adequate timing in view of the market maturity of the technology. While more technology-oriented mechanisms are needed during the first stages of technology development, market-push and market-pull instruments have to come to play at a later stage.

Third, environmental and administrative issues cover environmental, administrative, and social acceptance issues. For environmental issues, developers may face stringent and costly monitoring requirements in particular in relation to the size of the project. Regulatory authorities often adopt a conservative approach by enforcing extensive monitoring requirements on developments, when unsure of potential impacts. In terms of administrative issues, the usual concern is the presence of procedures to obtain full consent which is often lengthy and thereby delaying the project development. The lack of uniform procedures with regards to licensing and consenting also adds to the delay. Another constraint is the presence of social acceptance issues. Ocean energy deployments could experience significant delays if opposition from local communities are not correctly engaged. Therefore, consultation of the stakeholders is a must along with proper education on the benefits and risks associated with the project. From various literature on development, it is emphasized that the participants in these workshops are not inclusive to engineers and those from hard sciences. In fact, this paper is calling for an inclusive involvement of all stakeholders including social scientists and affected individuals in the community to avoid social acceptance issues and subsequently delay the projects once implemented.

Lastly, the grid availability in the proximity of proposed ocean energy projects is vital. Often, remote areas lack suitable grid infrastructure and require either network upgrades or the construction of new network lines, whose costs may fall on the developers. Further, grid integration should be seriously considered as a bottleneck. Hence, it is imperative to conduct feasibility studies under the guidance of the results of workshops and consultations.

Aside from addressing bottlenecks such as the development/ design of cost-competitive technologies, governments should actively engage in attracting investors to finance research, development and deployment. If possible in the case of Southeast Asian countries, Public-Private Partnerships should be encouraged between foreign investors, government corporations/agencies and even domestic private sectors. This kind of partnership is highly encouraged as reflected in the AOIP by 'developing a regional public-private partnership development agenda to mobilize resources for connectivity projects, including infrastructure projects in Indo-Pacific region.'

Lastly, to enhance the synergy and sustain the operation of the ORE projects, the developers must be willing to devise mechanism in the implementation of shallow charging regimes, where developers share the cost of new grid capacity with grid operators. Of course, the governments should be willing as well to share the burden at the early phase by providing incentives and support assistance to the developers.

Concluding Remarks

With the threat of climate change and the depletion of fossil-based fuel, countries in Indo-Pacific should be ready to embrace ORE as the source of energy to fuel their more demanding economic activities. Ocean resources are more predictable and reliable because, unlike wind, the endless flows of this resource create a reliable supply source for future availability. It is also energy-rich since moving water is more than 800 times denser than moving air, which multiplies the kinetic energy by the same factor and opens up the scope of huge amounts of energy.

While ORE is just one of the many possible collaborations between countries in Indo-Pacific, it is also a clear manifestation of the conflux between AOIP and IPOI that India and ASEAN can pursue soonest. By doing so, ORE will be able to support further the inevitable growth of digital revolution and in the regional efforts of addressing rapid urbanisation among others.

The ocean energy technology can help India and ASEAN countries stimulate innovation, higher economic growth and create new job opportunities as well as it helps to reduce carbon footprint. It will also help these countries to support its neighbouring states which have energy deficits, for their better economic growth and can guide them on their way to being self-sufficient in energy sector.[10] Thus, it is important that all stakeholders include India and ASEAN countries and should start to pay more attention to generating resources from renewable sources of energy – a resource that is unlimited and less vulnerable to the effects of climate change.

Notes

1. Refer, ASEAN Outlook on the Indo-Pacific, 2019.
2. Refer, Indo-Pacific Division Briefs, MEA, India.
3. Refer, Nakano, J. (2018).
4. Refer, Agundo, M. (2018).
5. https://www.drishtiias.com/daily-updates/daily-news-analysis/ocean-energy-as-renewable-energy.
6. Refer, Ocean Energy. Drishti. 2019.
7. Ibid.
8. Agundo, M. (2018).

9. Magagna, D. and Uihlein, A. (2015).
10. https://www.drishtiias.com/to-the-points/paper3/ocean-energy.

References

ASEAN (2019). "ASEAN Outlook on the Indo-Pacific", Association of Southeast Asian Nations (ASEAN), Jakarta, https://asean.org/storage/2019/06/ASEAN-Outlook-on-the-Indo-Pacific_FINAL_22062019.pdf

MEA (2020). "Indo-Pacific Division Briefs", Ministry of External Affairs (MEA), Government of India, https://mea.gov.in/Portal/ForeignRelation/Indo_Feb_07_2020.pdf

Nakano, J. (2018). "Energy Opportunities under the Free and Open Indo-Pacific Vision", Centre for Strategic and International Studies (CSIS), Jakarta, https://www.csis.org/analysis/energy-opportunities-under-free-and-open-indo-pacific-vision

Agundo, M. (2018). "Vast and Boundless: The Dawn of Sustainable Energy from Marine Environments in Southeast Asia". Singapore: Ocean Pixel.

Drishti (2019). "Ocean Energy", https://www.drishtiias.com/to-the-points/paper3/ocean-energy

Magagna, D. and Uihlein, A. (2015). "Ocean energy development in Europe: Current status and future perspectives". *International Journal of Marine Energy*, 11, 84–104.

SECTION V: Way Forward

16. ASEAN-India Partnership in the Post-COVID-19 and Way Forward

C. Uday Bhaskar

Introduction

The century-old association between India and Southeastern countries evolves over the years. From Dialogue partner to Strategic partnership, ASEAN and India have achieved many milestones. The unprecedented situation of COVID-19 pandemic has altered many global scenarios whereas it brings some cooperation more closer. To understand the present India-ASEAN cooperation, it is necessary to briefly scrutinise the Summit Statement issued at the end of the 36th ASEAN Summit in June 2020. It is a well-drafted and comprehensive document of more than 8000 words. It has 66 paragraphs as a matter of detail – and there is a section that talks about ASEAN and its dialogue partners in the early paragraphs. The relevant section notes:

> "We welcomed the holding of Ministerial meetings with Dialogue Partners, including Australia, China, the EU, Russia, and the U.S. via video conference to exchange views and explore cooperation to mitigate, control and respond to the impact of COVID-19...."[1], and India did not find mention.[2] However, in the latter part of the statement, there was brief reference: "We noted the progress in the implementation of ASEAN's free trade area (FTA) and comprehensive economic partnership (CEP) agreements with

major trading partners i.e. China, India, Japan, Korea, Australia, and New Zealand, and Hong Kong, China as well as engagement with new FTA partners." However, we are aware that in relation to the big-ticket trade issue of this decade – RCEP – India and ASEAN are not on the same page.[3]

Surprisingly, this 2020 document has a lot of reference to the COVID-19 pandemic and by extension, the impact on the comprehensive security of ASEAN as a collective. This is very valuable in terms of human security. Therefore, India should look at this prioritisation as the catalyst for 2021–22 apropos the India-ASEAN partnership.

The remarks made by the Hon'ble Deputy Prime Minister of Thailand at the inauguration of 6th ASEAN-India Think-Tank roundtable, where he spoke about this simple but powerful word *SHARE* and the import of each letter is significant. Dr. Jaishankar, Hon'ble Foreign Minister of India spoke about the need for out of the box thinking and pushing the envelope of partnership.[4] The two senior political representatives of India and Thailand (representing the ASEAN view) have given a political direction which needs to be taken forward. Therefore, the important question that arises before us is what is it that the think tanks can do now in order to take the bi-lateral cooperative effort even further given that India is a partner of choice for ASEAN in various areas.

In the following sections, the chapter discusses important aspects of human security in post-pandemic and the feasibility matrix of this security architecture. Lastly, the paper indicates issues of Indo-Pacific as a Way Forward.

Structure of Human Security in Post-Pandemic

The biggest challenge imposed by COVID-19 is a contraction of prosperity and economic growth across the board. It is accepted that there will be a visible contraction in global GDP and regional and individual nations GDP numbers will shrink relative to pre-pandemic estimates.[5]

In the Jakarta Post, the Indonesian Foreign Minister Ms. Sri Mulyani Indrawati, drew attention to the challenge Indonesia is facing because of COVID-19, particularly with reference to fiscal issues. She also emphasized the challenges of the political establishment in Indonesia to ensure that whatever was being implemented would have a human face i.e., it would be human centred and the need for Indonesia, along with its partners to take this idea forward. Therefore, when we talk about the impact of COVID-19, apart from national GDP numbers, citizen welfare would have to be protected even when per capita prosperity is going to shrink.[6]

Consequently, this overall belt-tightening will manifest itself in a wide-spectrum manner and national resource allocation priorities will change. Regionally, trade is now shrinking. The tangible figures that came out in June for India, indicate that in the first quarter the quantum of trade has shrunk. Similarly, across the board in ASEAN and in India, formal employment and informal employment has taken a big hit and this, in turn, impacts human security.

Working on human security as a component of comprehensive national security soon after the end of the Cold War has taken towards the early Indian formulation on this issue. This concept is what we refer to as 'yogakshemavaháh' – a term that is derived from the Arthashastra – a 3 BC treatise authored by Kautilya that dwells on well-being of the individual as the highest goal of governance and the kind of responsibilities that devolve on the ruler.[7]

This has been envisioned as 'Hexagon of Security' – a conceptual approach for individual nation-states and how this pursuit of comprehensive security could be harmonized both regionally and globally.[8] This hexagon has three primary components – being the political integrity and vitality of the state; complemented and supported by its economic and financial index of prosperity; and the third being the military or hard security capability to safeguard core ensure national interests. The two new elements for this hexagon are environmental issues and ecological concerns such as climate change and global warming (this has a great relevance for the maritime domain) and the last is the technology determinant –

given the quality and speed of technological innovations and breakthroughs that are radically altering domain status quo in an unprecedented manner.

Therefore, it is necessary to visualise the security hexagon for each of the ASEAN members and arrive at a determination about those areas or issues which could be prioritised for action or implementation in relation to India – either bilaterally or under ASEAN aegis. Think tanks could play the role of a catalyst and a resource centre for multi-domain harmonisation.

Working towards Feasibility Matrix

ASEAN and India can work on the equivalent of a desirability-feasibility matrix against the backdrop of the political compulsions of each individual nation-state and then attempt an implementation blue-print exercise across each of these arms of the hexagon. Whether it is about the political and diplomatic initiatives; or re-visit economic, finance, trade and connectivity issues which have been discussed at length (inconclusively?) or in review of hard security issues (military security, strategic concerns, maritime matters) and technology cooperation opportunities – there are distinctive areas of correspondence for India and ASEAN.

A certain degree of engagement and cooperation that is pre-COVID-19 can be seen at the bilateral level. The intellectual challenge for think tanks is to carefully review the ASEAN summit document and prepare a desirability-feasibility matrix for deliberation at the next think-tank network meeting. From the present perspective, managing the COVID-19 pandemic and ensuring timely vaccination for all citizens regionally is a high priority, so that the reality of a post-COVID-19 phase does not become elusive.

The India-ASEAN connectivity projects that signed long back but still not completed. And, we are still hoping that these projects would be realised in a short duration of time! Hence, from this experience we observed that the nature of the challenges that persist in ASEAN-India context is to swift implementation of projects; the reason behind this is as every country that is part of this project has its own constraints therefore the project is not able to move forward. Unfortunately, due to the pandemic, these constraints are going to become more acute because of the pressure on resources and capacity – whether it is financial or human.

Way Forward

Individual countries have outlined their own maritime vision which comes under the broader umbrella of the Indo-Pacific and India has reiterated the centrality of ASEAN in this formulation – the confluence of the two oceans. Further, the Indian Prime Minister had mooted the idea of SAGAR (which refers to the ocean in Sanskrit) but it also is an acronym for 'security and growth for all in the region.'

So, in the maritime domain, there are some low hanging issues for collective action that can build on the successes of the past. The recent oil spill outside of Mauritius is a good example of the need for collective effort when there are such exigencies in the maritime domain. We have individually pursued HADR, some bilaterally, some trilaterally and some like the QUAD that is still evolving. To conclude, the maritime domain may figure high on the desirability-feasibility matrix and India and ASEAN think-tanks could give this due attention.

Therefore, pollution in the Indian Ocean and the non-linear impact on climate change are a concern and threat to human security. India and ASEAN think-tanks could work on the current status of maritime pollution in the waters of the Indo-Pacific region and focus on plastic waste being dumped in the ocean. One area for some preliminary thumb-nail data collection is the quantum of medical waste generated by COVID-19 as part of protective equipment, gloves, masks and such are being dumped in the nearest sea/ocean by Indian Ocean littorals.

Assessing and meaningfully tackling oceanic pollution will call for a concerted regional effort and hence all the major stakeholders (India, ASEAN and dialogue partners) could be encouraged – at think-tank level – to prepare a status report on marine and maritime pollution. There are many issues that can be mapped by think-tanks in the first instance and then sent to the state machinery for appropriate action.

An objective and rigorous review of the previous five AINTT deliberations could be conducted with a single objective: how best to move from 'Think Tank' to 'Do Tank' and transmute this collective body into an effective regional group that can deliver results.

Notes

1. Refer, "Chairman's Statement of the 36th ASEAN Summit: Cohesive and Responsive ASEAN", page 2 (June 2020).
2. Note: The 17th India-ASEAN virtual Summit is due to be held later this year.
3. Refer, "Chairman's Statement of the 36th ASEAN Summit: Cohesive and Responsive ASEAN", page 16 (June 2020).
4. Refer, Remarks by EAM during the 6th Roundtable Meeting of ASEAN-India Network of Think Tanks (AINTT), MEA (2020).
5. Refer, World Bank (2020).
6. Refer, Akhlas, A. W. and Samboh, E. (2020).
7. Refer, Shamasastri, R. (1915).
8. Refer, Post-Cold War Security, *Strategic Analysis* (1997).

References

Akhlas, A. W. and Samboh, E. (2020). "Pandemic and Opportunity for Reforms in Indonesia: Sri Mulyani". *The Jakarta Post*, 21 August, https://www.thejakartapost.com/news/2020/08/21/pandemic-an-opportunity-for-reforms-in-indonesia-sri-mulyani.html

ASEAN (2020). "Chairman's Statement of the 36th ASEAN Summit: Cohesive and Responsive ASEAN". ASEAN, 26 June, p. 2. Association of Southeast Asian Nations (ASEAN), Jakarta.

MEA (2020). "Remarks by EAM during the 6th Roundtable Meeting of ASEAN-India Network of Think Tanks (AINTT)", 20 August, Ministry of External Affairs (MEA), Government of India, https://www.mea.gov.in/Speeches-Statements.htm?dtl/32904

Shamasastri, R. (1915). Concerning Discipline. *Kautilya's Arthashastra* (Translated by R. Shamasastri), pp. 31-32, https://ia802703.us.archive.org/13/items/Arthasastra_English_Translation/Arthashastra_of_Chanakya_-_English.pdf

World Bank. (2020). "The Global Economic Outlook During the COVID-19 Pandemic: A Changed World". The World Bank, 8 June, dhttps://www.worldbank.org/en/news/feature/2020/06/08/the-global-economic-outlook-during-the-covid-19-pandemic-a-changed-world.

PART II

Sixth Roundtable of ASEAN-India Network of Think Tanks (AINTT)
20-21 August 2020

Summary of the Roundtable

The ASEAN-India Centre (AIC) at Research and Information System for Developing Countries (RIS) in collaboration with ASEAN Studies Centre (ASC), Chulalongkorn University, Bangkok; Ministry of Foreign Affairs of the Kingdom of Thailand and Ministry of External Affairs, Government of India organised 6th Roundtable of the ASEAN-India Network of Think Tanks (AINTT) on 20-21 August 2020 via Video Conferencing. The theme of the roundtable focussed on "ASEAN-India: Strengthening Partnership in the Post-Covid Era". The roundtable provided scope to experts and scholars from ASEAN countries and India to exchange views and address the uncertainties due to COVID-19 and further strengthen the linkages in political, economic and socio-cultural areas between the two regions. The leaders of ASEAN and India, namely, H.E. Don Pramudwinai, Deputy Prime Minister and Foreign Minister of Thailand; H.E. Dr S. Jaishankar, External Affairs Minister of India and H.E. Dato' Lim Jock Hoi, ASEAN Secretary General, delivered the Inaugural Address, and released the fifth AINTT proceedings titled "ASEAN-India: Partners of Integration in Asia". Welcome remark was given by Dr. Mohan Kumar, Chairman, Research and Information System for Developing Countries (RIS), New Delhi and Dr. Suthiphand Chirathivat, Chairman, ASEAN Studies Centre (ASC), Chulalongkorn University, Bangkok. Dr Prabir De, Professor, ASEAN-India Centre (AIC) at RIS delivered the Vote of Thanks. More than 400 participants from academia, industry, government and diplomatic community attended the roundtable through video conferencing.

The roundtable was conducted in five sessions, each aimed at facilitating an in-depth discussion on the various aspects relating to the implications of Covid-19 pandemic and identifying the opportunities in the post-Covid-19 period by focussing on discussing the changes in the global order; potential scope of the emerging value chains; the significance of industrial revolution 4.0 in the new normal; complementarities and cooperation in the ASEAN Outlook of Indo-Pacific (AOIP) and India's Indo-Pacific Ocean Initiative (IPOI) and way forward in further strengthening ASEAN-India relations in the post-COVID-19 period.

Inaugural Session

H.E. Mr. Don Pramudwinai, Deputy Prime Minister and Minister of Foreign Affairs of the Kingdom of Thailand extended his opening remarks by emphasizing on the importance of culture of sharing in taking forward the ASEAN-India strategic partnership at this critical time. He expressed that the partnership can be threaded together by a powerful yet simple acronym "SHARE", which stands for S-Supply Chain Connectivity, H-Human Security, A Academics, R-Regionalism and Multilateralism, E-Environment. H.E. Mr. Don Pramudwinai, outlined the key areas of cooperation under the acronym "SHARE."

To strengthen supply chain connectivity, ASEAN and India should ensure unhindered flow of essential goods (particularly medical supplies), and therefore, facilitate investment and business travel. ASEAN and India should cooperate in integrating the key industries into the supply chain, redirect resources for enhancing digital infrastructure and creating a digital ecosystem, and enhance physical connectivity by completing and extending the India-Myanmar-Thailand Trilateral Highway project to ensure seamless movement of goods and people across the borders. For human security, ASEAN and India should work together to ensure food security for all. ASEAN and India should enhance cooperation in medical research and development as well as in medicine and vaccines. They should introduce new technologies such as climate-smart agriculture, application of robotics and drones in agriculture to increase productivity and meet global demand.

ASEAN-India partnership should focus on skill development of the workforce (especially MSME's) to get benefits from the 4th Industrial Revolution and the digital economy. Besides, it must also focus on ensuring women empowerment and providing skill development and financial access to women entrepreneurs. ASEAN and India should support regionalism and multilateralism by reinforcing the regional and sub-regional groupings such as ASEAN+1, Mekong-Ganga Cooperation (MGC), ACMECS, BIMSTEC and IORA further. ASEAN and India should work together in ensuring green and sustainable growth by reopening economies with re-invigorated efforts on environmental conservation. Lastly, H.E. Mr. Don Pramudwinai pointed that ASEAN and India need to continue sharing information, best practices, knowledge and experiences among health experts, academics and policy makers. This value of sharing must be maintained and reinforced even after COVID-19 pandemic comes to an end.

H.E. Dr. Subrahmanyam Jaishankar, External Affairs Minister of India, in his talk, highlighted that TRUST is the most valued commodity in international relations today. India and ASEAN need to work together more sincerely in searching collective solutions and in creating positive and practical models of cooperation to deal with all kinds of challenges. He pointed out that new thinking, fresh ideas, more imagination and greater openness are going to be the main drivers of social and economic order post pandemic. He added that think tanks must push this endeavour even further in the present world situation. Thus, we need to move beyond orthodoxies in trade, politics and security in this new world. H.E. Dr. Jaishankar emphasized on key areas such as people to people contact, health security, strengthening national capacities and de-risking critical aspects of societal existence, mitigating concerns about supply chain through greater emphasis on diversification and resilience and focus on employment generating economy called "Atma Nirbhar Bharat" or self reliant India.

H.E. Dato' Lim Jock Hoi, Secretary-General, ASEAN briefly shared ASEAN's response to the COVID-19 pandemic. To mitigate the ravages of the pandemic, ASEAN took various measures such as COVID-19 response fund to strengthen the public health capacity, Hanoi action plan on keeping the markets open and transporting essential supplies, standard operation procedure for public health and establishing a post-COVID-19 recovery framework to rebuild and reenergise ASEAN community. He added that India's assistance is important in dealing with the pandemic and he hopes to see India extending support to the ongoing initiatives. H.E. Dato' Lim Jock Hoi highlighted that people to people connectivity is the essence of ASEAN-India partnership which can be seen through various initiatives such as Nalanda Scholarships, Media Exchange Program, and ASEAN-India Student Exchange Programme, among others that contribute to the human capital development. He also added that the ASEAN-India FTA in goods must be reviewed to harness potential of bilateral trade and investment for mutual benefit. He also discussed that India's initiative of Trilateral Highway and its extension will pave the way for ASEAN-India transportation link and trade relation. In addition, he highlighted India's contribution in multi-sectoral development in ASEAN through the Mekong-Ganga Cooperation (MGC). H.E. Dato' Lim Jock Hoi also discussed about ASEAN-India Plan of Action for 2020-2025 that includes new areas of cooperation such as public health, smart cities, sustainable development cooperation and digital economy which is vital for ASEAN-India connectivity through multilateral forums.

Section I: Changing Landscape of Global Order and ASEAN-India Relations in the Post-COVID Era

Dr. Jayant Dasgupta, Member, Governing Council, RIS, New Delhi chaired the first session and gave the opening remarks for session I. In his talk, Dr. Dasgupta discussed about the impact of the COVID-19 pandemic on MSMEs, which contribute approximately

30 per cent to India's GDP and 40 per cent to India's exports. He added that the pandemic has impacted economic activities in both India and ASEAN and they need to work more closely to ensure new sources of growth and prosperity as global economic landscape is shifting. Dr. Dasgupta also pointed out that the pandemic has posed anti-globalisation and anti-multilateralism threat that may distort the GVCs even further or derail the emergence of new value chain. Thus, learning from best practices may help ASEAN and India in building a resilient and sustainable world post-COVID-19. Dr. Dasgupta mentioned that ASEAN and India can take advantage of the changing landscape of global order which offers new opportunity such as merchandise trade, value chain, public health, connectivity, digital economy including e-commerce, fintech, artificial intelligence, block chain, maritime resources, energy, etc.

Prof. Amitav Acharya, UNESCO Chair in Transnational Challenges and Governance and Distinguished Professor, American University, Washington, DC discussed about the current trends in the geopolitical landscape, and mentioned that COVID-19 pandemic is an accelerator rather than an initiator of the changes in great power competition, globalisation, global governance and ideology. He also added that COVID-19 has played a catalyst role in lowering global trade further which has had a catastrophic effect on supply chain. Moreover, with concepts like strategic autonomy and self reliance, governments would be looking inward for developing public health infrastructure which indicates that globalisation may take a new form i.e. more regionalisation. Prof. Acharya highlighted that global governance is weakening and we may see regional, multilateral, plurilateral health groups emerging. He also mentioned that ideology is becoming one of the principal factors of country's foreign policy indicating that the world may change towards less liberalised international order and will see more fragmentation and regionalisation, more competition. Talking about India, Prof. Acharya added that India has great potential to contribute in global governance and peace process as India's diplomatic approach enhances its ability towards future cooperation. Thus, to increase India's credibility in the global governance, Prof. Acharya suggested that India should focus on building diplomacy, trust, soft power capacity, governance capacity and handling transnational threat to further develop and strengthen economic, social and cultural links with ASEAN. He further emphasized on strengthening people to people connectivity in health, education and culture.

Prof. Amita Batra, School of International Studies (SIS), Jawaharlal Nehru University (JNU), New Delhi discussed about the change in the nature as well as the magnitude of global trade due to the pandemic and how India can cooperate with ASEAN to deal with the challenges while maintaining its national identity. Prof. Batra highlighted that there has been an unprecedented decline in global trade as countries have restricted trade in food products and other commodities and this has paved way for higher trade in medical supplies. She also mentioned that India and ASEAN need to come forward for cooperation to address manufacturing and distribution of vaccines by reviving multilateralism. In addition, Prof. Batra emphasized that India needs to take cognizance of the importance of regionalism and work more with ASEAN to strengthen its centrality in the region. She also pointed out that India and ASEAN should work to integrate with each other as a more dynamic region in developing national and regional supply chains. Thus, to strengthen India's relationship with ASEAN, Prof. Batra has put forward the recommendations of the revival of multilateralism through shared medical technology and knowledge or know how in manufacturing of vaccines; cooperation in providing flexibility in existing intellectual property rights agreements between ASEAN and India; focus on relocation and re-shoring of national and regional supply chains to ASEAN and India; shift from trading policy to industrial policy by reinforcing existing distributional unevenness through technology and globalisation and learn from Korea, Taiwan and Vietnam for data and technology governance and cooperate with them for betterment both during and post pandemic. Besides, Prof. Batra also suggested India to work on re-building and re-establishing confidence with ASEAN post-RCEP withdrawal in mega regional trade agreements.

Prof. Nanigopal Mohanta, Director, Centre for Southeast Asian Studies, Gauhati University, Guwahati discussed about the changes in the global political system and highlighted that even though the northeastern region is the drive engine of the Act East Policy, it is not getting adequate benefits from the policy. He also outlined four visible changes in the global political system. They are: (i) shift away from the centrality of geo-trade and geo-commerce of globalisation to a geo-strategic world with significant reliance on geo-technology; (ii) retreat from globalisation to regionalisation, regionalisation to sub-regionalisation and eventually towards localisation; (iii) transition from the US centric global order to a China centric world political economy; and (iv) decline in expense on defence by ASEAN due to the dominance of geo-strategic movements. Prof. Mohanta also added that India and ASEAN need to focus on the micro aspects of how people live their life rather than focusing only on the macro aspects. Thus, to enhance ASEAN-India strategic cooperation, Prof. Mohanta has suggested that India and ASEAN should focus on strengthening and reviving the traditional and historic relationship of communities living in the border areas through infrastructure, health and education facilities. He suggested enhancing Mekong-Ganga and Mekong-Ganga-Brahmaputra cooperation through research and sharing expertise in pandemic management, bringing cooperation in SMEs, food security and biodiversity for North-east India and strengthening connectivity by developing infrastructure at border points connected with Myanmar and other regions of South East Asia. He further added that timely completion and disbursement of projects is of critical importance in enhancing India's role as a serious player in the region.

Prof. Lau Sim Yee, Reitaku University, Tokyo and Columnist, New Straits Times, Kuala Lumpur discussed his recent study that captures the containment of COVID-19 in the ASEAN region using two sample sets. The findings from the first set of analysis substantiates that measures such as border control measures and strict domestic movement restriction have helped the ASEAN countries in reducing the containment of COVID-19. Thus, democracy may not necessarily be the answer to containing outbreaks and future prevention of other pandemics. The findings from the other set of analysis captures countries that lifted restrictions earlier and allowed free mobility of citizens for normalising social interactions and this resulted in reemergence of transmission. Prof. Lau added that the uncertainty has not diminished and therefore, ignoring clear and present danger of COVID-19 is not correct. Prof. Lau suggested establishing an "ASEAN-India Disease Control and Prevention Centre (AI-DCPC)" for public health emergency for preventing the COVID-19 pandemic and other public health challenges in future. Once AI-DCPC is established, ASEAN and India can expand the ASEAN EOC Network (The ASEAN Emergency Operations Centre Network for Public Health Emergency). Besides, AI-DCPC can further solicit cooperation from the established institutions of the similar kind in each dialogue partner (such as Australia, China, the EU, Korea, Japan, Russia, the US).

Prof. Carole Ann Chit Tha, Member, Myanmar Institute of Strategic and International Studies (MISIS), Yangon spoke about the changing landscape of global order amid COVID-19 and highlighted that we should turn the crisis into opportunity and make the best use of it. She added that the pandemic has stirred global diplomacy into a new direction that has strengthened the idea of digital governance. In addition, the strategic dimension has undergone major changes in Southeast Asia as well as India, with China's belligerent actions and US-China Cold War. Prof. Chit Tha asserted that the pandemic has offered India an opportunity to ramp up its public diplomacy in Southeast Asia by undertaking mutually beneficial collaborations and for broadening and deepening the scope of Act East Policy and securing future regional projects. On the other hand, she added that ASEAN need to foster closer engagement with dialogue partners and should not restrict its priorities to itself but also be accountable to the rest of the world. For strengthening ASEAN-India regional collaboration, Prof. Chit Tha suggested fostering

ASEAN unity, ASEAN centrality and its role as a primary driving force in the evolving of the region. He further suggested exploring trans-regional multilateral cooperation on COVID-19 in order to enhance ASEAN and India's preparedness to respond to infectious diseases like pandemics. India should also focus on adopting mutual best practices in the area of health security for the people. India and ASEAN should consider collaboration in pharmaceutical and vaccine research area.

Section II: Emerging Value Chains: Opportunities for ASEAN and India in the Post-COVID Era

Prof. Sineenat Sermcheep, Faculty of Economics, Chulalongkorn University, Bangkok chaired Session II and extended her opening remarks. She gave a brief background of the key issues and outlined the topics of discussion for the session. They included discussions on current scenario of ASEAN-India trade, opportunities and challenges of ASEAN-India trade and the way forward, strengthening ASEAN-India cooperation in building a more sustainable and resilient supply chain, promoting ASEAN-India trade and value chain through trade facilitation, digital connectivity, cross border service, logistic business and tourism, promoting start-ups or MSME participation.

Dato' Ramesh Kodammal, Chairman of Goldtex Group of Companies, and Chairman, ASEAN-India Business Council (AIBC), Kuala Lumpur spoke about trade and international linkages and highlighted the areas where India and ASEAN have potential to expand participation in the global value chains. He expressed that there are low linkages between trade and industry even in the presence of ASEAN-India FTA. Thus, India needs to integrate further with ASEAN to strengthen global value chains as ASEAN is much more integrated with GVCs. In addition, Dato' Ramesh Kodammal added that FDI in ASEAN is much more than that in India, which also spills over to its greater participation in GVCs. Moreover, countries like European Union, USA and Japan are likely to consider diverting some of the investments into ASEAN away from China due to the pandemic. Therefore, India's integration with ASEAN becomes ever more important. He also discussed about India vis-à-vis the RCEP, and how re-joining the RCEP will substantially increase India's participation in the global value chains. In order to achieve that India and ASEAN need to build industrial linkages and diversify their trade basket over the years. There must be a partnership to ensure sustainability. ASEAN and India should take advantage of the two markets for trading and building and strengthening relations in future.

He emphasized that ASEAN and India have potential to expand participation in the GVCs in electrical and electronic items, agriculture and agro-based products, pharmaceutical and medical equipment sector post-COVID-19. Apart from food security, ASEAN and India must relook at the facilitation and promotion of trade in agriculture and food. ASEAN and India must facilitate private sector investment in large food production to serve global and regional market. India and ASEAN should work to enhance trade and industrial linkages for sourcing intermediate products and services for GVCs. India can partner and link with SMEs in India and ASEAN to produce products for companies operating out of ASEAN. SMEs in India should work towards being more responsive in price competitiveness and quality. Building enhanced industrial linkages between ASEAN and India would broaden and diversify the trade pattern. From business point of view, India's re-joining of RCEP would substantially increase the potential for India's increased participation in GVCs. The two parties should review the ASEAN-India FTA for identifying the gaps to open trade opportunities and further relax trade barriers. ASEAN and India should re-engage, re-intensify and re-build trust to forge close relationship and increase trade.

Prof. Rupa Chanda, RBI Chair Professor in Economics, Indian Institute of Management (IIM) Bengaluru discussed about the emerging value chain opportunities post-COVID-19 and how India can increase its GVC participation by further building partnership with ASEAN post pandemic. She highlighted that India's backward and forward participation rates in the GVCs are low as compared to

ASEAN. In addition, India's backward participation rates in GVCs are high while forward participation rates are low implying that India is not as competitive and integrated in supplying intermediate goods to other countries. Therefore, this low participation rate indicates that there is untapped trade potential. Also, India's forward participation is higher with ASEAN than with the rest of the world, which presents an opportunity to deepen bilateral relations. She added that production hubs and supply networks are likely to realign post-COVID-19, which has implications for trade flows, GVCs, RVCs and also provide new opportunities for digitalisation, MSMEs, startups, new sectors/activities. Prof. Chanda pointed that the role of MSMEs in this is particularly important. She also asserted that investment is the key to strengthening these linkages.

ASEAN-India GVC linkages have potential for many sectors within and across manufacturing and services and there is a need for detailed examination of industries and segments. If we consider sourcing from ASEAN vis-à-vis from World, there is a lot of sourcing from ASEAN region and it is one of the areas for India and ASEAN for further cooperation. India and ASEAN can work on two-way sourcing as backward linkages for India and ASEAN are stronger than forward linkages. India and ASEAN should work towards improving their services value-added contribution content for better penetration in the two services markets. India should move away from the recent trend of increasing tariffs and being self-reliant to improve GVC participation. India should improve manufacturing capacities in network products where there is scope for intra-industry trade, low-cost logistics and enhancing FDI, including India-ASEAN FDI flows for GVC linkages. FDI linked manufacturing should be encouraged to FDI linked exports to deepen India's engagement and participation with ASEAN and world. India should make improvements in its ease of doing business for SMEs and MSMEs located in India and ASEAN to better penetrate into GVCs. Investment facilitation is equally important to enhance partnership between India and ASEAN as they are aligned with domestic policies. Also, India needs to identify specific segments of complementarity and overlap across industries within value chains to enhance ASEAN-India GVC linkages. India needs to align domestic industrial policies with trade implementation measures for enhancing GVCs.

Dr. Tham Siew Yean, Senior Fellow, ISEAS-Yusof Ishak Institute, Singapore discussed about the emerging sectors of GVC participation for both India and ASEAN. India's backward and forward GVC participation is lower than that of ASEAN. Dr. Tham Siew Yean mentioned that GVC participation of ASEAN countries varies depending on the development of the economy while India's participation is mainly in forward value chain. She highlighted that FDI along with trade liberalisation, low tariff, and low non-tariff barriers are important for GVC participation. She discussed that the presence of sensitive list and highly sensitive list in the ASEAN-India agreement is insufficient to facilitate GVC formation especially in the new product areas. Dr. Tham Siew Yean also expressed her views about India's participation in RCEP as all the key players (China, Japan and Korea) are present in the forum. Dr. Tham Siew Yean argued that India can identify the potential areas of exports using International Trade Centre's (ITC) export potential map to form new GVCs with ASEAN. She also suggested that India needs to reconsider joining RCEP and emphasized that 'Assembling in India' can be a part of the 'Make in India' campaign.

Dr. Saon Ray, Senior Fellow, Indian Council for Research on International Economic Relations (ICRIER), New Delhi discussed about the opportunities for India and ASEAN post-COVID-19 pandemic through the integration of GVCs. She highlighted that India's backward and forward participation in GVCs is very low as compared to ASEAN. Dr. Ray added that India has been increasingly importing from ASEAN while India's importance in ASEAN's imports is small but increasing. She also spoke about India's participation in GVCs under the context of the automotive industry and used the automotive industry to draw relevance for ASEAN-India GVC linkages. Dr. Ray has suggested that India and ASEAN can focus on developing RVCs further with India through the electronics sector, and can do the same in the pharmaceutical sector. Both should consider establishing necessary link between services and manufacturing sector. Besides, she also recommended reviewing the ASEAN-India FTA.

Section III: New Normal and Significance of 4IR on ASEAN-India Partnership and Future Collaborations

Dr. Mia Mikic, Director, Trade, Investment and Innovation Division, United Nations ESCAP, Bangkok chaired the Session III and delivered the opening remarks for the session. She expressed her views regarding the important role of digital technology in approaching the health, social and economic crisis that we are experiencing in the midst of the pandemic. Dr. Mikic was of the view that by learning to adapt with digital technology during the pandemic, we are already witnessing the transition towards the Fourth Industrial Revolution (4IR) which is much broader than advances in terms of digital technology. Dr. Mikic also mentioned that the relationship between ASEAN and India is not new and in the commercial sphere it was based in the context of Third Industrial Revolution (3IR), where we had very clear idea of specialisation and division of labour and benefits, etc. accruing from it. However, it started to change with ASEAN's increased participation in global value chains (GVCs). Now, it is time to shift the entire spectrum of partnership from 3IR base to 4IR base. To build the framework of this new partnership, she suggested that the need to find harmonious ways of putting physical, biological and digital world together which will enable in moving forward for living in the new environment.

Mr. Sovinda Po, Senior Research Fellow, Cambodian Institute for Cooperation and Peace (CICP), Phnom Penh discussed about the scope and potential of ASEAN-India Science, Technology and Innovation Collaboration and India-CLMV 'Digital Village' Project for strengthening the ASEAN-India relationship in 4IR. Mr. Po highlighted two major points in his presentation. First, he discussed that fund provided by India through ASEAN-India Science and Technology Development Fund (AISTDF) established under the

ASEAN-India Science, Technology and Innovation Collaboration in 2007 are limited given the coverage of activities (which includes joint projects like R&D, research and training fellowship, participation of ASEAN school children, innovation, workshops, seminars, etc.). In addition, participation of Southeast Asian countries in the ASEAN-India Innovation Platform established under AISTDF is low as compared to India. Second, the funds allotted by India for building digital villages in Cambodia under the India-CLMV 'Digital Village' Project is also limited and have not shown much progress. Given the coverage of activities in the collaborative projects, India should provide more fund to AISTDF and India-CLMV "Digital Village" Pilot Project. Southeast Asian countries should increasingly participate in the ASEAN-India Innovation Platform under AISTDF. With limited fund, focus should be on the niche areas of urgent need like agriculture development. The digital village project should incorporate the concept of "Digital Agriculture", where farmers can use latest technology to monitor their crops. Indian should focus on providing competitive package of internet services (better services and affordable packages) to CLMV countries for adopting technology from India instead of Huawei 5G.

Mr. Gagan Sabarwal, Senior Director, National Association of Software and Service Companies (NASSCOM), New Delhi highlighted that India is the only country in the region that offers skills, scale, price and TRUST for implementation and execution of 4IR in ASEAN. He discussed that COVID-19 has accelerated the 4IR and directed the focus towards supply chain continuity, reduced reliance on human capital, agility, and most importantly cyber security. Mr. Sabarwal also spoke about the change in manufacturers needs due to the pandemic. The manufacturers have set new priorities for plants and products such as workforce safety solutions, manufacturing engineering, plant remote monitoring and handling, plant automation and autonomy for reducing the overall cost of operations, flexible manufacturing for unpredictable demand, value engineering, product reprioritisation, product customisation, etc. There is a need to strengthen collaboration with government, industry and academia of India and ASEAN to accelerate ASEAN transformation to 4IR. By partnering with India, ASEAN innovation gets the scale needed to curate global industry to adopt this platform. Sharing of information, experience and best practices on formulating and implementing policies related to 4IR between India and ASEAN needs to be emphasized. Further, focus should be on forming B2B partnerships between ASEAN and India to ensure that the partnership is sustained. More focus and resources are required to create digital talent and cyber security.

Dr. Jayant Menon, Visiting Senior Fellow, Institute of Southeast Asian Studies (ISEAS), Singapore spoke about the macroeconomic issues such as employment, income distribution, labour mobility, etc. which arise with 4IR transformation and its implications in the ASEAN and India region. He discussed that the COVID-19 pandemic has simply changed the character and hastened the pace of realising 4IR with more reliance on technology, cyber security issues and so on. Dr. Menon focused on two implications of the 4IR transformation. They are: employment and income distribution. He pointed out that every IR comes with a fear of massive unemployment, however, each and every time employment and welfare increased and lives became much better as many new industries and jobs were created due to technological changes. Dr. Menon was of the view that 4IR will not be any less than previous IRs as GVCs highlight that all tasks cannot be automated and as long as some things cannot be automated those jobs will be required. Therefore, better payment opportunities will emerge as we witness an increase in productivity and the overall welfare and standard of living will increase. Dr. Menon raised concerns over the distributional impacts as inequalities within and between countries will rise, therefore, we need to have mitigating measures for these inequalities within countries and the newer countries need to catch up with technology if they do not want to lag behind. In addition, 4IR runs a big risk of further marginalisation of the communities that are already left behind in terms of development. He mentions that this is a real challenge that the region is facing.

To strengthen the strategic partnership between ASEAN and India, Dr. Menon had put forward several recommendations, such as the need to increase investment in training the workforce and making them adaptive to changes accompanied by 4IR, increasing national and regional level collaborations for accelerating 4IR transformation in India and ASEAN with changes happening at the national level. Addressing labour mobility from India to ASEAN is the key for realising 4IR as India has relatively young population and difference in skills (India has heavily invested in IT). Thus, the ASEAN member states can gain from mutual exchange if labour mobility is made free. ASEAN must also work on its skilled labour mobility. MRAs that are outdated and deals with occupational groupings that do not comply with 4IR must be re-assessed. To deal with the issue of unskilled labour mobility and migration, ASEAN and India initially need to work at bilateral level and then move to regional level and lastly at multilateral level.

Dr. Balaji Parthasarathy, Professor, International Institute of Information Technology (IIIT), Bengaluru discussed about the opportunities and policy challenges associated with 4IR and digital platform economy for ASEAN-India partnership and future collaborations. Prof. Parthasarathy pointed out that just like IR, Artificial intelligence (AI)/Machine learning (ML) has the potential of making an unprecedented transformation that benefits everyone in the long run. AI/ML has the potential to transform the economy by finding new applications and fusing with existing technologies to transform other pre-existing sectors of the economy. However, the long run benefits of 4IR depend on the short run management of AI/ML. He also discussed about the growth of digital platform ("work on-demand via apps" includes activities such as transport, cleaning and running errands) and the characteristics of work they offer in India and Indonesia (as these two are the single largest market for platforms in ASEAN), to highlight the shared policy concerns in the post-COVID-19 era. Prof. Parthasarathy highlighted that despite the growth in employment and the opportunities the platform economy offers, there are major concerns with platforms when it comes to employment relationship and mechanisms of work control. Thus, to build a collective framework for ASEAN and India in providing decent work for platform economy, India and ASEAN need to focus on the policies such as code of social security for "gig worker" (which empowers the government to frame social security schemes like disability cover, old age protection, etc.) that would help in the growth of digital platforms in the post-COVID-19 era. He also suggested that India and ASEAN need to create regularity framework for platform economy for better work environment and better services.

Section IV: ASEAN Outlook on Indo-Pacific (AOIP) and Indo-Pacific Oceans Initiative (IPOI): Complementarities and Cooperation

Dr Arvind Gupta, Director, Vivekananda International Foundation (VIF), New Delhi chaired Session IV and gave introductory remarks for the session. Dr. Gupta spoke about the AOIP and IPOI initiatives for Indo-Pacific that lays down ASEAN's vision for Indo-Pacific while the Indian outlook was defined by rules-based order by Indian Prime Minister. He added that a lot of changes have taken place in the COVID-19 era so far as the security environment is concerned. India is facing a triple crisis-health, socio-economic and most importantly security crisis at the India and China borders. Dr. Gupta mentioned that China's Belt and Road Initiative, maritime silk route project, naval modernisation with geopolitical implication and ascendancy in China's all-round assertiveness have impacted Sino-India relations and will deeply impact relations with ASEAN as well. He was of the view that geopolitical changes at the mega scale which are taking place in the Indian Ocean and Pacific Ocean will force countries to continuously revise their outlook of the region and deal with the changes. He also added that whatever may be the challenges, they have only reinforced the reasons why we need to have even deeper cooperation between ASEAN and India. At last, he added that given the long history of cooperation and strategic partnership, trust should be built further for mutual benefit.

Prof. Fukunari Kimura, Chief Economist, Economic Research Institute for ASEAN and East Asia (ERIA), Jakarta expressed his views on the Indo-Pacific idea from the economics perspective and said that we need more appealing aspects in the connection between India and ASEAN. He added that the dominance of politics and national security issues have complicated the cooperation between India and ASEAN in the Indo-Pacific but it still has a lot of potential. Prof. Kimura discussed that manufacturing production networks in the Indo-Pacific have so far been disappointing even though there is a lot of potential. Thus, unlocking this potential is important for economic integration and connectivity. He also pointed out that even though South Asia (India) is good in services, but we still need manufacturing as it will generate jobs for relatively poor people which will help in achieving inclusive growth. Prof. Kimura further discussed about the trilateral highway which is symbolic of interregional cooperation between south Asia and ASEAN. He further discussed about India's advantages in ICT (information communication technology) and the role it can play in tackling the big issues like personal data, competition, cyber security, and taxation in ASEAN.

To nurture the partnership between India and ASEAN, Prof. Kimura suggested that the upgradation of location advantages and reducing service link costs is vital for developing international manufacturing production networks in the Indo-Pacific. Addressing stability and inclusiveness by activating economic activities, making improvement in institutional connectivity, removing redundant restrictions on various modes of services trade will help in building the cooperation further. India can extend help to ASEAN in establishing an effective and efficient policy regime for the flow of data, and for promoting data-related businesses. India and ASEAN need to understand the importance of services and ICT in the medium and short run for connectivity development. Deeper integration in the Indo-Pacific must be realised to strengthen regional ties. India should attract production blocks to enhance its manufacturing base which will help in establishing stronger link between India and ASEAN.

Vice-Admiral Pradeep Chauhan, Director General, National Maritime Foundation (NMF), New Delhi highlighted that there is a clear congruence and complementarity between the functional framework of the Indo-Pacific perspectives of both ASEAN (AOIP) and India (IPOI) with the centrality of ASEAN as the foundational principle. Vice-Admiral Chauhan also added that there is predominance of inclusive development and prosperity, peace and stability, openness, transparency, dialogue and cooperation instead of rivalry and criticality of maritime domain in both India and ASEAN Indo-Pacific outlooks. In addition, the seven spokes of the web (Maritime security, Maritime Ecology, Science, Technology and Academic Cooperation, Disaster Risk Reduction and Management, Capacity Building and Resource Sharing, Trade Connectivity, and Maritime Transport and Maritime Resources) that define ASEAN and India's outlook in the Indo-Pacific region are highly correlated with each other. Vice-Admiral Chauhan emphasized that capacity and capability should never be mixed up and should be treated separately. In the past, these two terms have been used interchangeably which forced us to adapt to countries where capacity is in excess, which throw capacity into problem. In ASEAN, barring a few countries, capacity is not in excess but they do have capability. He was of the view that building infrastructure is not enough, and, ASEAN and India need to build bridges of trust for creating strong maritime connectivity by overcoming software challenges, etc. Thus, to strengthen the maritime cooperation and connectivity in the Indo-Pacific region, Vice-Admiral Chauhan had put forward the following recommendations:

- To build strong maritime connectivity, people to people connectivity and TRUST, ASEAN and India need to overcome various challenges through connectivity initiatives such as Belt-and Road Initiative, Blue Dot Network financing, providing inputs and investing in Asia-Africa Growth Corridor, establishing cross-cultural linkages and reviving historic ties through MAUSAM initiative.

- Utilize the experience from successful projects running under BIMSTEC and Asia Africa growth corridor to launch other new projects. This will give actual meaning to India's Act East Policy and AOIP.
- India's diplomatic, academic, science and technology, people to people and cultural outreach under SAGAR will help in assuring security and growth for all in the Indo-Pacific region.
- ASEAN and India need to develop time-bound roadmap along the lines of the deliverables of 'MPAC-2025' that includes not just 'hard' and 'soft' infrastructure, but also new initiatives to facilitate maritime tourism and people-to-people connectivity.
- ASEAN and India should develop cruise-ship tourism by reducing tariffs and promote Ro-Ro shipping.
- Need to develop strong Information and Communication Technology (ICT) infrastructure including hardware, software and skinware for utilising connectivity to its fullest.
- ASEAN and India need to work together more significantly on digital connectivity and climate change.
- ASEAN-India Network of Think-Tanks (AINTT) and academic collaboration with NMF is required for domain awareness through the functioning of information fusion centres and India's IOR IFC.
- Djibouti Code of Conduct should be the next avenue of approach for interacting with EU for signing 'White Shipping' data sharing agreements.

Dr. Premesha Saha, Associate Fellow, Observer Research Foundation (ORF), New Delhi highlighted that there are various similarities in the vision statement of ASEAN and India, indicating the existing complementarities. In addition, ASEAN and India have a diplomatic approach to the US-China trade war in the Indo-Pacific region, which provides a common ground for going forward. Dr. Saha was of the view that connectivity should be the focus in the region. She also added that maritime security is one of the primary challenges due to China's encroachment in the South China Sea.

Thus, it becomes extremely important to work on maritime law and look at the freedom of navigation in the Indo-Pacific region. To strengthen the connectivity between India and ASEAN in the Indo-Pacific, connectivity initiatives such as maritime summits, Indo-Pacific structural meet, disaster management collaboration and strengthening existing mechanisms can help in deepening India-ASEAN cooperation. Platforms like maritime law workshop and maritime security workshop should start between India and ASEAN to strengthen maritime cooperation. Collaborative initiatives/actions can be taken between India's NDMA and ASEAN's coordinating centre for humanitarian disaster management for managing disasters and learning from each other's experience. Coalition for disaster resilient infrastructure is another avenue for ASEAN countries to work along with India. India and ASEAN can form Blue Economy task force to deal with plastic debris, IORA fishing and sustainable use of marine resources. India and ASEAN can come together through coast guards to supply offshore coast guard vessels, to build ships, to conduct collaborative cleaning exercises. India can participate in ASEAN Coast Guard Law Enforcement Forum which is another platform where all the coastguards of the ASEAN countries work. India and ASEAN should work towards developing people-to-people connectivity by exchange of officers through training programmes from naval board colleges and defence universities of India to ASEAN. They can also explore developing information sharing centres for maritime domain awareness, host maritime law workshops to work on the freedom of navigation between India and ASEAN, conduct maritime security workshops between India and ASEAN and strengthen and revive the existing mechanisms (plurilateral, trilateral and unilateral initiatives) between ASEAN and India.

Prof. Joefe B. Santarita, Dean, Asian Center, University of the Philippines, Diliman discussed about the ASEAN outlook of AOIP and IPOI and highlighted the potential of Ocean Renewable Energy (ORE) (form of marine resource energy that pertains specifically to energy drawn from the power potentials of the ocean) in his presentation. Prof. Santarita pointed out that India and ASEAN have cooperated in energy generation. However, bulk of the cooperation is based on fossil-based energy extraction. He pointed out that energy access remains to be a challenge despite the improvements. In the ambit of sustainable development, there is an urgent need to explore energy sources from fossil-based to renewable sources of energy such as solar, wind, etc. and now marine resources. Stakeholders in India and ASEAN need to pay attention to generating energy resources from renewable sources of energy which is unlimited and less vulnerable to the effects of climate change. He also added that India's long coastline can be used to harness ocean renewable energy and Southeast Asia's archipelagic region holds immense power potential.

Thus, there is a need for collaboration in synergising ASEAN and India Indo-Pacific visions to make it more operational. India and ASEAN should synergise their efforts in joining and extracting ocean energy resources through public-private partnership, attracting investors to finance research, design and development, share expertise through academic institutions and an alliance of best engineering centres specialising on ocean engineering must be encouraged. Both India and ASEAN should conduct collaborative workshop of experts to address various bottlenecks (such as technology development, environmental and administrative issues, etc.). Governments should support the development of cost competitive technologies and educate local communities and address social acceptance issues. They should devise mechanisms in the implementation of shallow charging regimes. Emphasis should be given to India-ASEAN renewable Ocean Initiative. Government and private organisations can invest to maximise the potential of ocean energy (just like in the case of solar energy) and create a reliable supply source for future availability. Ocean energy technology can help India and ASEAN in stimulating innovation, creating economic growth and new jobs for energy deficit nations and guide their way to being self-sufficient in energy sector as well as reduce their carbon footprints.

Section V: Way Forward

Dr Mohan Kumar, Chairman, RIS chaired the way forward session and briefly discussed that there is a need for achieving greater strategic convergence and coherence between ASEAN and India because of the challenges of real politics, geopolitics, COVID-19, etc. posing in Asia. According to him, there is an imperative need for both India and ASEAN to adjust, accommodate, and alter positions if necessary, because of the changing situations and dynamics that we are seeing of not just COVID-19 but other concerns as well. He pointed out that we need a political, strategic or security architecture in Asia that is more cohesive and will react to the dynamic situation around us. To achieve this security architecture in terms of trade, investment and a resilient supply chain, Dr. Kumar highlighted the discussions from the previous sessions that emphasized to review the India-ASEAN FTA on goods, prepare both ASEAN and India to deal with 4IR, digital commerce and digitisation of the economy, flexible labour mobility or professional mobility between India and ASEAN so that things can be taken to the next level. He also highlighted the discussions on connectivity (air, surface, digital and maritime). To strengthen the strategic partnership between ASEAN and India, Dr. Kumar suggested expediting the completion of the ongoing connectivity projects, strengthen the disaster resilient infrastructure and focus on the issues like climate change, counter terrorism and cyber security.

Amb. Preeti Saran, Member, Governing Board, Indian Council of World Affairs (ICWA), New Delhi shared her outlook on ASEAN-India relationship and highlighted several aspects for building on the gains made in recent years from this strategic partnership. She pointed out that India has always been the strongest proponent of ASEAN's centrality and unity in the Indo-Pacific region and a prosperous and dynamic ASEAN will be instrumental in reviving the region after the challenges posed by the COVID-19 pandemic. At the same time, it is important for ASEAN countries to access and ask themselves whether it is in their interest to have India as a partner to sustain this multipolar Indo-Pacific of plural, rules-based, open, transparent democratic country. Amb. Saran highlighted that ASEAN and India have issue-free relations without any stress or anxiety with no territorial disputes, no overlapping maritime claims, no code of conduct to negotiate, except for a vast pool of goodwill on both sides and deep commitment to uphold international laws which is a great beginning to assess where we can move forward. She added that the COVID-19 pandemic has taught us to remain vigilant, self-reliant and important avenues of future collaboration and cooperation have opened up between India and ASEAN not only pandemic but also healthcare cooperation, cyber threat, information warfare and potential threat of biological warfare. Amb. Saran has put forth the following recommendations to strengthen the ASEAN-India strategic partnership:

- India and ASEAN need to work on cyber warfare, information warfare and biological warfare under the ambit of our political pillar.
- India can work with ASEAN in experience sharing, research and development including foreign affordable vaccine and other life-saving medicines or medical kits, low cost ventilators and training of health care workers.
- Since USA and Europe are looking to diversify away from China, India and ASEAN must seal this opportunity together for mutual benefit and should work towards building new value chains, and economic cooperation, therefore becomes top priority.
- Addressing rules of origin provisions under FTAs can potentially increase the scope of regional cooperation through various trade agreements.
- India and ASEAN should undertake specific action-oriented projects such as hydrological surveys, marine degradation related projects particularly those caused by man-made activities like illegal fishing, illegal construction islands, and destruction of marine life.
- Consider coordinated patrolling in high seas to prevent such illegal actives including trafficking of humans, drugs and other goods.

- We should consider more serious information and experience sharing on aspects of sustainable exploitation of rivers and harnessing them for our mutual benefit under the Mekong-Ganga Cooperation (MCG).
- BIMSTEC, another sub regional cooperation, is also an important forum and we must look on to it as it bridges South and Southeast Asia.
- We should go back in history and civilisation in taking forward cultural connectivity through people-to-people contact between India and ASEAN.

Dr. Zaw Oo, Executive Director, Center for Economic and Social Development (CESD), Yangon expressed his views about non-traditional security threats and India-Myanmar trade relations during the COVID-19 pandemic crisis. He highlighted that Myanmar can put forward its support to India in its food security scheme, provided that there is guaranteed trade and removal of quantitative restrictions on Myanmar's agricultural exports by India. He added that India should adopt a more resilient trade approach during the pandemic for the sake of Myanmar's farmers' income. Dr. Zaw Oo pointed out that India's assistance to Myanmar and other ASEAN countries is essentially important in building digital infrastructure and mitigating various challenges during and post the pandemic. He also discussed about connectivity projects and his outlook favours such projects as they address the underlined causes of avenue conflicts in that area. He also suggested enhancing the cultural links between India and Myanmar for attracting tourists from ASEAN. He suggested that the pandemic can be used for strengthening the partnership and overcoming the challenges between ASEAN and India. Dr. Zaw Oo suggested following recommendations as way forward:

- Think-tanks and policy makers must come up with regional mechanisms to deal with the second wave of COVID-19 for enhancing the regions preventive capacities, trust building measures and strengthening partnership.

- India should remove quantitative restrictions on food exports from Myanmar for the sake of humanitarian considerations and adopt a more resilient trade approach during the pandemic.
- India and Myanmar can work on an agriculture bilateral trade agreement which may be expanded to ASEAN-India trade agreement with a special focus on agricultural trade to address food security challenges under the COVID-19 crisis.
- ASEAN and India can work on specific action-oriented projects (such as Kaladan Multimodal Project) which do not cause any debt burden and can also balance other mega connectivity projects that lead to economic development of the region.
- Myanmar and India can work bilaterally on cultural cooperation projects like Buddha Gaya which attracts ASEAN tourists for religious tourism.
- Given that India has digital solutions for agriculture, education, etc., it should provide assistance to Myanmar and other ASEAN countries in developing digital infrastructure (e-education and e-government platforms) to reduce the digital divide within the region.

Commodore C. Uday Bhaskar, Director, Society of Policy Studies (SPS), New Delhi highlighted some of the opportunities and challenges of the ASEAN-India cooperative partnership that Think Tanks can take into consideration. Given that India has no mention in ASEAN's vision for 2025 (36th ASEAN Summit Statement), Commodore Bhaskar pointed that it provides an opportunity to India to make it more relevant and be a part of the partnership prioritised by ASEAN. He also talked about his "Hexagon of Security" formulation and identification of equivalents to desirability feasibility matrix which can be harmonised with the equivalent of ASEAN's vision for 2025. He also pointed out some takeaways for addressing maritime issues in the Indo-Pacific region. Commodore Bhaskar suggested following points at the Think Tank level:

- India and ASEAN countries should prepare a "Hexagon of Security" individually and see how it can be harmonised both regionally and globally.
- ASEAN and India can work on an equivalent of a desirability feasibility matrix by focusing on issues at the bilateral level and identifying how much can be harmonised with the equivalent of ASEAN's vision for 2025.
- ASEAN and India Think-Tanks should identify areas and come up with desirability blueprint along with feasibility (i.e. taking forward politically supported identified area).
- ASEAN and India Think-Tanks need to collectively revisit the low hanging issues in the maritime domain by taking account of feasibility of their capacity for addressing them.
- ASEAN and India Think-Tanks need to work on the current status of maritime marine pollution in the Indo-Pacific region for finding the amount of COVID-19 pandemic waste (as part of protective equipment, gloves, masks, etc.) dumped in water.
- ASEAN and India Think-Tanks should map the issues in the maritime domain and figure out how much can be sent to the government for appropriate action.
- ASEAN and India should review the previous AINTT deliberations to check what has been achieved and what is not achieved.
- Think Tanks in respective countries can move to Do Tank or Do Group for implementing the AINTT suggestions.

Mr. Kavi Chongkittavorn, Senior Fellow, Institute of Security and International Studies (ISIS), Chulalongkorn University, Bangkok discussed that more action is required to be taken for cementing ASEAN and India relations. He added that ASEAN and India should prioritise completion of the stalled plans and focus on action rather than too much talk and plan. He suggested that India should reconsider RCEP. Mr. Chongkittavorn recommended that ASEAN and India must complete the fourth five-year plan that includes strategic plans rather than re-inventing the wheel of objectives. ASEAN and India need to elevate their partnership and plans from strategic to comprehensive strategic partnership level.

Concluding Session

Dr. Suthiphand Chirathivat, Chairman, ASEAN Studies Centre (ASC), Chulalongkorn University, Bangkok chaired the concluding session and highlighted some of the major outcomes from the two-day roundtable discussions on strengthening ASEAN-India partnership in the post-COVID-19 period. Dr. Chirathivat said that Trust, ASEAN centrality and unity is the core of achieving strategic convergence between ASEAN and India. He also highlighted that COVID-19 has accelerated digitization and changed the way we rely on technology. Therefore, there is a need for altering the traditional ways of using technology and establishing a common platform where ASEAN and India cohesively work on innovation and catch up with 4IR. Dr. Chirathivat also pointed out that strategic issues like South-China Sea and energy cooperation should not be neglected. He expressed his views about taking steps for making these outcomes concrete and adapt to the new ways of doing exercise.

Dr. Piti Srisangnam, Associate Professor, Director of Academic Affairs, ASEAN Studies Center, Chulalongkorn University, Bangkok extended the vote of thanks to all the participants and organisers and summarised the policy recommendations from the two-day roundtable discussions. He emphasized that ASEAN and India can veer the crisis into opportunity through rise in demand and supply for new products and services, opportunity to build stronger and healthier regional value chains, a collaborative strategy to utilise each other's advantages. Associate Prof. Srisangnam added that ASEAN and India need to have a new mindset through constructive dialogue and consultation, information exchange/sharing/management, people-to-people connectivity, education and cultural exchange, and sincere political will. To bring this into action, ASEAN and India should strategise on confidence-building and preventive diplomacy without interference from external powers and recognise the vitality of ASEAN centrality for collective bargaining and building relationships based on mutual trust to convert crisis into opportunity.

Finally, Dr. Piti Srisangnam extended the Vote of Thanks on-behalf of the ASEAN Studies Centre at Chulalongkorn University, Bangkok and Dr. Durairaj Kumarasamy, ASEAN-India Centre (AIC), RIS, New Delhi delivered the Vote of Thanks on-behalf of AIC and RIS.

Key Recommendations for Actionable Projects

---

1. ASEAN and India must focus on completion of its 4th ASEAN-India Plan of Action (POA) and both the partners need to elevate their partnership from strategic to comprehensive strategic partnership level.

2. India and ASEAN can work together to develop affordable vaccines and other lifesaving medicines or medical kits, low cost ventilators and training of healthcare workers. In case a vaccine is developed in some other country but could be manufactured in India under license, India could take the lead to persuade other nations through the WHO/WTO to relax the IPR related patent conditions for manufacture of the vaccine in India (which incidentally has the largest manufacturing capacity for vaccines in the world) so that the vaccine could be supplied to third countries at a reasonable rate without wastage of time.

3. ASEAN and India shall establish ASEAN-India Covid Control and Prevention Centre for Public Health Emergency and to provide healthcare for the COVID-19 affected victims, which would help knowledge sharing and dissemination in the region.

4. ASEAN and India have unmet trade potential and offer scope to expand GVC participation in the sectors such as electrical and electronic items, agriculture and agro-based products, pharmaceutical, medical equipment and digital services in manufacturing in COVID-19 period. To improve the GVC

participation, India should engage in 'Assembling in India' as a part of the 'Make in India' strategy and improve manufacturing capacities in production networks to enhance the scope for intra-industry trade and low-cost logistics. Besides, digitisation could provide opportunities for MSMEs in integrating the manufacturing and services sectors, thereby unlocking GVC potentials.

5. Digital technologies need to be introduced in the field of agriculture. India's 'Digital Village' programme in CLMV should also include agriculture. Capacity in digital techniques and platforms in the field of agriculture should be enhanced. It also requires creating a pool of 'Digital Talents'. India may consider extending necessary assistance to Myanmar and other ASEAN countries for developing the digital infrastructure and providing digital solutions for agriculture, education, e-government platforms.

6. Untapped opportunities of India-ASEAN e-commerce need to bring out to the next higher level through (i) sustainable Fintech, helping people to do financial transactions just by using a smart-phone; and (ii) set up of an ASEAN-India e-Commerce Online Market. This will allow India and ASEAN to sell directly their products, thus strengthening MSMEs' participation and inclusiveness.

7. COVID-19 has fast-tracked the process of digital connectivity in a remarkable way. However, it has also generated growing cyber threats. Hence, cyber security should be one of the priority areas of cooperation between India and ASEAN.

8. Collaborative initiatives/actions shall be taken between India's NDMA and ASEAN's Coordinating Centres for Humanitarian Disaster Management (AHA Centre) for managing disasters and learning from each other's experience. Coalition for Disaster Resilient Infrastructure is another avenue for ASEAN countries to work along with India.

9. India and ASEAN shall form the Blue Economy Task Force to deal with plastic debris, hydrological surveys, marine

degradation related projects particularly those caused by human activities like illegal fishing, illegal construction islands, destruction of marine life and coordinated patrolling in high seas to prevent such illegal activities including trafficking of humans, drugs and other goods, IUU fishing, etc.

10. Think-tanks of India and ASEAN need to work on the current status of marine pollution that concerns the Indo-Pacific region particularly to find how much of the waste generated by COVID-19 is dumped in nearby water.

11. India and ASEAN can come together through Coast Guards to supply offshore coast guard vessels, to conduct collaborative cleaning exercises, to foster the exchange of officers through training programmes from naval war colleges and defense universities of India to ASEAN, developing information sharing centres, making India participate in ASEAN Coast Guard Law Enforcement Forum, etc.

12. Emphasis should be given to India-ASEAN Renewable Ocean Initiative, a conflux of IPOI and AOIP, by investing in technology and stimulating innovation through PPP to unlock the potential of ocean energy to create a reliable source for the future and to reduce carbon footprints.

13. Platforms like maritime law workshop and maritime security workshop should start between India and ASEAN in order to strengthen maritime cooperation.

14. India needs to spell out details of the Indo-Pacific Oceans Initiative (IPOI) and also accommodate ASEAN's invitation to join RCEP. Commonalities in various Indo-Pacific visions should be spelled out with actionable agendas.

6th Roundtable of the ASEAN-India Network of Think-Tanks (AINTT)

ASEAN-INDIA: STRENGTHENING PARTNERSHIP IN THE POST-COVID ERA

20-21 August 2020
Through Video-Conference

AGENDA

[Indian Standard Time]

DAY I: 20 AUGUST 2020

09.30 – 10.00	**Registration / Log-in to Webex**
10.00 – 11.00	**Inaugural Session**
10.00 – 10.10	**Welcome Remarks**

- **Dr. Mohan Kumar,** Chairman, Research and Information System for Developing Countries (RIS), New Delhi
- **Dr. Suthiphand Chirathivat,** Chairman, ASEAN Studies Centre (ASC), Chulalongkorn University, Bangkok

10.10 – 10.40	**Opening Remarks**

- **H.E. Mr. Don Pramudwinai,** Deputy Prime Minister and Minister of Foreign Affairs of the Kingdom of Thailand
- **H.E. Dr. Subrahmanyam Jaishankar,** External Affairs Minister of India
- **H.E. Dato' Lim Jock Hoi,** Secretary-General of ASEAN

10.40 – 10.45   Break

10.45 – 11.00   Inaugural Session (continued)
- Online release of 5th AINTT proceedings [*ASEAN and India: Partners in Integration in Asia*]
- Vote of Thanks by **Dr Prabir De**, ASEAN-India Centre (AIC), RIS, New Delhi

11.15 – 13.00 Session I: Changing landscape of global order and ASEAN-India relations in the Post-COVID Era

Chair: **Dr. Jayant Dasgupta**, Member, Governing Council, RIS, New Delhi

Speakers
- **Prof. Amitav Acharya**, UNESCO Chair in Transnational Challenges and Governance and Distinguished Professor, American University, Washington, DC
- **Prof. Amita Batra**, School of International Studies (SIS), Jawaharlal Nehru University (JNU), New Delhi
- **Prof. Nanigopal Mohanta**, Director, Centre for Southeast Asian Studies, Gauhati University, Guwahati
- **Prof. Lau Sim Yee**, Reitaku University, Tokyo and Columnist, New Straits Times, Kuala Lumpur
- **Prof. Carole Ann Chit Tha**, Member, Myanmar Institute of Strategic and International Studies (MISIS), Yangon

Q&A

13.00 – 14.00   Break

14.00 – 15.30 Session II: Emerging Value Chains: Opportunities for ASEAN and India in the Post-COVID Era

Chair: Assist. **Prof. Sineenat Sermcheep**, Faculty of Economics, Chulalongkorn University, Bangkok

Speakers
- **Dato' Ramesh Kodammal**, Chairman of Goldtex Group of Companies, and Chairman, ASEAN-India Business Council (AIBC), Kuala Lumpur

- **Prof. Rupa Chanda,** RBI Chair Professor in Economics, Indian Institute of Management (IIM) Bengaluru
- **Dr. Tham Siew Yean,** Senior Fellow, ISEAS-Yusof Ishak Institute, Singapore
- **Dr. Saon Ray,** Senior Fellow, Indian Council for Research on International Economic Relations (ICRIER), New Delhi

Q&A

DAY II: 21 AUGUST 2020

09.00 – 09.30   Registration / Log-in to Webex

09.30 – 11.00 Session III: New Normal and Significance of 4IR on ASEAN-India Partnership and Future Collaborations

Chair: **Dr. Mia Mikic,** Director, Trade, Investment and Innovation Division, United Nations ESCAP, Bangkok

Speakers

- **Mr. Sovinda Po,** Senior Research Fellow, Cambodian Institute for Cooperation and Peace (CICP), Phnom Penh
- **Mr. Gagan Sabarwal,** Senior Director, National Association of Software and Service Companies (NASSCOM), New Delhi
- **Dr. Jayant Menon,** Visiting Senior Fellow, Institute of Southeast Asian Studies (ISEAS), Singapore
- **Prof. Balaji Parthasarathy,** International Institute of Information Technology (IIIT), Bengaluru

Q&A

11.15 – 13.00 Session IV: ASEAN Outlook on Indo-Pacific (AOIP) and Indo-Pacific Oceans Initiative (IPOI): Complementarities and Cooperation

Chair: **Dr Arvind Gupta,** Director, Vivekananda International Foundation (VIF), New Delhi

Speakers

- **Vice-Admiral Pradeep Chauhan,** Director General, National Maritime Foundation (NMF), New Delhi

- **Prof. Fukunari Kimura,** Chief Economist, Economic Research Institute for ASEAN and East Asia (ERIA), Jakarta
- **Dr. Premesha Saha,** Associate Fellow, Observer Research Foundation (ORF), New Delhi
- **Prof. Joefe B. Santarita,** Dean, Asian Center, University of the Philippines Diliman

Q&A

13.00 – 14.00   Break

14.00 – 15.15 Session V: Way Forward

Chair: **Dr Mohan Kumar,** Chairman, RIS

Speakers

- **Amb. Preeti Saran,** Member, Governing Board, Indian Council of World Affairs (ICWA), New Delhi
- **Dr. Zaw Oo,** Executive Director, Center for Economic and Social Development (CESD), Yangon
- **Mr. Kavi Chongkittavorn,** Senior Fellow, Institute of Security and International Studies (ISIS), Chulalongkorn University, Bangkok
- **Commodore C. Uday Bhaskar,** Director, Society of Policy Studies (SPS), New Delhi

Q&A

15.15 – 15.30   Concluding Session

Chair: **Dr. Suthiphand Chirathivat,** Chairman, ASEAN Studies Centre (ASC), Chulalongkorn University, Bangkok

Vote of Thanks by

- **Assoc. Prof. Piti Srisangnam,** Director of Academic Affairs, ASEAN Studies Center, Chulalongkorn University, Bangkok
- **Dr. Durairaj Kumarasamy,** ASEAN-India Centre (AIC), RIS, New Delhi

Remarks

H.E. Mr. Don Pramudwinai
Deputy Prime Minister and Minister of
Foreign Affairs of the Kingdom of Thailand

This is perhaps the largest congregation of virtual participants that I ever had previously – mostly ASEAN Meetings. As I count on the screen, we have about 25 small windows and perhaps many more outside of the screen. Certainly, it is my pleasure to be with you. I perhaps should start by extending our greetings to you all from Bangkok.

Your Excellency, my Colleague, Mr. Subrahmanyam Jaishankar, Minister of External Affairs of the Republic of India
Your Excellency, Mr. Lim Jock Hoi, Secretary-General of ASEAN,
Dr. Mohan Kumar, Chairman of RIS
Dr. Suthipand Chirathivat, Chairman of ASEAN Studies Centre, Chulalongkorn University
Distinguished Academics, Colleagues and Friends

Again a very good morning to you all from Bangkok. It is a great pleasure for me to be with you all today at this 6th ASEAN-India Network of Think Tanks. I offer my opening remarks in many capacities: as co-host of this conference; as Country Coordinator for ASEAN-India Dialogue Relations; and as a close friend of India, bound closely to Thailand by historic, cultural, trade, and multifarious links.

We are meeting at an unprecedented time in the history of the world, and the daunting challenges that we face require new and innovative solutions. Today's Forum, therefore, provides a timely opportunity for us all to brainstorm ideas among the astute and knowledgeable think tanks, academia and policy makers gathered here, as we look to ensure the good health, safety and well-being of our peoples.

Distinguished Colleagues,
It has become clear that the world is no longer what it used to be just six months ago. The geo-political landscape is shifting. We are redefining "normal". Multilateralism is being challenged, while the value of regionalism has been reinforced. In the midst of it all, the importance of partnerships is more apparent than ever if we are to address the genesis of the current crisis.

The COVID-19 outbreak continues to take a heavy toll on our economies and peoples' welfare. The IMF has projected economic growth for ASEAN at minus 2.9 per cent, the first contraction in many decades, dating back to the Asian financial crisis back in 1997. And according to the World Bank, an additional 11 million people will fall into poverty in the East Asia and Pacific region.

Despite these monumental disruptions, what has proven to be enduring for ASEAN and India are our common aspirations. The two of us are inextricably interconnected and have, for centuries, flourished and been nurtured by those connections.

The visions we have for our regions have converged on many core principles that have much in common. The future of the ASEAN Outlook on the Indo-Pacific and India's Act East Policy, as well as the latest Indo-Pacific Oceans Initiative, continue to be predicated on peaceful, stable and prosperous regions.

Distinguished Colleagues,
Against the backdrop of this pandemic, the value of sharing and caring have been increasingly reinforced across the globe. Those with the capacity to give have stepped forward to share their surplus

with those in need. The culture of sharing is critically important, particularly during times of crisis, to ensure that no one is left behind.

This brings me to offer my reflections today on how the ASEAN-India Strategic Partnership should be taken forward at this critical time, threaded together by a simple yet powerful word spelled S-H-A-R-E, or SHARE.

Now let us begin scrutinising the first letter, S, that refers to Supply Chain Connectivity. As key players in the global supply chain, ASEAN and India need to ensure that the flow of essential goods, in particular food and medical supplies, is unhindered, and that investment and business travel can be facilitated. As India is seeking to become a stronger, more self-reliant country under the "Atmanirbhar Bharat" initiative, ASEAN stands ready to work with India in supporting our key industries and integrating them into the global supply chain.

Owing to the impact of the pandemic, we have witnessed in recent months remarkable two-digit growth in digital-related businesses. ASEAN and India should therefore redirect their resources to enhancing digital infrastructure and creating digital ecosystem conducive for new growth.

Physical connectivity will also be key in ensuring the seamless movement of goods and passengers across borders. I, therefore, look forward to the timely completion of the India-Myanmar-Thailand Trilateral Highway Project and its possible extension to Laos, Cambodia and Viet Nam. Once completed, it could become one of the world's most important land bridges for trade and transport, connecting the Northeastern part of India, the deep sea port of Dawei in Myanmar, the new Eastern Economic Corridor (EEC) in Thailand, and the Danang Port in Vietnam.

Now the next letter, H, in SHARE refers to Human Security in all dimensions. It is widely argued that countries could perhaps have responded more effectively to this crisis had they invested more in their health systems. As a long-time promoter of Universal Health Coverage or UHC, Thailand would be pleased to share our experiences on UHC, spanning nearly twenty years, as well as on the network of Village Health Volunteers. The latter has greatly contributed to enhanced capacity for Thailand in controlling the current pandemic.

Given India's renowned capacity as "Pharmacy of the World", we look forward to enhanced cooperation on medical research and development as well as on medicine and vaccines. We also support the ongoing efforts among leading global laboratories and vaccine institutes on mass production and distribution of anti-viral medicines and vaccines such as Remdesivir and Covishield. Once available, these vaccines should be made global public goods, accessible to all at an affordable price, in particular for lower to middle income countries.

The World Food Programme has forecasted that an estimated 265 million people in low- and middle-income countries could face acute food insecurity by the end of 2020 due to COVID-19. ASEAN and India are among the world's largest food and agricultural producers and should work to ensure that food safety is there and it is secured for all. New technology, such as climate-smart agriculture and the application of robotics and drones in agriculture, should be widely introduced to increase productivity and meet the world's demand. This is another area where we should work together.

Now the third letter, A, in SHARE refers to Academics. Academics and think tanks make a vital contribution to human capital development. Even before the pandemic, development gaps already existed and were deepening in many countries due to technological transformations. We should, therefore, equip our people, especially the MSMEs and the workforce, with the necessary skills that will allow them to benefit from the Fourth Industrial Revolution and the digital economy. Women's empowerment and supporting women entrepreneurs through skills training and financial access will also be crucial as they now constitute the majority of the new workforce.

I am pleased that a set of recommendations will be prepared today's at Forum and look forward to engaging in a lively discussion, along with other ASEAN Foreign Ministers, at the upcoming ASEAN Post Ministerial Meeting with India in September.

The fourth letter, R, in SHARE refers to Regionalism. ASEAN and India must stand firm in promoting regionalism and multilateralism as they have served as a solid foundation for the global economic growth over many decades. The ASEAN+1 framework, including with India, as well as other sub-regional groupings, such as Mekong-Ganga, ACMECS, BIMSTEC and IORA, should be further reinforced. And as India is a major economic player in the region, it goes without saying that the door to RCEP will always remain open to India, whose participation would contribute to the region's advancement and prosperity.

As Thailand will take up the Chairmanship of BIMSTEC during the year 2021-2022, we wish that the BIMSTEC members, including India, would carry on our important work on the BIMSTEC FTA which was initiated over a decade ago. We also wish to bring the attention to India that you might want to become the Chairman of the Asia Cooperation Dialogue, or ACD, after Turkey, for the year 2021-2022. Just make your move, and the Chairmanship will be falling on your lap.

Finally, the last letter, E, refers to the Environment. The COVID-19 pandemic has given us a silver lining for the environment, allowing it to rest, recuperate and rejuvenate itself from human practices that have long damaged our natural resources. We should look into how we can balance reopening our economies and societies with re-invigorated efforts on environmental growth and environmental conservation, and thus ensuring the path for green and sustainable growth. India's Blue Economy initiative, therefore, deserves our serious deliberation. Other related issues of climate change, haze, natural disaster and marine debris are areas that ASEAN and India can jointly cooperate.

Distinguished Colleagues,

As we look ahead to the post-COVID era, it is apparent that no single country can overcome this pandemic alone. ASEAN and India will, therefore, need to continue sharing information, best practices, knowledge and experiences among our health experts, academics and policy makers. This value of sharing must be maintained and reinforced even after the COVID-19 pandemic comes to an end.

The five letters of the word SHARE, which I have just outlined in my remarks, are all key issues that you will be discussing at this important forum. Let me conclude then, with one parting wish – that we use this current crisis as an opportunity to build back better, together. I am confident that through this, ASEAN and India can become a cohesive and responsive community that leaves no one behind and remains resilient to future challenges.

I thank you.

Ladies and Gentlemen, Colleagues, thank you.

Remarks

H.E. Dr. Subrahmanyam Jaishankar

External Affairs Minister of India

Your Excellency Deputy Prime Minister and Foreign Minister Don Pramudwinai,
Dignitaries from ASEAN and India,
Ladies and Gentlemen.
A very good morning to all of you.

It gives me great pleasure to address this Sixth Roundtable of the ASEAN-India Network of Think Tanks (AINTT). Let me begin by congratulating H.E. Don Pramudwinai for his recent elevation as Deputy Prime Minister, I believe this is the first time we are speaking since then, and I would also like to thank him for his very thoughtful opening remarks. I also appreciate deeply the presence of the Secretary General of ASEAN today at this event.

AINTT was established to provide policy inputs to our governments on future directions of our cooperation. I think it is fair to say it has seen some success in this regard, but I would urge the think-tanks today, specially ours, to push the envelope even more in the present world situation. Even in normal times, there is a need and space for new ideas. Because, obviously, not everything can be generated within Governments alone and we have seen fresh thinking in the past coming from scholars, media, businesses and civil society. What I can say with some emphasis is that they are probably more welcome today than before.

The world faces an unprecedented challenge. And believe me, the term "unprecedented" is not an exaggeration. None of us has seen a crisis of this proportion before, or indeed uncertainty of this level. How, when and with what result this pandemic will end is still a very open question. Even after several months, the true extent of its destruction in terms of losses of lives and livelihood remains unclear. We cannot pretend that this is just another happening, only bigger. On the contrary, the impact of the Coronavirus has been beyond our collective imagination. Current estimates put the cumulative loss in the range of US$ 5.8-8.8 trillion or approximately 6.5-9.7 per cent of the global GDP. The contraction of the world economy being predicted will surely be the largest since the Great Depression. It is against this background that your discussions today should examine our shared prospects.

The contemporary relationship between India and the ASEAN was founded very much on our shared interest in globalisation. In Asia at least, the ASEAN were pioneers of that process and helped bring India into it. But as it comes under stress today, we need to go beyond its economic and even social definitions. Globalisation may be reflected as trade, travel and financial flows. But in reality, it is something very much larger. In fact, what the pandemic has brought out is the indivisible aspect of human existence that underpins globalisation. Whether it is climate change, terrorism or indeed pandemics, these are not challenges where those affected have a choice. The limitations of purely national responses or sometimes living in denial have become evident. It, therefore, underlines the need for the international community to work together much more sincerely in search of collective solutions.

The irony, however, is that just when multilateralism was most in demand, it did not rise to the occasion. If we saw little leadership, it was not just due to the admittedly anachronistic nature of key international organisations. Equally, it reflected the intensely competitive nature of current international politics. Indeed, if one goes beyond organisations and structures, this was even more evident in the individual behaviour of many states. Therefore, the big issue that confronts the thinking world is not simply the state of the economy, the damage to societies or the challenges to governance. It is actually a debate on the future directions of global affairs and what kind of world order – or disorder – we are going to live in.

As a result, the commodity that is perhaps most valued in international relations today is that of trust. We had already seen in many quarters national security being redefined to include economic security. More recently, this then led to questions and concerns about technology security. The pandemic has now added to that the importance of health security. In fact, the concept of strategic autonomy that was once fashionable in a unipolar world has now assumed relevance once again in terms of global supply chains. Whatever we may profess, the actions of nations during times of crisis determines how the world really perceives them, and they did bring up many of the risks inherent in the current global economy. Consequently, concerns about supply chains are sought to be mitigated at the very least through greater emphasis on their diversification and resilience.

For exactly these reasons, it is incumbent on all of us to think through these challenges and come up with a more positive and practical model of cooperation. And it is not as though the world lacks good examples even during times of crises. After all, there were many who also shared what they could at this time, whether it was in terms of medicines, supplies or resources. In fact, through their actions what they demonstrated was a need for broader rebalancing as well as a more generous and equitable world view. For India today, this means among other things the urgent requirement to strengthen its national capacities. It also underlines the importance of de-risking critical aspects of societal existence, specially health. And at the same time, complementing the domestic priority of building an employment generating economy, not just a profit generating one. We call it Atmanirbhar Bharat-self reliant India.

Ladies and Gentlemen,

The ASEAN is one of the cross-roads of the global economy. India is the fifth largest economy in the world. We are not only proximate to each other, but together help shape Asia and the world. It is important that at this juncture, we put our heads together. There are conceptual issues to debate including Indo-Pacific. The Indo-Pacific Oceans initiative that we have tabled needs elaboration. As global relationships alter, we too need to take stock. Security, connectivity, economy and politics will jostle for space in your discussions. My remarks today are only meant to remind you all, how much the big picture has changed. As we come out of this pandemic, let us be clear on one fact. The world will never be the same again. That means new thinking, fresh ideas, more imagination and greater openness. We need to go beyond orthodoxies, whether of trade, politics or security. These are domains that all of you debate regularly and I am sure today you will have a very productive discussion.

Thank you very much.

Remarks

H.E. Dato' Lim Jock Hoi
Secretary-General of ASEAN

HE Don Pramudwinai, Deputy Prime Minister and Minister of Foreign Affairs of the Kingdom of Thailand
HE Dr Subrahmanyam Jaishankar, Minister of External Affairs of the Republic of India
Excellencies, Ladies and Gentlemen,

Good morning. To our Muslim friends, I wish you good blessings as we welcome the Hijri New Year. I am delighted to join you all for the 6th Roundtable of the ASEAN-India Network of Think Tanks. I commend the RIS and Chulalongkorn University for convening this Roundtable virtually to ensure that the important dialogue between ASEAN and India continues unimpeded by COVID-19.

Allow me to convey our heartiest congratulations to the government and people of the Republic of India on the occasion of the 74th Independence Day last Saturday. In addition to renewing our warm and long-standing friendship, I would like to reaffirm our solidarity with the people of India as we join hands to overcome the COVID-19 pandemic.

I also take this opportunity to warmly congratulate His Excellency Khun Don on his recent promotion as Deputy Prime Minister of the Kingdom of Thailand.

Excellencies, ladies and gentlemen,

Before I address the important subject of the ASEAN-India partnership, allow me to briefly share some of ASEAN's responses to the COVID-19 pandemic. The socio-economic impact on the ASEAN region is severe. For the first time since the 1997 Asian Financial Crisis, the region's economy is expected to contract by 2.7 per cent. As of 18 August, the ASEAN region has reported 376,070 confirmed infections and 9,132 fatalities.

ASEAN was able to mitigate the ravages of the pandemic with immediate and expeditious interventions at the earliest stages of the outbreak. Initiatives to strengthen public health capacity and response and in place, such as the COVID-19 ASEAN Response Fund to assist in the provision of essential medical supplies, personal protection equipment and, when it is developed, vaccines. A Regional Reserve of Medical Supplies is also in the works. In addition, ASEAN is drafting a Standard Operating Procedure for Public Health Emergencies which would provide guidance to address the current and future disease outbreaks.

The adoption of the Ha Noi Plan of Action on strengthening ASEAN economic cooperation and supply chain connectivity demonstrates ASEAN's commitment to keep markets open, and ensure smooth flow of trade, especially essential supplies. To facilitate the region's wider reopening, ASEAN is also discussing modalities to establish travel corridors which would restore regional essential travel in a measured and safe manner.

As ASEAN has one eye on containing the virus, it has the other focused on developing a post-COVID-19 recovery framework. This framework is expected to provide recommendations to pave the way for ASEAN's recovery. More importantly, it will provide possible pathways for ASEAN to rebuild and re-energise the ASEAN Community-building process.

Needless to say, India is very much a part of our work together in dealing with the impact of the pandemic, as well as in ASEAN's post-COVID-19 vision. We hope to see India lending support to some of the initiatives that I've highlighted.

Excellencies, ladies and gentlemen,

Within the short time of my remarks, I am unable to do justice to the breadth and depth of the ASEAN-India partnership. Let me begin with what I think is the most important and invaluable aspect of our unique partnership: its people.

The people-to-people connection is the essence of the partnership. The free-flowing and exchange of socio-cultural ties of yesterdays have stood us in good stead and have provided the foundation for the dynamic and resilient ASEAN-India partnership. The songs and dances, the chai tea, philosophy and religion are not just edifices of culture. These manifestations of history and personal connections create ties that bind the people of ASEAN and India in friendship. A major thrust in efforts to strengthen bilateral ties has to be in fostering better and deeper understanding of our societies and culture. One example of such initiatives is the ASEAN-India Media Exchange Programme which support ASEAN journalists to spend time in various parts of India to better understand the culture, society and politics of India.

Similarly, the "1,000 IIT Fellowship" Programme launched by Prime Minister Shri Narendra Modi at the 25th Anniversary ASEAN-India Commemorative Summit will provide a cohort of ASEAN's brightest graduate students the unique opportunity to experience India's rich culture and diversity as they embark on their doctoral studies at the prestigious India Institutes of Technology. India's generosity is also seen in the Nalanda University Scholarship Programme which funds post-graduate students from ASEAN in areas of liberal arts, philosophy, history and spiritual studies. In addition to promoting people-to-people interactions and cross-cultural understanding, these programmes contribute to ASEAN's human capital development.

The ASEAN-India Students Exchange Programme (AISEP) is yet another fine example of the commitment to ensure that different generations of Southeast Asians continue to have a personal connection to India. Indeed, youth engagement has been a long-standing ASEAN priority and the ASEAN-India Youth Summit is helping to sow the seeds of friendship and building connections among future leaders of ASEAN and India.

It bears reminding that the traffic has not been one-way. Tourist arrivals from India constitutes the fourth largest group of inbound tourist to ASEAN. The region welcomed more than 4.6 million tourists from India in 2018, a development spurred in part by better air connectivity between ASEAN and India. At the end of the day, these people-to-people interactions translate into better understanding of and respect for our cultures which in turn, help to build confidence and trust to bring ASEAN and India closer as friends and partners.

Excellencies, ladies and gentlemen,

The ASEAN-India friendship is founded on strong fundamentals and even brighter opportunities. India is ASEAN's sixth largest trading partner with bilateral trade reaching a highpoint of US$ 81.8 billion in 2018. While India's share of ASEAN's total trade stands at 2.2 per cent, it should be noted that bilateral trade has improved 209 per cent in the last decade. This is a strong foundation to build on. In this regard, the review of the ASEAN-India Trade in Goods Agreement (AITIGA) should result in a meaningful and mutually beneficial outcome to harness the full potential of bilateral trade, as it serves as one of the primary trade frameworks linking ASEAN and India.

India's leadership in driving the India-Myanmar-Thailand Trilateral Highway Project which would be extended into Cambodia, Laos and Viet Nam would pave the way for closer ASEAN-India transport links and trade relations, in addition to advancing ASEAN connectivity. In the sphere of multi-sectoral development, the Mekong-Ganga Cooperation is a showcase of India's contribution in assisting ASEAN to narrow its development gap.

Beyond trade, development and connectivity, I am delighted to share that the expansive ASEAN-India partnership has been progressing seamlessly: 77 per cent of the Plan of Action to Implement the ASEAN-India Partnership for Peace, Progress, and Shared Prosperity has been either acted on or completed. This goodwill and momentum will be sustained and expanded in the ASEAN-India Plan of Action (2021-2025) that is currently being finalised. I am pleased to note that the new POA will include new areas of cooperation such as public health, smart cities, sustainable development cooperation, and digital economy, that will be vital to the well-being and prosperity of our people.

Excellencies, ladies and gentlemen,
The future of ASEAN and India is invariably linked with the wider geo-economic and geostrategic landscape. ASEAN provides the indispensable bridge for India to be connected to the region's plethora of multilateral fora. Within these processes, India's diplomatic voice and strategic weight is highly valued and had made a meaningful impact to ensuring East Asia and the wider region remains a stable, forward-looking and rules-based community. As an original participant of the Regional Comprehensive Economic Partnership Agreement (RCEP) since negotiations was first launched in 2012, the RCEP remains open for India that would contribute to the advancement and prosperity of the region.

Excellencies, ladies and gentlemen,
Notwithstanding the COVID-19 pandemic, the region is not all gloom and doom. We are confident that COVID-19 will only be temporarily set back, and would not derail our commitment for a deeper and mutually beneficial partnership. India is a trusted and valued partner, and we would like to see India draw closer to the region, not just in the realm of socio-cultural relations but also in the political, strategic and economic spheres. In this respect, I very much look forward to the experts' deliberations and proposals from today's Roundtable, and I wish all of us a fruitful discussion.

Thank you.

Glimpses of the Roundtable

6TH ASEAN-India Network for Think Tank
ASEAN-INDIA: Strengthening Partnership in the Post-Covid Era
Day 1: 20 August 2020

6TH ASEAN-India Network for Think Tank
ASEAN-INDIA: Strengthening Partnership in the Post-Covid Era
Day 2: 21 August 2020